IGNITE
Possibilities

Other internationally best-selling compilation
books by IGNITE for you to enjoy

———————

Ignite Your Life for Women

Ignite Your Female Leadership

Ignite Your Parenting

Ignite Your Life for Men

Ignite Your Life for Conscious Leaders

Ignite Your Adventurous Spirit

Ignite Your Health and Wellness

Ignite Female Change Makers

Ignite the Modern Goddess

Ignite Love

Ignite Happiness

Ignite Your Inner Spirit

Ignite The Entrepreneur

IGNITE Possibilities

INTRODUCTION AND
FEATURE CHAPTER BY **JB Owen**

Founder of Ignite and JBO Global Inc.

PRESENTED BY

AMY HACKETT-JONES • AMY LIN • ANDREW KAP • ANNABEL WILSON
ASHLEY PATTERSON • ATTA EMAMI • BARBARA DRTINA • BEEJAL COULSON
DERRICK HILL • DIANA LOCKETT, M.SC., R-EYT, • DONNA LOCKETT, PHD
DR. GERALD CURRY • FRANCIS PICHÉ • GUY A. FORTT • HEGE ELARA SALVESEN
JB OWEN • JIMMY HAYS NELSON • KATHERINE VRASTAK • KIRUSHA KULCAR • LINDA M PARKER
LISA LYNN EVELETH • MARINA SIGALOVA • MARSHANELLE HORNE APRN FNP-BC
MEGHAN HUTHSTEINER • MELODY D. BYRD • NOA TAKARROUMT • PAT LABEZ
RENEE DUTTON • RYAN WILLIAM MANNION • SAM HUMPHREY • REVEREND SHEILA BLACK
SORANA PASCARIU • TAMMY MCCANN • TRACI HARNELL • TRACY STONE • DR. YASMINE SAAD

PUBLISHED BY IGNITE AND PRINTED BY JBO GLOBAL INC.

Published and printed by JBO Global Inc.
5569-47th Street Red Deer, AB
Canada, T4N1S1 1-877-677-6115

Cover design by JB Owen
Book design by Dania Zafar
Designed in Canada, Printed in China
ISBN 978-1-7923-4175-5

First edition: May 2021

Ordering Information: Quantity sales. Special discounts are available on quantity purchases by corporations, associations, and others. For details, contact the publisher at the above address. Programs, products, or services provided by the authors are found by contacting them directly. Resources named in the book are found in the resources pages at the back of the book.

Dedication

This book is dedicated to every single person on the planet, all 7,862,831,932 who were listed among the world's population when this book was printed in May of 2021. It is our intention that all people, of all races, creeds, customs, and inclinations, are blessed with the opportunity to make what is possible in their lives. What's possible is possible for all of us. Now, more than ever, every human on this Earth should be living within the realm of what is possible for them. Imagine the world we would live in if every man, woman, and child were smack-dab in the center, gloriously enjoying what is possible for them.

May your life be filled with Possibilities.

Possibilities belong To You.
By Peter Giesin

Your dreams belong to you, exclusively...
No one else has a reason to fight for them, like you do.
No one else can see the possibilities that for now only exist in your imagination, like you can.

Waiting for something or someone to make it happen is a wish.
But doing something about it is a choice...

The moment you take responsibility for the purpose of your life,
The life of your dreams will come to be.

The more you work on your passions and believe in yourself,
The more momentum you build,
And the more unstoppable you become.

No matter how long it takes, or how impossible it may seem,
Keep going,
Keep believing,
Make your stand.
For you have something special to offer that no one else can.

TESTIMONIALS FROM AUTHORS

"Giving life to my story in IGNITE Possibilities has been a personally profound experience. Moreover, the response received of its impact has been truly heartwarming. Being part of the IGNITE community has been such a wonderful journey and I look forward to more writing with such a powerful platform."

— Pat Labez

"I enjoyed every step of writing with IGNITE! Every 'Writer's Nest' and 'Candlelight Session' was brilliant! IGNITE editors and the team were so helpful at getting your juices flowing and so positive about your capabilities in this journey. I loved the entire experience!"

— Lisa Lynn Eveleth

"JB's energy is infectious and her vision is compelling. Working with her and the IGNITE team is a joy and encourages a metamorphosis of the Self. The supportive journey the team guided me through from the original idea for my story through the resistance lurking in the corner of each twist and turn as I sat down to write empowered me to embrace those blocks in my path, love them, and let them leave of their own accord, enabling me to tell a part of my story that I'd found so difficult to tell."

— Amy Hackett-Jones

"The process has always been so easy. I think it's the best program on the planet to share a personal message to the world and get published in such an easy way."

— Francis Piché

"My experience writing with IGNITE has been positive, uplifting, enjoyable, and empowering. I am a much more confident person and writer than I was four months ago when I first started the process. All of the editors are fabulous, kind, and genuinely care about their writers and their stories. Writing for IGNITE is much more than simply having a book or chapter published. The wide array of classes and abundant opportunities for networking are transformational. Thank you IGNITE!"

— Renee Dutton

"Writing with Ignite was eye-opening and pleasant. I no longer operate in fear."

— Ashley Patterson

"I am still pinching myself that this is really happening. I have always dreamed of being an author, I love to read and wanted to someday put my story to print. I had no idea how to make this happen until a friend and soror of my sorority told me about IGNITE. I made the contact and everything was amazing from that point forward. The whole experience was pleasurable and allowed me to release the fear of writing. JB and the team of editors were phenomenal. They guided me through the process and made this experience treasurable. Because of them, I have found the author inside of me that has been waiting to emerge."

— Marshanelle Horne APRN FNP-BC

"Prior to writing my chapter, I had settled into the safety of my own inner world like a spiritual hermit, hiding my Self and hoarding information. I felt for some time that I had a message or two but thought I would just wait until telepathy becomes more commonly used before sharing it! I am thrilled that I became an *Ignite Possibilities* author instead and can now reach the people who need my stories. The IGNITE process helped me make it to the finish line and cross an item off my bucket list. Heartfelt thanks to my fellow IGNITE authors Amy, Marina, and Giselle for your ongoing support and friendship."

— Kirusha Kulcar

"It's a privilege to participate in this amazing journey with my fellow Ignite authors. The IGNITE team, community, and support structure helped me to unpack and liberate a dark chapter in my life beyond my wildest expectations of this team. The IGNITE process is powerfully impactful. I hope everyone enjoys this book and gets a chance to experience the IGNITE journey as an author."

— Atta Emami, MBA, IMC, MSc.

"The experience of writing your story and sharing it with the world is made so simple and utterly doable with Ignite and the incredible team JB has put together. The process is so well thought-out, planned, and executed that it is a joy; and in fact, the journey is one where you learn how to pour your story out, connect with your readers, share vital and inspirational learnings with them, and form wonderful connections with your co-authors along the way. All this comes with the support, motivation, and uniquely fizzing energy of the indomitable Pink Billionaire and Queen of Possibilities, JB Owen."

— Tracy Stone

"This is my second Ignite publication. I love the opportunity to write a single chapter and have it come to life through the eyes of the skillful editors, JB, and her team in a short time frame. If you have a story to tell, IGNITE has a team to help you get it published and you will forevermore be part of the amazing IGNITE family."

— Diana Lockett, M.Sc., R-EYT

"I have never been so excited to be in my first compilation book series, called *Ignite Possibilities*. Kudos to JB and lovable husband Peter to Ignite all of our possibilities and help us achieve greatness."

— Guy A. Fortt

"I would like to take this time to share what an incredible experience it has been to write my story with the Ignite community. I have never published a story before. In fact, I didn't even like journaling, but I felt so empowered writing my story and learned so much. This wasn't just a writing experience. There is so much support, personal growth opportunities, global connections, and inspiration in weekly Zooms. Speakers are brought in to inspire and teach us. I have made so many new friends around the world. The editing process was painless and JB herself does the final edit. Thank you to IGNITE for igniting my writing abilities. I can't wait to do more with you."

— Barbara Drtina

"As a published academic writer and clinician, the thought of sharing my personal story was very vulnerable and uncomfortable. As a latecomer to the process, with only three weeks to move through the writing and editing process, it felt quite daunting. JB and her editors and staff were incredibly responsive, supportive, and helpful. Although I did not have the time to engage in most of the learning opportunities, I could feel the energy in the field and allowed it to inspire my process. I am so grateful for this experience."

— Donna Lockett, PhD

"Thanks so much to JB and team for being so responsive and supportive as I wrote my chapter for your book. I'm very much used to writing and publishing in my own unique style, and your team managed to honor that while still helping me fit my story to your dynamic format."

— Andrew Kap

"The journey with JB Owen and all of the IGNITE team has been an extraordinary experience for me! I took the "solo" book writing course with JB and was thrilled to be invited to write for the "Possibilites" book. The love and support of JB and all of the IGNITE staff editors provided such confidence for me, and helped me to realize my true potential as an author, and my impact in the world. I am excited to share this launch with all of the other authors and to read their beautiful and heartfelt stories. I am also delighted that this is an excellent segue for me to write and publish my own book! Thank you."

— Reverend Sheila Black

"I am immeasurably grateful for the editors at Ignite. They have allowed a girl who gets paralyzed from writing a business correspondence out of fear of improper everything to become a woman who feels like she's had the best therapy and writing course over her entire, ENTIRE, education! Writing wasn't just telling a story. It gave me my life back. The editors stood not in front or behind but right next to me. They gave me tools that they KNEW would work to get me writing like a veteran novelist. If it wasn't for this platform and their dedication to follow through with their mission to Ignite every life in the world, I never would have gotten back to a place of fearlessness… I made a conscious choice where I fully committed to the certainty everything is possible and didn't look back once! I found a place to call my home in every aspect and the irony is, it's the place where I was the most terrified to go. Thank you for believing in me and thank YOU for committing to doing something bigger than you for the greater of this world."

— Meghan Huthsteiner

"I am very grateful to all the Ignite Team for making my first publishing such a positive experience. Project Leader Traci Harrell was so encouraging, supportive and helpful in the pre-editing stage too. I really value all the editing sessions I received from Alex, Michi, and JB Owen and final edit by Andi; which truly brought my story alive, better than I imagined or could have done on my own. Much gratitude for this success!"

— Katherine Vrastak

Contents

WHAT IS AN IGNITE BOOK?

Inside the pages of this book, you will find a part of you. Your story, your thoughts, your worries, wishes, ideas, and dreams will be reflected in a story shared here by one of our authors. We know this because Ignite stories represent the human emotions in all of us. They are Universal and common. They reflect what all of us feel and touch upon the very essence that makes us human; in our human experience.

The very word *Ignite* signifies the goal of our books and describes the intention behind the stories that are shared inside. We see our books as gifts to the world. Every one we publish is done so with the idea of inspiring, uplifting, and igniting the reader in the process. We believe we are a bridge for all human connection, and that each story is a beacon for what is possible for every person on our earth.

As you begin reading the upcoming pages, you will find that every story starts with a *Power Quote*. It is a self-affirming, self-empowering, self-inspiring statement designed to awaken you. It is designed to uplift you, push you forward, and encourage you to break outside your comfort zone. Power quotes are phrases that you can use when you need encouragement or a dose of hope. They are meaningful statements intended to provoke thought, Ignite ideas, spark action, and evoke change. Every power quote written in Ignite is that which is already within you so that you can be all that you desire to be.

Below the power quote, you will find each author's personal *Intention*. These are the personal insights and genuine wishes the author wants to share with you. They are the reasons they have written their story, filled with both purpose and meaning. Each author has the desire to *Ignite* something special in you and they share that eloquently in their intention. They want you to know right from the beginning what they feel their story will do for you.

After the intention you dive right into the Ignite *Story*. It is a genuine account of how the author went through their life to emerge a greater expression of themself. Through their unique experiences and circumstances, the authors explain how their Ignite moments transformed them, awakened them, and set them on a new trajectory in life. They reveal their honest feelings and share their personal discoveries. They give you an insightful account into the moment that resulted in magnificent change and elevated their consciousness.

We all have *Ignite* moments that change us, define us, and set us forth on a wonderful new journey of inner exploration. These stories are derived from those very moments and told in the most endearing and heartfelt way. They show that *life-altering* situations are designed to impact us in a way that ultimately inspires us to love ourselves more and appreciate those around us more completely.

Once you have completed the story, you will find a list of *Ignite Action Steps*. Each author shares a powerful, doable action that you can take to move toward greater fulfillment and adopt new habits that will benefit you. Each action step is an effective idea, unique process, and powerful practice that has been successful in their lives. The hope is for you to implement them in your life and then use them daily to manifest positive change. Each Ignite Action step is different and unique, just like you are, and each has proven to have amazing results when done diligently and consistently.

As you sit down to read this book, know that it is not required to read it in the traditional way, by starting at the beginning and reading through to the end. Many readers flip to a page at random and read from there, trusting that the page they landed on holds the exact story they need to read. Others glance over the table of contents, searching for the title that resonates with them. Some readers will go directly to a story recommended by a friend. However you decide to read this book, we trust it will be right for you. We know that you may read it from cover to cover in one single sitting or pick it up and put it down a dozen times over a long period of time. The way you read an Ignite book is as personal as every story in it, and we give you complete permission to devour it in whatever way fits you.

What we do ask is, if a story touches you or in some way inspires you, that you reach out and tell the author. Your words would mean the world to them.

Since our book is all about Igniting humanity, we want to foster more of that among all of us. Feel free to share your sentiments with the authors by using their contact information at the end of each chapter. There isn't an Ignite author who wouldn't love to hear from you and know how their story impacted your life.

We know that the phase 'Ignite moments' will now become a part of your vocabulary. You'll begin to think about your own impactful moments and the times in your life that Ignited you in a new way. If sharing your story feels important or writing your Ignite moment is percolating to the surface, please reach out to us. We believe every person has a story and everyone deserves to be seen, heard, and acknowledged for that story. If your words are longing to come forth, we want to support you in making it happen. Our desire is to Ignite a billion lives through a billion words, and we can only do that by sharing the stories from people like you!

As you turn the page, we want to welcome you to the Ignite family. We are excited for what is about to happen; because we know the stories in this book are about to Ignite you. As you dive into the upcoming pages, a million different emotions will fill your heart and a kindred spirit will be established. We know that this will be a book that both awakens and blesses you. May you be honored, loved, and supported from this page forward and all your Ignite moments be one of exceptional change.

INTRODUCTION
BY JB OWEN

Welcome to a book like no other. I have to be honest and say that I do not think there is another book on the market that speaks solely about possibilities in this way. *Ignite Possibilities* is incredibly unique in that it has been birthed during a time where the most important thing on the planet for all of humanity, in my opinion, is *manifesting what is possible*. As we adapt to the swirling mix of needs in this ever-changing world, what is needed is to press forth with the notion of what IS possible for all of us. People need to believe that *all* is possible so that we can make this world a greater place for everyone. If you look at all the major needs in the world, you will probably agree that making peace possible, making inclusion possible, ending world hunger, saving the polar ice caps, and ensuring a hundred other deeply needed and life-altering necessities are all possible... *truly matters*. If we can reach those major initiatives and overcome those milestones, then the world would be a much more glorious place for all of us to live in. With possibilities at the forefront, our lives will be richer, our hearts supported, and each of our intrinsic human needs will be fulfilled.

I took this idea of possibilities and made it personal, and I put it upon myself to spearhead this cause. I set out to inspire as many people as possible with what is actually possible. Thirty-six people heard my call and came together to share their passion for what is possible for them, for you, and for all of us. They embraced the dream of Igniting possibilities in everyone. Somewhere in their lives, something profound became possible. Whether it was forgiving a transgression, saving a life, overcoming a crippling belief, or awaking an injured heart, each and every author featured in this book has experienced a powerful moment in their life when they moved from what one might consider a notion of the impossible to a mindset where everything is totally possible. In fact, we refrained from even using the word impossible. Instead, we reframed our perception of what was possible and in doing so, we all found within ourselves abilities, ambition, excitement, and opportunities in such a way it changed us on a cellular level.

How is *that* possible you might ask? To be changed on a cellular level? When one redefines themselves in a new way, the body, mind, and spirit shift into becoming what you desire that new way to be. A once bitter, angry person may begin feeling light, alive, and free meaning that the very fiber of their being has been transformed. They function differently. They sleep, eat, laugh, and love in a new way. And science has proven that how you think is how you are, and how you are is what you become. This transformation affects everything, which means even your cells function differently. They awaken, heal, and thrive. To go from homeless to saving lives and becoming a hero means that on the very deepest level, change took place. To face death and prevail… to give up on life and then come back and persevere… to have everything you own taken from you and then have it come back better than before… means that every part of your internal makeup has shifted from what was to what is new. That's a cellular transformation!

What is exciting is that this book is filled to the brim with examples of just that: individuals making the move from what was to *what can be*. Possibilities ring loud and plentiful in every story as the authors walk you through the journeys they took to create what is possible for them. Their tenacity, drive, and personal convictions are woven throughout every story. You can read their inner thoughts and discover what paths they took to make possible what they wanted. They tell of the seed that was planted and then the faith that grew. They outline the steps they encountered and then share the climb toward possibilities that ensued. It isn't all rainbows and sunshine though; there are certainly hardships and trials. But like many times in life, there is the triumph at the end and the authors get the reward and experience the joy in reaching the place they aspired to be.

What is great about these stories is that they are all *our* stories. They are the stories of each and every one of us throughout the world. We all go through the process of unknowing, being unsure, and treading lightly toward our dreams. We worry. We fear. We waffle. We try, fail, and then try again. We wish life was different than it is. We conceptualize, create, and then curate our ideas before, after, and all the while we are going after them.

Humans are a fickle breed. We question the very things that we are entitled to and push away what we most need. We ask too many questions and worry about who's watching, who might steal our ideas, or how many people will like or dislike us along the way. The ego, the monkey-mind, the critic, the inner child, the badass, and the skeptic all get in the way of unleashing all the wonders of what is actually wanting to be formed into possibilities.

That is why this book is so vital at this time. We are living through a time in history where nothing is as it seems and nothing will ever be as it was. The world IS changing. People are being forced to think in a way they have never had to before. Humans are being pushed and corralled into confines and conformity. Old freedoms are obsolete and new indulgences are being put into question. It isn't what we want; and yet, here we are. That is why I feel compelled to offer an alternative idea. One where we all live in the very center of what is possible. Where we get to *have* what we desire. Where *impossible* becomes obsolete and everything that is possible for every person on the planet is supported, encouraged, and revered.

I invite you to release the mental shackles of what has not been possible for you up to now and turn up the dial on what is possible for you going forward. At this very moment — wherever you are in the world, in your life, in your home, and however old or young you are — you have the ability to activate your possibilities. And not just one possibility, ALL possibilities! Everything you dream of — all your desires and what you wish for — lies at the heart of this belief. Knowing, trusting, and embracing the very essence of possibilities is the magic of Igniting them. This book and all the stories in it are designed to turn you into a believer of unlimited possibilities and show you just how possibile all that you hope for is. Everything is truly within your reach.

This book began with a dream. A dream of mine to Ignite humanity with the idea that if each and every one of us was living in the very center of what is possible for us, our world would be a magnificent place. Imagine how people would treat one another if we were all encouraged to be manifesting possibilities for ourselves and for each other. Imagine the things we would create, the problems we would solve, the goals we would accomplish, and the smiles we would instigate. Our world would be so much more enjoyable if each and every one of us had permission to go after what was possible. Our lives would be richer, our families more connected, our children more in tune with their future.

Generations would flourish, sickness would disappear, life would blossom, and the utopian Nirvana we all dream of would appear.

I want to inspire that kind of movement, and this book is the chrysalis to that. I hope that it becomes like the butterfly for you that will metamorphose from the caterpillar of what once was, into what can be. This book is the lighthouse at the edge of the raging sea, designed to be a beacon for those who see how possibilities will pave the way to the promised land for all 7 billion people on this planet. Let us each choose to create a place where we all are living the very essence of our greatest possibilities. May those possibilities germinate and create new possibilities, which will in turn bolster and birth even more. If we want anything on our planet to be contagious, it has to be possibilities! This book is the beginning of that. You reading it is the start of that. These authors writing about it is the affirming of it. Ignite Publishing distributing it is the activation of it. And, as you share these stories with others, you will become the multiplying of it. Possibilities are here to stay and it is my greatest wish that when you close this book, you decide to step into everything that is divinely possible for you.

Much love, JB

Awaken What's Possbile

Enraptured with all things possible, I am delighted to share that my team and I have created the Realm Of Possibilities, an online virtual environment to bring people together to enjoy the best empowerment content on the planet in an interactive arena where conscious people can share and connect with one another to collectively raise the vibration of the planet. If you'd like to join us, please go to https://connect.igniteyou.life and sign up.

Inside What's Possible is a podcast I host to interview individuals that have overcome hardships and have activated possibilities in their lives. They have moved beyond limitations and challenged the impossible to make it possible. If you have a story like this and would like to be featured on my podcast, please email me at info@igniteyou.life and share.

The Possibilities Principles is the newest solo book I am writing. It is a book designed to awaken what is possible in each and every one of us through powerful techniques and tangible action steps. For many of us, activating possibilities is not a muscle we have been using. This book will change that. It will inspire you to think more grandly and create a whole new possibilities mindset. Look for *Ignite What's Possible* in the spring of 2022.

The Possibilities Institute is the big dream of building a place, a physical building, that will become a haven for possibility thinkers and visionaries from around the world. I aspire to create somewhere people can come to discover what is possible on a global scale. Part museum of possibilities and part think tank for possibility discussion, The Possibilities Institute will be a mecca where young and old can be transposed into the realm of all that is possible on this Earth, from yesteryears to light-years ahead. Proceeds of our books sales go toward the formation of The Possibilities Institute.

Possibility Planning is the big BHAG (Big Hairy Audacious Goal) to define a new outline of what is possible for all people on the planet. It is an education system designed to teach people how to think in possibilities from the moment of conception, through school, into their careers, and as they choose their life partners, hobbies, future endeavors, and retirement; all from a place of what is possible for them. It is a lifestyle plan to inspire people to show them how, in every stage of their life, what is possible *is* truly possible. It is designed to bring possibilities to the forefront for all of us.

As you can see, 'possibilities' is now my mission and I look forward to all the delightful ways our paths will cross as you step into your greatest experience of what is possible for you.

"Anything and everything IS possible for you" ~ JB Owen

Ignite Possibilities in YOU

This is your time.

Right here, right now, something cataclysmic is about to happen…
Your mind is going to awaken and your spirit is
about to come alive to what is possible for you.
Your heart is going to feel enlivened and
your emotions will be joyously turned on.
Something rare and special is about to transpire
and you are at the very centre of it.
Get ready…
because
anything and everything
is about to become
possible for you.

You have read a lot of books, been to many places, heard others speak, and learned many things. All of it has led you to this moment. As you read the many words inside this book, it will Ignite something new inside of you. That ignition process will awaken something greater that will lead to a deeper desire. Over time, that burning desire will inspire action, and those actions will produce great results. It is a powerful equation that, once ignited, cannot be quenched.

It is the life of possibilities; and once it has been birthed, a ripple of events will happen to make it all transpire perfectly for you.

A lot of people believe this truth about possibilities. Others do not. Some have lived unexposed to possibilities and are not privy to the power of them. Others have seen its strength and witnessed its unwavering potential. Possibilities has not been a buzzword like consciousness, wellness, and spirituality have been over the recent years. These three ideals have been the dominant direction that the human race has leaned into as of late. They have awakened many hearts and lifted many minds. They have indeed driven humanity to where it is today and shifted the planet on a massive scale.

Now, it is time for what is next.

POSSIBILITIES

In a time riddled with confusion and the unknown, people need more than ever to have something new to inspire them. Instead of living in what we've been told and being caught up in what once was, the world needs to look at what is *possible*. The possibilities that live inside of each of us will be the map to our future; a future for all. Your gifts, talents, ideas, and possibilities are what humanity needs to move forward. All the things you aspire to create and dreams you hold dear are exactly what people need. You have so much to offer; so much to give. There is a burning light in you that will shine the way for others. How you proceed will affect how others proceed.

There was a time when we each wanted what was best for us alone and material goods plus accumulation sat at the forefront of our actions. That has all changed. Each and every person on the planet now has the opportunity to live at the helm of their masterfully-given possibilities. All of us, including you, have the ability to change the trajectory of our world by tapping into and living out exactly what you were designed to do; bolstered high by all possibilities.

I invite you to Ignite Possibilities in you *right now*. Awaken what is possible for you. As you proceed though the next few pages, you will begin to uncover what is indeed possible in your life. The self-reflective journaling exercises that follow will help you uncover the many possibilities available right now and awaken new ideas that will foster even more possibilities yet to come. When it comes to activating all that awaits you, doing this work is vital. Possibilities are swirling all around you. If you put out your hand and turn it upward, it will be instantly filled with an unlimited abundance of possibilities. If you close your eyes and turn your face upward, you will be showered with them. If you get up and walk forward, a hundred doors will open to all the possibilities that are waiting for you.

This knowingness about possibilities is how you can begin to shift your mind when it comes to creating possibilities in you. Just as we had to listen to the soul as we meditated and trust the Universe as we spoke, we now must shift our thinking to the infinite and never-ending supply of possibilities in our midst. Possibilities can be plucked from the air in front of you and placed in your pocket. They can be grabbed in an instant and fused into our minds. Possibilities swirl inside our imagination only to be manifested in our reality moments later. They are a massive power source we have not yet tapped into as a human race… until right now.

Understanding the greatness of what is possible for you and mapping out what it is you desire to make possible is a defining moment in your life; and here you are!

This book and the work you are about to do in it begin the quest to Ignite all people on the planet so that we can live in the very center of what is possible for us. Like a massive tornado with its calm point in the center, you too have the power to create that kind of force in your life. You just have to access it and harness it first. You need to define what is possible for you and clearly state your intentions. Then, allow the rest to take place. Intentions plus knowing, conviction with emotion, and belief attached to clarity makes up the winning recipe for possibilities to manifest.

Let's create your Possibility Recipe

We all have our reasons for wanting the life we do. We have grown to where we are right now through facing a lot of situations along that way that have molded our understanding and brought us to this point. Imagining our perfect life is a common habit for many of us. We want certain things, choose certain paths, and say yes or no without often knowing exactly why. Our human minds think in facts and figures. The brain was designed to solve problems, so to keep itself busy and important, it often creates problems it has to solve. Possibilities do not fit neatly into predefined categories. Possibilities unfold like petals unfurling in the sun. They are like whispers that travel on the wind. Possibilities surpass what we 'know.' They come from a higher place. They are divine and sacred, and they are specific to you.

In a world of billions of people, there will never be and can never be a person just like YOU. Your authentic self is an unstoppable force working to accomplish your goals, dreams, and what is possible for you. Being fully aware of just how amazing you truly are is the key to unlocking what is possible for you. Understanding your intentions and why you do the things you do will be the building blocks to your next steps. Knowing your intentions and comprehending the emotions that drive them will solidify your belief in them and bring clarity and conviction to your possible next steps.

The journaling prompts below are designed to assist you in beginning to recognize your unique possibilities and what matters most to you. Let them guide you to a new understanding of what's fully attainable as you craft your own unique possibility recipe.

What is truly important to me?

_____

_____

_____

_____

_____

_____

What do I really enjoy doing?

_____

_____

_____

_____

_____

_____

When am I having the most fun?

_____

_____

_____

_____

_____

_____

I'm proud of how inventive I am when I...

_____

_____

_____

_____

_____

_____

I make things possible for myself when I...

_____

_____

_____

_____

_____

_____

I see possibilities in me most often as I…

_____

_____

_____

_____

_____

_____

If anything were possible, I would…

_____

_____

_____

_____

_____

_____

Identifying what you value and what matters most to you is an important part of defining the possibilities you can manifest. The intention behind your desires and *why* you want what you do is a driving force.

Ask yourself right now:

What do I want to make possible in my life?

_____

_____

_____

_____

_____

Why is this so important to me?

_____

_____

_____

_____

_____

_____

You have just defined what matters most to you, what you value, and what you'd like to make possible in your life. Now we get to think even broader to see how making something possible for *you* makes something possible for *others*. Your possibilities ignite a chain reaction of possibilities for others. Your ideas, crafts, products, non-profits, businesses, and brands along with your words, gestures, compassion, understanding, and exuberance *all* have an energy force that has perpetuates endless expansive opportunities to Ignite the world.

IGNITE POSSIBILITIES IN OTHERS

When we look beyond ourselves and see greater possibilities for others, we pave the way for more and more people to step into what is possible for themselves. We allow possibilities to blossom and create a harvest of possibilities for every single person on the planet to enjoy. Our possibilities shine a light by which others can find their way.

You wouldn't be reading this book if you didn't already believe much of this. Inside of you, possibilities have already mustered and it is no coincidence that you are here. Your mind has been awakened to what is possible for you and you have attracted this book into your life. That is how possibility creation works. Through a trillion micro-actions, the Universe has conspired proudly to bring you to this moment where you are reading this right now. And in your soul, on a cellular level, things are magnifenclty changing! You and the very essence of your Being is formulating what is next for you, beyond what you have known up until now. Possibilities are so plentiful that how you see yourself right now cannot even comprehend the potential of who you will grow to be. In fact, what you make possible in your life today will be the hinge that opens the door to what is possible for your future and the futures of all those who encounter you.

Take a personal moment to define how your possibilities make possibilities for others. See the exponential effect of what you set in motion and how it will intrinsically uplift and impact those in your vicinity. Then go a step bigger and envision how they will impact all of humanity.

My Possibilities will help others in the following ways…

_____

_____

_____

_____

_____

_____

My Possibilities will change things for others in the following ways…

_____

_____

_____

_____

_____

_____

My Possibilities will Ignite possibilities for my family in the following ways…

_____

_____

_____

_____

_____

_____

My Possibilities will Ignite possibilities for my friends in the following ways…

_____

_____

_____

_____

_____

_____

My Possibilities will Ignite possibilities for my community in the following ways…

_____

_____

_____

_____

_____

_____

My Possibilities will Ignite possibilities for humanity. Here is how...

_____

_____

_____

_____

_____

_____

It is a magical thing when the rainbow of possibilities is set free. By doing this exercise and digging deep within, you have unleashed the next realm of possibilities. Do not take this lightly, for what you decide *will* become truth. Be intentional, careful, and heartfelt. The world is your oyster, so become a pearl diver. Reach as high as you can, seek all the golden layers, and bask in the sparkle dust.

What needs to be in place going forward is that what's possible for you can no longer remain just in your imagination or just a dream. What you see as possible in your life has to be a *conviction* from this moment onward. You have to know with every fiber of your being that what you desire desires you! Your dreams want to be actualized! They want *you* to be the one to bring them into life. Nothing comes into your mind without the belief that you will be the one to bring it to fruition. All ideas and wishes are centered in the very under-standing that if you wish it to be so, then it shall be so. This is a basic principle of possibilities. You thinking about it is not a coincidence; it is you calling into being. It is ready. It is here. The moment I spoke about at the beginning has already happened. What is possible for you has been Ignited into being.

IGNITE POSSIBILITIES IN HUMANITY.

Knowing how 'possibilities' work, you now have all the permission you need and any encouragement you desire to summon forth even more possibilities on a global scale. Each one of us has the ability to be an instigator of love, peace, joy, happiness, inclusion, connection, support and any other possible positive possibility ever imagined. We have the capacity to expand the framework of old paradigms and bust the seams of any limitations. The big goal for all of us should be to make possibilities the newest and most important trend. Everyone should be talking about it, Twitter should be trending on it, news reports should be reporting it. Memes, YouTube videos, Facebook ads, Apple iPhone apps, and the hottest designer clothing should all be sporting it. Everywhere we turn, what is right in front of us should be what is possible for us so we can create a better nation, forge more collective bonds, and unite all people in ways we have never done before.

WHAT IS POSSIBLE IS POSSIBLE FOR ALL OF US.

You opened that idea the moment you opened this book. You allowed the breath of possibilities to fill your home and latch on to your heart. Now grab hold of it, squeeze it tight, and ride the glorious wave it takes you on. Kick up your heels, throw back your head in abundant laughter, and squeal with delight. Possibilities are the most wondrous thing we have and they are given to all of us.

May your life be richly filled with all that is possible for you, for me, and for everyone.

THE POSSIBILITY PROMISE

I promise to ignite possibilities in myself,
in others,
and in all of humanity.

I promise to live my truth,
my light,
and my divinity.

I promise to walk each step with intuition,
conviction,
and pride.

I promise to foster possibilities in my children,
their children,
and all the children I meet.

I promise to cherish possibilities;
the ones that arrive,
the ones that I see,
the ones that awaken every part of me.

I promise to grow possibilities on this Earth,
throughout this world,
And in humanity.

I promise when I am done,
possibilities will ring true
endlessly in me.

JB Owen

"Anything and everything IS possible."

My intention is to write a story that truly inspires you. I want to share a moment in my life that profoundly changed me in the hope that it does the same for you. I wish that, by sharing my story, something magical Ignites inside you. Allow my excitement and discovery to be a flame that lights yours. We all have powerful moments that define us and refine us; may this story of creating what is possible be an inspiration for you to manifest and awaken all that is possible for you.

Anything *IS* Possible

I didn't know it at the time, but my story of wondrous possibilities began in Prague, Czechoslovakia, on a beautiful fall day in November. I was lying in bed in my elegant hotel room, nestled under the blankets, wrapped up in one of the fluffiest down comforters I had ever seen. In my marshmallow-like haven, I was staring up at the intricately carved ceiling, circling a glittering antique chandler. My husband and I were drinking champagne and eating a delectable array of European cheeses, meats, and delicacies arranged on a hearty charcuterie board. I was feeling amazing, having just returned from a most captivating evening performance of Mozart's classics at the stunningly refurbished Opera Hall. Life was delightful and the tingly feelings of bliss and contentment filled the room.

I was staring at the blooming rosettes carved into the ceiling and pondering my thoughts because my husband had just asked me what I wanted to do for my 50th birthday. It was still eight months away, but the big half-century mark was coming and in our relaxed state of indulgence, he inquired how I wanted to signify the auspicious occasion. Fifty seemed unfathomable to me. I actually had to stop to wrap my mind around the fact that I *was* soon to be 50. It was hard to imagine. I felt nothing like a 50-year-old. In my mind I was still 36: young, free, and dynamo. Fifty felt heavy and old, and I wanted nothing to do with it. But the question lingered in my bubbly-infused mind and I began to think, "What should I do to mark my 50th year?"

I didn't want to go skydiving; that seemed a bit extreme. I had been to the Great Wall of China, the Roman Colosseum, and the Eiffel Tower. I had worked on a cruise ship in my 20s, so no thank you to cruising. I had floated on a gondola in Venice, traversed by zip line in Costa Rica, swam with the sharks in Bora Bora, and cuddled with a koala bear in Australia. Going sightseeing somewhere didn't feel like that was a fit. Purchasing something extravagant wasn't a need. I lay there wracking my brain as to what would indicate that I had hit that monumental milestone.

As my husband topped up my glass, I sank deeper into the crisp cotton sheets and took in the rich aroma of the fig jam and caviar. I was marinating on what *was* going to be meaningful for my birthday. What would truly be special and epic? I started to scan my life and all that I have done, asking myself what had been the most enjoyable experiences. That led me to think of all the things I had wished for since I was a kid. I mentally traveled back in time to see what goals I had aspired to accomplish ever since I was little and asked myself what wish had slipped through my fingers and not been fulfilled? And then it hit me.

My entire childhood, I was into fashion, lavishly dressing up both myself and my dolls. I learned to sew very young so I could make my elaborate designs. I effervescently poured through fashion magazines until piles of them took over my room. At 16, I started modeling for fun and all I could think of was my desire to walk the glamorous Paris fashion shows and be on the cover of the prestigious Vogue™ magazine. At 17, I went to the big city to see a talent agent and kick off my career, and that was when I was told I was too fat to be a model!

"You'll never make it," he said, flicking his hand in the air a-la-mode. "You're too fat. You don't have what it takes. You might as well give up now; this isn't the life for you."

I walked out of his office and did just that. I gave up, gave in, and gutted any desire I had of becoming a model. He planted a seed of doubt in me and, like a curse of black magic, my mind was filled with thoughts of self-doubt and inadequacies. I steered my life away from modeling and went into fashion design instead. I forced myself to be happy with making clothing and parked away any desire to ever model again…

…until that moment in Prague.

With champagne bubbles and the air of possibilities swirling around me like the costumed clad dancers at the Opera, I thought about how I had let go of that dream like a child drops a ragged, unwanted toy. I didn't fight back. I didn't rally, lose weight, or show him I *could* do it, I simply *gave in*! I walked away and left my glittering dream to tarnish like an old penny does on the ground at a dirty subway stop.

I am not sure if it was the elixir of the alcohol, the fragrance of the rose-chocolate truffles, or the floating feeling from the feather-thick bed, but something stirred inside of me at that moment. Something surged forth like an excited colt, pushing through a membrane of ancient doubt. I decided to make becoming a fashion model at 50 possible for me.

I left Prague inspired and flew home with images of photoshoots, couture fittings, and sky-high Louboutins preculating in my future. I wanted to resurrect my dream from when I was 17; reaching for the brass ring to restart the light-filled carousel of ambition that had been dormant since my youth. I was going to knock on every door, turn over every rock, and do whatever it took to fulfill my idea of being on Vogue and strutting my walk at Fashion Week. I told my husband and my kids, and posted it boldly on social media: for my 50th birthday, I wanted to be a 50-year-old cover girl!

'*Road To Vogue*' became my new tagline and was #hashtagged everywhere. I started working out, dieting, calling agents, making logos, printing T-shirts, and declaring my desire to meet Vogue's Anna Wintour as soon as she would take my calls. I left dozens of messages, sent hundreds of emails, and took pictures in my bathing suit each month to track my slimming-down progress. I knew I was going to do whatever was required to make it possible. Nothing was going to stop me. Birthed in my mindset was the new belief that *anything and everything IS possible* if you choose it.

Of course, Anna never called; nor did Lagerfeld, nor Dior. The agents weren't getting back to me and the town I lived in seemed galaxies away from Paris or New York. And then the pandemic hit, clamping down on not just my but *everyone's* dreams. For months, I kept my hopes kindled, plastering my wall with an eight-foot vision board, amping up my social sharing, and starting a *Road to Vogue* blog. My birthday was looming, we were all sheltering-in, no more going to the gym, and the shortages of food had me eating processed concoctions I hadn't digested in decades. Yet, I was determined to prevail.

Still 16 pounds overweight and with 50 just two months away, I felt I had to do something to keep my illustrious dream alive. One day, while taking out the garbage, I noticed the tandem bicycle that was hooked on the side of the wall in our garage. My husband and I had not ridden it in over a year. I stared at it intently. It was like the bike was speaking directly to me. Its cobwebbed frame and dusty handlebars were screaming at me to take it for a ride. It pleaded like a puppy wanting to be let outside and set it loose. As I stared at it, I imagined my husband and I pedaling freely on the open road, riding with the wind in our hair. Pumping our legs. Filling our lungs. The sense of excitement I felt and the freedom it provoked was utterly alluring. That's when I got a bold idea: I decided I was going to cycle with my husband across Canada!

It didn't take long to get everyone on board. My family was used to my big visions and wild decisions. My husband and two daughters rallied with me as we mapped out the route, tuned up the bike, and packed the motor home for a two-month excursion biking 5,000 kilometers across five provinces to the eastern side of Canada. I was elated with the prospect of seeing my majestic homeland. I also wanted to push myself in every way to see what was truly possible. Many said I was crazy to get on a bike, cycle the highways, and risk the danger of being run over by semitrucks or other vehicles. Some said it was reckless and irresponsible to leave my home and business to venture out and travel during a pandemic. I decided this was my *Road to Vogue* and I was going to make my dream possible no matter what!

I didn't listen to the naysayers nor the critics. Instead, I dialed into the burning desire I had within. I heard the voice that said, "You got this. You can do this. And yes, it *is* possible." With only a month of training and a whopping amount of belief, my husband and I set off enthusiastically on the extensive ride across the great land of Canada.

The adventure was life-changing! From the vast yellow and purple fields of lavender and canola in Saskatchewan to the sparkling blue lakes that dotted across Ontario… from the lush green forests of the national parks to the raging ocean waves crashing off the east coast… my mind was tantalized, my body enriched, and my spirit awakened. Every single moment was magnificent. I saw colors in flowers I had never known, felt salt-air crisping on my lips, and watched in splendor as the awe-inspiring sunsets graced our evening rides in colors one can barely describe. It was a cornucopia for the senses and a painter's palette of visual delights. Every day was special. Each night when I lay in bed feeling the burn in my leg muscles or the sting of sunburnt shoulders, I felt closer to myself than I had ever had before.

On the tough days, when the rain beat down, seeping through my helmet, wetting my hair, and running down my neck into the back of my jacket, I cringed but toughed it out. When the hills were so long and arduous that I didn't think we could do it, I'd bellow out a rhyming singsong from my childhood to help get us to the top. When the tanker trucks raced past us, so close I could feel their draft suck us forward, I squealed with delight. When the cattle trucks passed by, leaving a trail of raw manure wafting through the air and into our nostrils, I'd sputter and gasp for fresh air, but we laughed it off. It was all just part of the trip, part of the process, and part of the dream. A myriad of things are part-in-parcel of the experience when we are determined to make something unique possible.

Early in our riding, we fell. A slippery patch of gravel in the fresh rain had us losing our footing and as we were on a tandem bike, both my husband and I went down. My daughters saw the whole event and my youngest was most concerned. She came running to my aid with an ice pack and blanket, worried I was hurt. And although my elbows and knees were bleeding, I was okay. I told her, "I signed up for this adventure and everything that came with it. Whatever happens is meant to happen, and I will get through it because I know this is for me."

My conviction was unwavering and once I said those words, I knew deep in my core that I would endure all of it. Whatever was thrown at me, whatever unfolded, however it went, I knew that by saying, "I signed up for this," I could do it. I would make it to the end.

We often don't know the wheels that are put in motion when we speak our truth. We can't see all the magical moves that are made on the big chessboard of life. We don't foresee the cosmic connections that are formed or the moving parts that make way for our dreams to materialize. We just believe. We choose, we decide, and then we faithfully pursue with all our might so that it *will* come true. I didn't know at the time of dreaming this big dream what I was setting in motion and making possible for me. I didn't know what I had called forth to come to me, nor did I realize the magnitude of what the Universe was doing to conspire devotedly on my behalf. While planning the trip and researching the ride, I had no clue of what I was making possible going forward. I didn't see the courage, pride, and blessings I was bringing forth. I didn't have an inkling of how saying yes to the ride was saying yes to all that was possible for the rest of my life.

On a freezing cold day riding through a mountain range, I came face to face with the very limits of my strength. Riding in a foggy rainstorm with visibility less than 10 feet ahead, I pushed my abilities to their very brink. The climb was steep, taking every once I had in me. The rain was coming down in the most torrential way and the tires spun and slipped on the drenched asphalt. The hairpin turns on the down slopes were so whited out by the fog that we had to ride the brakes nonstop. Trucks passed by, spraying sheets of water that almost knocked us into the ditch. My hands were ice cold from my soaked gloves. Water was dripping off my nose, my chin, and from the rim of my helmet into my straining eyes. Thank God I was on the back of the bike because I had to close my eyes, gasp for breath, and hang on with all my might as my husband took the brunt of the wind and water for me. Our follow vehicle had gone ahead, but they returned to look for us as the weather was so bad, they had grown concerned. As they approached, my daughter yelled at us to rack the bike and get in. I shook my head in disagreement and shouted, "I'm not stopping!"

I don't know why I refused. The conditions were hellish and with the single-lane traffic, imposing guard rails, zero visibility, and wet roads, we were facing the height of danger from every direction. It was the most treacherous situation I have ever put myself in and the most harrowing conditions two people on a tandem bike should ever want to face. Shouting into the pouring rain, my husband asked me why I refused to quit. I didn't have an answer. I just couldn't stop… I just wouldn't stop… I just had to keep going, keep pushing, keep doing it no matter what.

When the rain finally subsided and we made it through the mountain pass, we stopped at the next town. I laughed out loud as we approached the city's welcoming sign. It was a massive wood structure, towering above me with the word 'Marathon' boldly painted in bright tourist colors. The town was named Marathon! I couldn't stop laughing at the irony, the symbolism, and all that I had been through to get to that sign on that day, on a tandem bike, at 50! It was as if my entire life had been a marathon. It felt as if the race of my existence had been pushed to the pinnacle and arriving in Marathon signified my arrival into who I was born to be. It wasn't just a bike ride or an idea. It wasn't a magazine cover or a single catwalk, a pound on the scale, or a perceived idea. All the things that I thought were markers in my life were actually guideposts to my bigger destiny.

I'll confess I left Marathon a different person. So much had converged inside of me that I saw what was possible going forward. I realized that by making my ride possible, I had opened an entire treasure trove of what was possible for me. I didn't know when I started what I was making possible, but what I learned is that when you make one thing possible, you awaken anything and everything else that is possible.

You just have to take your shot. Leap full-out and capture your dream! You have to believe it *IS* possible and then make it so. There is nothing out there designed to stop you. Everything is there to mold you, guide you, and enliven you to what is possible for you! Push past your fears and limitations, ride your heart out, and climb that hill! What you want — wants you! When you make one thing possible, you make it *all* possible. Everything and anything *IS* possible for you! Your possibilities are just waiting for you.

IGNITE ACTION STEPS

See yourself doing your dream. Visualize your aspirations in such splendor that even Michelangelo would be jealous. Imagine yourself there. See the road, the path, the journey, and then see the finish line and you standing there. Flood yourself with all the feelings you will have when you get there. You need emotions and sensations to get the heart, mind, cells, and soul working in unison. Wrap yourself in all the beauty of your wishes and get a 360-degree view of all you desire. To truly reach what is possible for you, you have to immerse yourself in it. All of it, emotional, physically, mentally, and spiritually. Make one thing possible, and let that be the gateway to all that is possible for you.

JB Owen – Canada
Speaker, Author, Publisher, CEO of Ignite, JBO Global Inc. & Lotus Liners
www.jbowen.website
www.igniteyou.life
www.lotusliners.com
f *jbowen*
jbthepossibilitymaker

TRACI HARRELL

*"Trust your truth when it speaks to your heart and take action;
then you can make anything possible."*

**To the reader I offer my tale of purpose, peace, and power as a gift with
the goal of fueling your personal transformation and elevating your mind,
heart, and life to a new level of belief, action, and accountability. You can
'Ignite Possibilities' to accomplish anything in your life. Transformation
comes as you trust the truth when it speaks to your heart, and then act
on it. It is my sincerest intention that you will join me on a journey of
exploration, transformation, and inclusion — filled with facts, feelings,
spirituality, and practicality — to unlock a lifetime of infinite possibilities.**

TRUST YOUR TRUTH TO MAKE ANYTHING POSSIBLE

Have you ever imagined what your life would be like if you knew with
complete certainty that you could make anything possible? What if someone
had shared with you as a child that you had the answers inside of you to direct
your life — that you could tap into an internal power to *create* the life that you
desired? Would you be bolder and braver? Would you have less doubts, fear,
and hesitation about what you could make possible in your life?

For me, the answers were always, Yes. As a child, I learned about three key
principles that I surrendered to completely. The first, "Your thoughts become
things," so guard your mind. Second, "Your heart is your guide," so listen to the
truth inside of you. Finally, "You can achieve anything," so take action every

day to create the life of your dreams. These beliefs changed everything for me. They started my transformation into a person who fully believes anything is possible, despite all obstacles.

I was in the first grade when I learned that we all have creative powers that can shape our life experiences. First-grade Traci was adorable — carefree, innocent, and optimistic about everything. She loved flowers, wild birds, and butterflies (I still do). She was smart and sassy with a sweet smile and a heart of gold. She loved to wear her hair in two long ponytails, which her mother or sisters always adorned with matching bows or ribbons. Little Traci was not a girly-girl at all, but she liked her hair looking cute. She didn't play with baby dolls and would much rather be outside climbing a tree, playing in the garden, or skateboarding. But her biggest passion was reading; being transported to faraway places and discovering deep life lessons between the covers of her books. First-grade Traci was always happy because in her mind, there was no reason not to be; after all, she was a child of God (we all were). She trusted that she was loved and that the Creator was watching out for her.

I had learned early in life, in a backyard Bible Study, that the Creator of the Universe lived inside of us all, which meant I had a similar creative power within me. This created three lasting beliefs for me: 1) I was loved, never alone, and meant for something great; 2) the Spirit inside my heart would always show me the right thing to do; and 3) I could accomplish anything my little heart desired by tapping into this hidden power. This made me feel virtually invincible, completely confident, and filled with high expectations. Even in the first grade, I knew that I couldn't just use my powers for myself; I had to use my powers for something 'Bigger Than Me.'

When I first learned about the concepts of purpose, peace, and power, it was my mother, Daisy Charles, and my grandmother, Vertie Warren, who clarified and exemplified the fact that it was all *Fueled by Faith*. These ladies were the 'Queens of Igniting Possibilities.' In our house, we couldn't even say the word *"can't." Can't* was at the top of my mother's list of the worst four-letter words. She shared age-old wisdom about our beliefs, like "Whether you believe you can or can't accomplish something — you are right." As her shortcut to get her point across, Mom would often say, "Can't never could do nothing," and that always made me smile. Together, they also explained how the Power of Faith works. We are rarely shown exactly how we will achieve our goals, but that's the point… the power comes from the belief and trust – and knowing there is a higher force at work helping us to achieve our goals, if aligned with the true purpose for our lives.

I had learned that our Inner Spirit often only reveals that next right action for us to take. All we have to do is 'step out on faith' and do what we know in our hearts is right. When the truth speaks to you, you just know it. The trick is in actually following the truth without doubt or hesitation when it speaks to our heart. You can pray or meditate in silence to ask for confirmation, but trust is key. You must expect God and the universe to support you on your journey. I have gathered decades of research and scientific evidence that supports this phenomenon. I used to put the *Faith Factor* to the test with big things and little things alike. Each time, things would always work out in my favor, even if it didn't appear that way at the time. Eventually, no 'tests' were necessary — I just believed.

Like the time I almost drowned in a neighborhood lake. I remember the day clearly. It was a hot summer day in Florida, just beautiful, not a cloud in the bright blue sky. I was at Turkey Lake Park in Orlando, with my older siblings and some of their friends. We were in the water just playing around and cooling off. I had wandered off a little deeper than the others, just exploring a bit. I was walking out, testing the boundaries, to see how far I could go before the water got past my shoulders. Suddenly, my foot stepped into an underwater hole or I slipped off a ledge. All I remember was falling forward fast, head first, deep into the water. I recall going down quickly and seeing strange things in the darkness until I hit the bottom of the lake. I was 10 years old and maintained an inner peace, even though I was underwater for what seemed like forever. I either blacked out or blocked the memory because the next thing I remember, I was lying on the shore. My siblings were kneeling around me in a circle and looking quite worried. They seemed frozen for a moment, silent and still… then I heard one of them say, "Traci, we are glad you are okay, but please… whatever you do… don't tell Mama." I paused, smiled, and said, "Tell Mama what?" We all laughed. That was a close one for me. It could have been the end. I wasn't afraid (well maybe for a minute), but in my heart I knew I would be saved. My sister's friend Donna gets the credit for going in after me. She was a hero that day. She took immediate action; it was clearly a Divine moment. I knew I would be okay. Inside, I had perfect peace. I was meant for something great, and I was grateful.

I was a Black girl born in the South in 1969, just one year after Dr. Martin Luther King, Jr., was assassinated. As I grew up, he became my hero. He was a man of God and a Civil Rights leader who also believed that no matter what happened to his people, he had faith that things could, and would, get better. I knew that someday I would make things better, too. I didn't know how or when, but I knew societal impact was my destiny. We all have a purpose in life and when we find that purpose, we must just surrender to our Higher Power, then listen and allow that voice from within to guide us.

My core values include: Peace, Joy, Justice, and Progress. The topics of Racial Equity, Justice, and Inclusion were always something that deeply impacted me. This was an area where I really put my faith to the test. So many things happened to my people, to Black people, that just weren't right. When would this get better? I have been traumatized over the years from seeing Black people like George Floyd murdered on TV, to having my own devastating experiences of exclusion at work, to enduring threatening looks from my own neighbors. The optimist in me often bottled it up inside and tried to find something positive to focus on. I had no choice but to believe that things would get better.

When I think about the key milestones in my journey for Racial Equity and Inclusion, I realize that my heightened awareness started back in school when I first saw a documentary during Black History Month about the murder of 14-year-old Emmett Till. His courageous mother had experienced an atrocity and wanted the world to bear witness to what had been done to her child — torture and an actual lynching. Like countless times before, the killers were not convicted. There was no justice, and I had no peace, and neither did so many in the Black community. That was the moment when I knew I would never want to have children in this country. The pain and fear of protecting my child from psychological, emotional, or physical harm would be too great to bear. We can't keep our children safe. We can't even keep ourselves safe from harm. It can all be too much.

Another mother who triggered my trauma response — while also showing a queen's quotient of grace — was Trayvon Martin's mother. Trayvon was an unarmed teen that was brutally murdered in my hometown, near Orlando, Florida. My best friend lived just five minutes from where he was gunned down. He had been walking home from the store carrying skittles and an iced tea when he was followed and killed by a dude from the neighborhood watch who thought he looked 'suspicious.' Despite community outrage and months of peaceful protests, his murderer was set free under a 'stand-your-ground' law. The injustice of it all was again too much to bear, but that was all we could do: suck it up, hold it in, and pray that it didn't happen to another child… to your child.

Sometimes it feels like the message to all our children is that we don't matter. But our lives DO matter. Our safety matters. If I could talk to first-grade Traci, I would assure her that no matter what happens in this world, she absolutely matters.

I realized that I have been building the mental and spiritual fortitude to amplify this message for over 40 years. I still believed that anything was possible. Each day, year after year, my *faith and beliefs* grew stronger, although I didn't always see the desired manifestations in my life. I still allowed my life to be led by faith, and that made all the difference. Despite so many challenges and heartbreak, I have led a happy and productive life because I both believed and acted on what felt right in my heart.

My *beliefs* shaped everything for me. And my family, faith, and favorite authors helped to shape my understanding of those beliefs. The ultimate truth I relied on for everything was my belief in God. I have also read over 1000 books, which contributed to my unshakeable belief that we all possess creative powers in our hearts and minds to shape our future and impact the lives of others. For first-grade Traci, the only knowledge she needed was the power of Faith and the Belief that good will conquer all. It was simple.

I truly couldn't understand why everyone didn't think this way. Why wasn't everyone confident in their abilities to change their lives... to positively impact the world... to Ignite Possibilities? I felt lucky and blessed to have started gathering this insight so early in life, but I also felt a tremendous responsibility to share it. I would find my point of activation in a place I didn't expect.

As a young adult, I hoped that by going into Corporate America, I might gain some expertise that would help to change lives in my community. I also thought I would experience less exclusion and be somewhat safer around people who seemed to say the right things. Unfortunately, the racial injustice and exclusion in society also happens in business, just in a different way; and we aren't talking about it like we should. There are known challenges of exclusion that anyone in a minority position may experience, including Unconscious Bias, Similarity Bias, Unequal Performance Standards, and a Lack of Leadership Accountability. When we experience these things, when we don't feel *valued,* don't feel *safe*, and we don't have *trust*, we walk a tightrope with an unbearable load on our shoulders. When you add in the compound trauma of the societal injustices, it goes beyond being 'too much.' It can destroy your faith, break your heart, and crush your spirits.

I have always been the type of leader who will fight harder for someone else than I will for myself. Over the years, I have encountered many young professionals who came to me for support and advice as an experienced leader and community advocate. They often shared that they were feeling 'unwanted,' 'uncomfortable,' and others were 'tormented' based on experiences of bias and exclusion in business. Their stories were consistent with all my research. I knew that I had to stand up for what was right. I always took extra leadership roles, internal and external, to fight for inclusion and make things better for the next generation. My purpose was clear; but progress was not what it needed to be. This was 'Bigger Than Me.'

The moment that changed everything for me happened five years ago. I was sitting in my office across from a young girl who said she wanted to commit suicide because she was about to be fired. Overall, it was a great company with good leaders, but there is a 'system' that she was caught in (that we were all in), and I knew I needed to be part of the solution. The experience she shared was traumatic for her… and for me, too, just listening. I hoped I could make a small difference. I couldn't help Emmett. I couldn't help Trayvon. But it wasn't too late for me to help this girl. She was the first in her family to go to a full-time university (like I was), and the first to 'make it' by getting an amazing high-paying job in Corporate America. There is a huge community responsibility and burden that comes with being 'the first.' We laughed and cried together, and she felt relieved — freed of her shame… and empowered. I offered to call her mother. I wanted her family to know that she was not a failure. She had not failed her family or her community; we had failed her. The 'system' had failed us all.

That moment changed me. My mission is to do more to make Inclusion possible. We *all* carry this responsibility; we are ALL part of the system. I was now putting my actions into overdrive to fulfill my destiny… our shared destiny… to *'Lead Change and Build Legacy.'* I have been perfectly groomed for this journey. So many people continue to experience the same trauma of *exclusion*. I know we can do better… together.

This was going to be remarkable and transformational. I was ready. I knew how to tap into my inner power and to let the Spirit guide me to take action. I was confident and fearless, which is what the combination of purpose, peace, and power produces. I had to fight for what was right. First-grade Traci still believed in the goodness of others. She believed that if we really wanted to see a different outcome, together we could drive change. My core values of justice and progress demanded action and accountability. I was inspired and fully committed. If not me, if not you, if not us… then who? If not now, then when?

So, I started a quest, one that is already making a real difference. We now focus on bringing the right leaders together who are truly ready to transform hearts and minds — those ready to focus on Awareness, Action, and Accountability. I am now living out my purpose and my passion: "We are helping Leaders to change the status quo at a systemic level by increasing their ability to lead authentically, learn collectively, and build collaboratively™" with a process called, *Embracing Transformational Leadership with Heart & Soul*™. We are inviting leaders around the world to join our Inclusion journey as part of the *Bigger Than Me Movement*™. We have even started our next compilation book titled *How to Ignite Inclusion*. Nothing feels better than being completely on purpose and doing what you love while leading change and building legacy. Miracles are already flowing, which is my confirmation that I'm aligned with my destiny.

If I could go back to talk to first-grade Traci, I know she would be proud. I am still optimistic and positive. I still love flowers and seek joy. Most importantly, I still Believe. Inclusion IS possible. Together, we CAN be the change we want to see. Let's do this!

You have the same power inside of you. When your purpose is clear, it's easier to stay focused on your values and to listen to the Truth of your heart. When you hear that voice from within, surrender to it. Whether you believe in God or something else, all you need to know is that there is a universal force synergistically working for your good. On your journey of transformation to Ignite your Possibilities, know that you were meant for greatness. Embrace gratitude as a regular practice. Amplify your expectations fueled by faith. Take action to manifest miracles and power in your life. Go! Ignite Your Possibilities!

IGNITE ACTION STEPS

- **Find your purpose and passion, then follow your heart.** You can find your purpose when you explore what you are most passionate about, combined with what you do well, and where you can contribute to the world.
- **Spend time in nature and in silence to replenish your peace and power.** The first step to activate your power is to believe that you have an inner strength that is available to you. Then, faith is needed to sustain your next right actions.
- **Know that you have the truth and power inside of you.** When you follow your heart and take action, anything is possible. You've got this!!

Traci Harrell – United States of America
President, It's All Bigger Than Me Consulting
Founder, It's All Bigger Than Me Ministry
www.ItsAllBiggerThanMe.com

FRANCIS PICHÉ

"Your greatest hidden treasure is your power of creation. Unlock it, reclaim it, and choose what makes your heart come alive."

My intention is to show you that unlimited possibilities exist when we follow our heart and unlock our power to create. Nothing can stop us from creating the life we want. The miracles in your life are a direct correlation between choosing what makes your heart come alive and honoring the truth of your gifts. The treasure in you can either light up the world or be dimmed by your self-limiting beliefs. It is entirely up to you to choose how you want to use your creative power. My hope is that you will become what you envision and feel deeply in your heart; that you will have the courage to choose who you want to become.

REAWAKENING YOUR CREATOR WITHIN

"I have homework for you. It's a challenge and you are not going to like it. Will you commit to it?" I sat across from my life coach, Gary, ready for him to push me toward all I was eager to accomplish. "What!? Yes!" I replied with a tone of frustration. I didn't know what the challenge was, but I knew I could trust my coach.

"I want you to do nothing for three days." I was taken aback. "Nothing? What do you mean nothing?" I felt I would lose so much time. After so much procrastination, I had just committed to take action on a new business idea.

"Yes nothing. No journaling, no reading, no audiobook, no training…

nothing!" Gary repeated. He was calm, but my mind was still racing. "Well, what about my clients?" I asked urgently. I was a real estate agent and prospecting to generate business was crucial for survival.

"Only if you really need to, but nothing else." He laughed. "You are sneaky!" he said, acknowledging my struggle to adjust. I tried to make sense of his unexpected proposal, which I had already accepted beforehand.

"Wow, what am I supposed to do then? Meditate, see friends, or go explore nature?"

"Yes to all of that," he replied with a smile.

It was almost five years ago that I had arrived at Gary's office, determined to focus on my life's mission, not on my recently broken-off second engagement. My ex-fiancé and I had revived our relationship because we never forgot the love we felt and rekindling it was exciting. But my wounds were cut open again. I'd had enough of my misery with love and I was looking to numb the pain. All I wanted was to think about something else, me, and finally work on my life's purpose. Mission first, I thought. Relationships will come after.

To find my purpose, I thought that I just needed to focus on my strengths. I was great in sales, leveraging my 16 years of experience and the many accolades for my communication and speaking skills. I knew that I was equipped to help people gain influence through sales and communication training. I had invested so much time and money in coaching: business, communication, online marketing, and even voice coaching. On top of that, I was passionate about happiness. So, why not create an online program around it? It was logical. You focus on what you are good at and the harvest will come. I felt that it was a better choice than being dedicated to a career in real estate — a career I no longer loved. All I had to do was make the magic happen!

My mission, although unclear, *had* to come first. That's the mindset I had when I entered the room at my coach's office. After I shared my thoughts about my purpose with Gary, he asked me a powerful and disturbing question, "What about your big dream, Francis?" My teeth clenched with resentment. His question confronted me and I didn't like how uncomfortable it made me feel.

Although everything I said made sense to any stranger, Gary knew me better and was able to read between the lines. As much as I wanted to push back and ask why we were talking about this NOW after all those years of coaching, I knew that he knew I was selling myself short; playing small. My soul's potential was way bigger.

"Now that you have agreed to the challenge," he said, "I want you to open your agenda and write in exactly five years from now, 'This is the day that I die.' Now the question is, what will you do until then Francis?" My heart knew the answer immediately. And like a needle oscillating between two magnets, it was polarized, and instantly pulled in one direction.

He followed this with more questions: What's the point of living? What will be your legacy? Who do you want to be with? Who do you want to become? I heard my heart speaking out, ready to announce the real things I had been wishing for. I opened my mouth to answer, but Gary raised his hand and stopped me, saying, "I don't want the answer. Tell me in three days."

My mindset when I left his house that day was completely different to the one I entered with, and it changed my life forever. I took the challenge to heart. His questions resonated in my consciousness for three days. During those three days of stillness and living fully without a to-do list, I gave so much space to my mind to download the proper information from my heart.

Everything slowed way down. I still remember the observation my friend Ali made while we were having a coffee on a Friday afternoon: 'Wow you look so calm brother." And in response to his special request: "Are you free to stay a little longer? Do you have time?" I responded with, "Plenty!"

I took the time to walk on the street and a sense of serenity and reverence for life filled my heart. I felt the gifts from the present moment. I noticed the essence of life and I started to envision my dream with excitement and love.

I saw myself conducting entertaining interviews of famous people, talking on big stages, and filling millions of hearts with inspiration. I saw how impactful I could be globally and the legacy I could leave. For the first time, it was not about the money. I thought, "If I can do this and make enough to pay my bills, I will be so happy!" Excited and enlivened, I desperately wanted to write down these ideas. But I couldn't because I was following the rules of the challenge. I was scared of losing my thoughts so I decided to trust that my intuition would help me crystalize the essential ideas.

This challenge marked the debut of my journey to build the life I had always imagined. It provided so much clarity, conviction, and new perspective, and became the genesis of my new company. The ignition of energy I felt from having a clear purpose fueled vigorous action toward my dream. I decided to create a documentary to illustrate the element most necessary to create the life we dream of. I called it *Resilience Element*.

I incorporated my new business, hired a graphic designer, created a new logo, got it trademarked, and built the website in a few short weeks. I was in flow. I was even invited to speak about resilience at various events and audiences seemed to resonate with the idea. The Universe was conspiring to help me realize my dream. I was elated.

I was still a real estate agent but I noticed it no longer made my heart come alive. I felt so vibrant working on *Resilience Element*. I envisioned the company helping people reawaken their inner power and mastering their mindset to transform their life, all underpinned by an engaging, conscious, social, and technology platform offering transformative content, events, and documentaries. How could I not be thrilled with this?

My problem was that it wasn't financially sustainable. I had already decided to sell my condo a few years back to give myself the opportunity to go for my dreams. As my money depleted, fear started creeping in. I felt that I couldn't fully focus on one career. A dream takes time to build but the pressure made me nervous and even nauseous. I felt desperate to get more real estate sales just to survive. It felt heavy to sink back into the mire of something I was trying to leave behind. Doubts crept in about revealing my dream to others who expected me to stay grounded, and well-meaning support from those who wanted me to be realistic began to chip away at my confidence.

Still determined, toward the end of 2017, I took a leap of faith and hired a local filmmaker to create a promotional video to invite support for my crowd-funding campaign. My objective was to create a documentary trailer as a demo for filmmakers interested in creating the whole project. With gusto and excitement, I asked friends if they would be willing to donate their time to attract donations. I forged through and promoted my mission with live videos on Facebook™. The project didn't hit the target but raised approximately $8,000. I needed more capital and my friend JoAnne helped me vet the filmmaker who would create a trailer with a bootstrap budget, and also offered to use her own credit card, with the understanding I would pay her back. The financial pressure was multiplying exponentially.

We moved forward with the strategy to film the interviews in New York in July. I saw an opportunity to be in front of Lindsey Stirling in her live show in New Jersey so I purchased the 'meet and greet' VIP tickets for me and my film crew. My fear of rejection paralyzed me, stopping me from asking her to join my mission. Click! The photo with Lindsey was done and we were gone. I was a bit depressed my insecurities had held me back. My heart knew that I was playing small — it created an inner conflict each time I didn't fulfill my true potential and embrace my fears. So, I resolved that I would connect with her again and next time I would do things differently.

While the post-production work on the trailer was progressing nicely, I reconnected with a friend who was a successful serial entrepreneur from Montreal. He was interested in investing in my company and offered his social platform as the backbone of our mobile-based technology. Thanks to his expertise, we were well-positioned to attract venture capital. A few months later, I had a sealed partner agreement in my pocket and I felt almost invincible. I knew I could count on their financial commitment to attend international events and retreats to observe what the marketplace had to offer. With faith, I cranked the credit cards once more until I could get the investment money from the partners. My self-confidence paid off fast in terms of connection. It was filled with magical synchronicities that led to the meeting of our company's existing President and our Chief Resilience Officer.

The book *The Alchemist* tells us, "Every search begins with beginner's luck. And every search ends with the victor's being severely tested." In 2020, the pressure to fund the various initiatives started to take a toll on my psyche. COVID hit and although the partners promised over $190,000, some kept delaying their scheduled commitments to pay. I had gone ALL IN and I was frustrated by the lack of commitment from my partners. I had to be creative to sustain my living, and debt started to accumulate on all my credit cards and line of credits. I told myself one more month and I will be fine. One more month here and there but it never happened. All that time. All that worry. All that unnecessary suffering and wasted emotion, tearing down my energy and my usual positive outlook. I felt locked in and financially wounded. The fear of spending an extra dollar on things dragged me down. It was an awful feeling of lack; of shame and failure, and I physically trembled at times in fear of not being able to sustain myself.

I was barely surviving scrutinizing each expense. Never in my life had I had to be so careful. I almost wanted to purge each time I was at the cash counter… hoping and praying the transaction wouldn't be rejected. My load of debt to my parents was already maxed out. I felt engulfed with guilt and regret from the choice I made to go all in. I was plagued with questions. Why was I so committed while others weren't? How could I survive this without going back to real estate with my tail between my legs, so embarrassed that I had not kept my promise of company success to my financial backers? Then one day, I realized I had spent all of my effort trying to force the outcome of receiving the due money. The only reason why I didn't impose the terms and conditions of the agreement was, again, my fear of losing their support.

By the end of 2020, my fear actualized and I didn't get the finances I was promised. I felt betrayed, and was tired of chasing money. I felt I would let down the few amazing partners who had gone all in with me, but I had to do the right thing. I had to face my fear and give the partners who hadn't paid, a choice to either fulfill their commitment or be taken away from the project. I felt a weight lift instantly as I made the choice to swallow my pride, be vulnerable, and move forward. As I came into this knowing, letting go of the anchor I had been dragging behind me, I felt a sense of release. What might have been anger was replaced with conviction, and would eventually give way to gratitude for the lesson I had been allowed to learn through this experience. It was a critical moment for me and a huge lesson of leadership. Surprisingly, the remaining partners were very supportive and that gave me wings. I was able to emerge from the deep sea and not be swallowed by it. I was determined to pursue my mission; to create the future I desired, just as I had created the setbacks in the same way.

The best life lesson had just emerged: you are ultimately the creator of your own life. I got to understand the power that nobody can take away from me: my way of *BE*ing that creates everything. I accepted 100 percent responsibility of the temporary defeat. I embraced it and I owned it. I knew it was just a question of time. I became friends with my fears and I knew that the only reason why I didn't succeed was because I put myself in purgatory waiting for an outcome to show up. I realized that I mostly lived in fear the entire year and what had manifested mirrored my thoughts and emotions.

Instead of being upset, I regained energy. My conviction about my mission never faltered and kept me alive. I was willing to do whatever it took to continue even if it meant using my pension funds that I was told to NEVER touch. As I put my attention and energy on possibility, not scarcity, I began to feel and expect success.

Today, I am grateful for the lesson. I understand and I know deep in my core the unstoppable power of creation that I have, which we ALL have. The most intense setback I ever had resulted in the most beautifully rewarding lesson I could have ever imagined. I grew to be bigger than my fear of failure, my challenges, and my external circumstances. I hold the *BE*lief that I will reach my mission and this is why dreams are possible.

It can take time or we may fail, but we will always get an invaluable lesson if we stay committed to walking on the path of our dreams. Putting our fears to the side feels like unlocking the secret code and hearing the "click" to open the magic vault of happiness where all the wondrous treasures of life are waiting for us to enjoy. We think of possibilities. We are the possibilities. With a fulfilled heart, we become creative and we find all the solutions that already existed for us to discover. We have elevated our consciousness to find them. Like Einstein said: "No problem can be solved from the same level of consciousness that created it."

So now my friends, what do you want to create with the time you have left in your life? You either wait or you create. You choose. Who will you choose to become?

IGNITE ACTION STEPS

Conviction: Ask yourself who you would truly want to become if you only had five years left to live. Let your heart speak. Forget about the how and take small steps daily toward your goal.

Certainty: How would you feel if your dream or goal was already accomplished? Start by taking inventory of what you are already grateful for in your life and involve all your senses while imagining your new possibilities. Feel worthy of them.

Courage: When obstacles present themselves on the path, know that life is presenting a gift such as a lesson that will help you move forward. Think about a major challenge you already had in your life and find the silver lining. You can expect the same benevolence. Remember your strength and surround yourself with people that believe in you. Don't be too hard on yourself. See your future self giving you a big hug for the breakthrough you are about to have.

Francis Piché – Canada
Resilience Into Results Mindset Coach
www.francispiche.com

SAM HUMPHREY

"Failure isn't the end of the road; it's really the beginning."

I hope to inspire people by demonstrating that no matter what your challenges or obstacles are in life, nothing is impossible. All you need is self-confidence, determination, a lot of hard work, and a single opportunity. My hope is that I can empower you to achieve anything your heart or mind conceives. You can experience the most unforgettable moments and live life without regrets. Nothing can stop you.

FROM NEAR DEATH TO HOLLYWOOD

My life has consisted of extreme highs and lows, a nonstop roller coaster; a journey of living and dying. In my first six weeks of being alive I was challenged with survival. Since then, I've been in and out of the hospital more times than I can count. I shouldn't even be alive today!!

There were many complications prior to my birth. In the last month of pregnancy, my parents and doctors discovered that I was not growing. Upon delivery I was placed into an incubator. The doctors expressed their concerns about my life expectancy. One doctor had said to my mom, "I don't know what the future holds for your baby." My parents were stunned, they didn't know how to accept the news; to my mom, it sounded as though I was going to die at any moment. And I was.

Despite my circumstances, I prevailed. At the age of 3, I was diagnosed with a very rare genetic condition called 'Acrodysplasia,' which can also be referred to as 'skeletal dysplasia.' To put into layman's terms, it simply means my bones don't develop to that of a "normal" person my age and I am, and always will be, smaller than most. As a kid I didn't understand any of this. All I knew was that I was very different. As I got older, I still didn't really understand why I was so different. I felt unattractive and ugly. My teeth were so badly deformed due to my condition and I hated my smile. Everyone would tell me I was unique and special, but I didn't care.

I didn't want to be special or unique; I just wanted to fit in. I didn't understand why I couldn't be normal... I often asked myself how I could be accepted and loved by others, being the way that I am.

I grew up in a Christian home and spent the bulk of my time at church. I was taught that God never makes mistakes and that he is perfect, but at the time I couldn't understand why he would create me to be and look so different. If he was so loving and just, why was I burdened with these challenges? I thought that I was a mistake. I have a loving family who supported me and treated me the same as any other member in the family (for the most part). At home, I felt safe and comfortable. To my family, I was simply short, though it wasn't always easy to pretend that life was normal. I can remember moments when I felt so alone; no one could understand me or the emotional pain I was burying inside. There were moments at home when, as an adult, I still felt very different and small; like when people came around to the house that didn't know me and started talking down to me or using language that you would use to speak to a 5-year-old. Because of this I never wanted to meet new people, which made me a very reserved kid; I was tired of not being treated or accepted for who I was.

Growing up with my condition was tough. My family did their best to create a normal environment at home, which for them they didn't really know any different; there were obvious adjustments that were made around the house to make life easier for me. For example, the kitchen was arranged so that I had plates, bowls, cups, and other everyday things accessible to me.

Acting was a natural fit for me. My first love of acting came when I was just 5 years old; my family friends' kids (Olivia and Ben), my older brother and sister (Josiah and Esther), and I were putting on these mini productions for our parents. I also wanted to join the army during that time. I pretended to train for the physical exam and was excited to be a soldier. At that age the possibilities of what I could be were limitless; anything was possible.

At age 8, I saw Hugh Jackman for the first time, acting in X-MEN™ on the big screen and at home on the TV. I made fake claws from cardboard and wanted to be Wolverine. I ran around my house pretending to fight like him.

Running around yelling, stabbing, and slashing at the pretend enemies. From that day, he became my role model and inspired me to pursue acting and follow in his footsteps as an actor, producer, and philanthropist, though it would take me a long time to actually do that.

I was a very shy kid though that was the least of my problems. I was always sick and this affected my education. My family and doctors were confused by many of my physical and mental developmental issues because although Acrodyplasia does affect my entire physiology and overall health, it couldn't explain all of the symptoms I was having. Around the age of 15, the doctors in Australia finally gave me a diagnosis for why I was so ill all the time: Crohn's disease, yet another incurable mutation. I was already dealing with so much and on top of all this I now had an additional and very serious health issue that would present further challenges for me to live with.

Then came high school and my challenges were only about to multiply. It's like someone flipped a switch and the intensity of being a teenager increased. I was already different and was dealing with challenges like coming to terms with my own mortality or feeling attractive to the opposite sex. I felt anxious, unworthy, depressed, not accepted, suicidal. I was so caught up in who did and didn't like or love me, it felt like a matter of life and death. I didn't feel like I belonged in the world.

High school was a very emotional period, both physically and mentally. I was not a "normal" teenager. Anyone who knew me in high school would say that I was a very happy, friendly, down-to-earth, confident, and easygoing kid. On the surface that was my disguise. Because I was an actor, being able to hide my realness and vulnerability came naturally. No one knew that I was unhappy. No one knew that I thought of suicide. They never knew the pain behind the smile or the sadness and depression underneath the laughter. While I was smiling, confident, and full of joy at school; on the inside I was filled with fear and self-doubt. Having missed so much school because of my Acrodysplasia and desperate not to be left behind, my feelings were amplified times ten.

My siblings were both academically bright, and that only added more pressure on me to succeed. With all that my family had to do to support me, I felt like a burden. I still sometimes feel like that today.

One of the symptoms of my diagnosis was delayed maturation, so I looked and sounded years younger than my teenage classmates. No one wanted to date me; I was 16 but sounded and looked like I was 8 years old. No girl wants to feel like they're dating a kid, let alone deal with the judgmental stares/opinions that society would perceive about the relationship. My voice sounded like a chipmunk and I was less than three-feet tall. I was the cheery best friend to girls but never the one they dated.

I struggled to accept myself, the way I looked and felt about my image. I couldn't look in the mirror without wanting to change everything about myself. I would smile in the mirror, at friends in school, and in photos for social media, but it was a fake smile and I didn't love the smile I saw smiling back at me. Behind that smile was a lot of pain. I couldn't accept myself, and it was reinforced by strangers' comments, stares, and whispers; I was my own worst enemy. Not receiving the love that I wanted and feeding lies to myself that I wasn't good enough... didn't have anything to offer... couldn't measure up to others (especially my siblings)... no one would love me... or want to have a family with me... led me to a very dark place during my teen years. I tried several times to commit suicide. I couldn't see a reason to continue on. My life seemed to have run its course. If what the doctors said were true, I didn't want to keep being a burden on my family or pointlessly existing only to die a few years later. If I was going to die, I wanted to end it on my terms.

When my family discovered how many times I had tried to end my life, they were shocked. They knew I was struggling, but didn't know my desperation. They had this perception of who I was and I didn't want to destroy that. When you're struggling and in a vulnerable position, no one wants to show that. Everyone wants to seem like they have it all together. Everyone kept telling me that I was such a strong person, being able to deal with this. I didn't want to ruin that. I was just trying to get through one moment, one day, one emotional crisis after the other, hoping eventually I would get to the end of the tunnel and it would all be okay. The only way for me to feel like there was going to be a light at the end of it all was to fake it until I made it.

After graduating high school at 18, I seemed to be thriving. I simply kept looking forward to being grateful and having an attitude of extreme gratitude for both the big things and especially the little things. I worked several jobs including admin, cleaning, retail, sales, education, and finally hospitality at a casino in Melbourne, Australia, but while they paid the bills, none of these satisfied or stimulated my creative mind.

Growing up in the shadow of my older brother was tough. I was always known as 'Josiah's brother.' He ran a very successful tech development company called "Appster." Over the years, we would have many one-to-one deep talks, where he would give advice and share his experiences to inspire and push me. He never sugarcoated or pulled his punches during these talks. He said you've got to take risks and give it everything you have. Similarly, my youth pastor would say, "The only way to know if you're going to be an actor is to give it a real shot." While I dabbled at acting, I let my fear of failure hold me back. If I didn't try that hard, then I couldn't really fail.

One day, my brother and I were sitting in my dad's car outside my brother's office building in Melbourne. It was late afternoon and we were waiting for Dad so we could go out for dinner. I was in the front passenger seat and my brother was in the back. He was living in the city then and we didn't see each other that often, so we were just chatting and catching up when Josiah suddenly asked me, *"If you had all the money and time in the world… What would you do?"*

He already knew the answer before he even asked the question, but I had never allowed myself to admit it.

The answer came automatically: "I would be an actor."

He knew this already, and after sharing with him yet again, he started laying it on heavy: what was I doing? I wasn't taking the risks. What had I really done to make it happen? I knew I should be doing certain things, but I wasn't doing them because I didn't want to fail. He was driving home what I already knew, and I started to get emotional. His probing questions made me realize I wasn't really trying. It finally clicked inside my head: *I was born to be an actor.*

I began to change my mindset. I admitted to myself that acting was my true passion, my biggest ambition, and what I had dreamed about since childhood *was* a possibility for me. Since I was born, doctors had told my parents that my future was very uncertain and it was unlikely that I would live past my 18th birthday; if I did, they said, *"We are unsure of the quality of life he will have."*

I was determined to make a career from acting, and I wanted to live my life with no regrets. At 22 years old, I outlived what the doctors had expected: being alive. This was the year where it all changed. After quitting my job in hospitality, I refocused my vision and ambitions. I wasn't gonna waste any more time on things that weren't propelling me forward. I remember standing in my bedroom looking out the window and I had this intuitive feeling. I told myself: *"I will work with Hugh Jackman and walk the red carpet one day."* I didn't have a clue how I was going to make that happen, no idea where or when, but I just knew I was going to do it.

In pursuit of my dream, I invested every dollar I had (about $3,000) into shooting a showreel called *Ricochet*. I believed without a doubt that this was the right move. Shortly afterward, a very close friend, Olivia Shvias, chose me as a young person to follow in a documentary as part of her not-for-profit orga-nization, *Attitude Live*. The organization documented my life as an individual with a rare ability pursuing my ambition to be an actor. They filmed behind the scenes while I shot my showreel and lined up a mock audition for the famous TV series *Neighbours* in Australia. At that audition, I impressed the casting director so much that they decided to create a role specifically for me: "James Udagawa," a young finance whiz kid.

I believed in my skills and talent and everyone called me 'a natural,' however, this was my first professional audition with a casting director. Up till then, most of my experience was from studying drama during high school and attending a few minor certificate-level courses and workshops. I had no major formal training with drama-theatrical schools. The audition for *Neighbours* validated my talent because I was now a *professional working actor*. That validation was the confirmation I was hoping for; that I had a lot to offer with my unique gift for acting, film production, and my authentic charismatic personality. I started to believe in the possibilities that could become available for me, helping me to accept myself for who I am.

I began auditioning for more parts and roles, aspiring for bigger films and projects. Within a few weeks of being cast in the role on *Neighbours*, I was at home watching TV. I heard a 'ping' and glanced at my phone. It was an email notification saying, *"We just heard back that Sam has been approved by the studio for the role of Charles Stratton/Tom Thumb! Sam is going to get an offer."* I had just landed my first major role in a Hollywood feature film, Hugh Jackman's *The Greatest Showman*. I was completely stunned, my mind began racing a million miles an hour. So many thoughts running through my brain, trying to process the news and holding back waves of constant nervousness; such a surreal feeling. I could hardly believe it as I told my family. It was my dream coming true!! Being cast as Tom Thumb *aka* Charles Stratton next to Hugh Jackman surpassed my wildest expectations. This was my time to shine, my big break. I was off to Hollywood.

For seven months, I was acting alongside some of the best people in the industry. I was living full-out. It was mind-blowing to be working with them, as one of their co-stars and colleagues! It goes to show that determination, commitment, and belief can make anything possible.

The next thing that I made possible was getting my 'MILLION DOLLAR' smile. After *The Greatest Showman*, I had earned enough money to pay for my teeth to be fixed. I felt truly confident in not just the external way I looked, but internally. I could feel the shift in my mindset. I could look in the mirror with a newfound sense of love for myself; I loved my body and my smile even more. I remember having a conversation with my sister on the phone, telling her that my new smile endowed me with the confidence to embrace whatever possibilities this world could throw at me.

I am now a positive, confident, strong, and resilient person. I have fought my way through all those character-building challenges — all the impossibilities that I thought were my destiny — to not only survive but to thrive. I now see unlimited possibilities for my life going forward. What I thought was once impossible for someone dealing with such overwhelming odds to simply live was now a reality and many more possibilities lay on the horizon; my story really is climbing from near death to Hollywood.

You can experience the most unforgettable moments and live life without regrets. Nothing can stop you. If this world wasn't designed for you, change it. Redesign it. Any little dream is possible. As PT Barnum says, "We *can* live in a world that *we* design."

IGNITE ACTION STEPS

It takes a lot of self-confidence, determination, and hard work to be ready to embrace the opportunities that present themselves to you. Every day, I try to live by these five rules for mental health to keep my confidence and determination high.

- Express extreme gratitude every single day.
- Spread love to both self and others.
- Be positive with your attitude and outlook.
- Self-care is vital. It's not selfish to take care of yourself.
- Speak positive affirmations. Words have power.

Sam Humphrey – New Zealand & United States of America
Actor, Producer, Motivational Speaker, Author, Rare Advocate
© *@thesamhumphrey*
🅕 *Sam Humphrey*

ANDREW KAP

"Feel good for just five minutes a day, and watch the magic unfold."

It is my sincere intention that what I share with you today provides you with a brand new perspective on gratitude you never would have otherwise discovered. Surprisingly enough, this is the key to dramatically improving your quality of life through just five minutes of focusing on whatever makes you feel good each and every day. Inviting wonderful possibilities into your life really is that easy. And it really is that simple. Take it from me, you'll be absolutely overjoyed when you get there.

TURNING MY WORST WEEK INTO MY BEST LIFE

Does the Law of Attraction actually work?

If you've ever found yourself going down the rabbit hole of self-improvement, I can almost guarantee that's a question you've inevitably asked yourself at one point or another. And if you still don't have an answer, sit back, relax, and allow me to help clear a few things up for you.

Before diving in, just to make sure we're on the same page, I should probably admit I know this whole idea of the Law of Attraction can sound a bit ridiculous, especially the first time you hear it.

I mean, really, "Thoughts become things?"

"Like attracts like?"

"What you think about creates new possibilities?"

It doesn't exactly line up with everything we're taught by our parents or teachers growing up. With decades of conditioning telling us the opposite, one can't be blamed for having their doubts. I know I had a few of my own when I learned about this concept of 'thoughts becoming reality' for the very first time.

I was a young entrepreneur working over 100 hours a week, desperately hoping for a way to succeed and get my business off the ground. It was not uncommon for me to spend my Saturday nights typing away on my computer all night with a cold slice of pizza waiting next to me. I can still hear the awkward clacking of those old keys, and without a steady salary or dependable mentor to rely on, I found myself looking everywhere I could on my own for a helpful answer.

Books. Videos. Programs. You name it, I tried it. I explored esoteric points of view, new models of thinking, and every personal development modality I could get my hands on. I had so many books and papers lining my shelves, I can't even remember the color of the shelves themselves because they were always cluttered with some new idea I was looking into.

I would spend countless hours flipping through page after page, trying to glean all the useful information I could. For me, the Law of Attraction wasn't this one-size-fits-all answer to every one of life's riddles. Instead, it was simply one of many ways I was trying to 'fix' my life. And while I couldn't quite get it all figured out, even through all the doubt, something about it rang true. It resonated with me in a way that everything else I was learning about didn't.

All I knew was there was more to all of this than I was seeing at the time. As I looked deeper and deeper into it and started 'working' with it, I began discovering (and even creating) a whole bunch of 'manifestation methods.'

If you've never heard of a manifestation method before, I define it as a gratitude, scripting, or visualization technique that's designed to help energetically instruct the Universe (through the frequencies of your thoughts and the Law of Attraction) to 'magnetically' attract and give you whatever you want or focus on.

Unfortunately for me, this so-called 'law' of attraction just wasn't very reliable. Nor was any method I tested out. Sometimes they would work, and other times they wouldn't. Some days I'd get what I want, and other days everything would go completely wrong, and I'd end up doubting myself even more.

I couldn't figure out why it was so inconsistent, and I was practically pulling my hair out. All I knew was that I could never count on it when I really needed it. Whenever I circled a goal or a 'deadline' on my calendar — it would never actually happen for me. Whenever I needed something specific to occur, it didn't.

Worse yet, on those rare occasions when things actually began happening for me the way I wanted, my momentum would always fizzle, I'd inevitably lose my motivation to keep doing whatever method I was doing, and I'd find myself right back at square one.

It was only years later that I realized that the Law of Attraction wasn't inconsistent after all; *I was*. It wasn't exactly an easy lesson to experience, especially since the door was about to close on about 90 percent of my life — in the span of only one week.

By that point, I'd been struggling with those 100-hour work weeks for almost six years. Every argument I had with my girlfriend of three years was over my not being around enough and not spending enough time with her because I was always burning the midnight oil on my business.

After all those years of letting my obsession with success ruin nearly everything in my life, it was becoming clear to me that this insatiable drive for more was going to end my relationship as well. Because by now, my girlfriend had completely lost her patience with me, and she was just about ready to find someone else to be with instead.

I saw the writing on the wall, decided to finally end this vicious cycle of nonstop failure, and pulled the plug on my business. I completely closed everything down. I willingly threw it all away. I made a commitment to myself that I was finally going to give my girlfriend everything she needed to keep us together. Bad news for me, though, was that my decision was too little too late because three days later, she ended things with me over a text.

Now I had nothing. No business. No relationship. No life.

I woke up every day feeling lonely, confused, and depressed. I had no idea how I was ever going to turn things around in my life. Every other breath was a sign of despair. I was completely hopeless. But it was at that rock bottom point that everything somehow shifted for me — where I finally had my own personal Ignite Moment.

Because one day, seemingly out of nowhere, a profound insight occurred to me.

I thought to myself, "You know, Andrew, that Law of Attraction deal seemed to work whenever you actually stuck with it. What if the answer this whole time was just to keep going? What if you started again and this time, you simply never stopped, and you even made the methods easier to stick with? What would actually be possible?"

Now normally, an out-of-the-blue thought like that would have left my head as soon as it arrived, but this one stuck to me like glue. I could feel my chest effortlessly expand, my lungs filling with the air of genuine renewal. This feeling was unlike anything I'd ever experienced, and I couldn't look away. But the sad truth was I was also so angry at myself and frustrated with where I was in my life, that I had nothing else to do but finally listen for a change. Now I was ready to do those methods that had worked so well in the past, and I was willing to do them every single day. I was all in!

Lucky for me, since this new commitment required only five minutes a day, I was JUST motivated enough to finally stick with it once and for all. Only this time, I didn't put a deadline on anything. I didn't have any requirements for when things would change or how they might happen. I just decided that I was going to do my part for as long as it took, and I was going to trust the Universe to do the rest.

THAT'S when everything finally changed for me. That's when new possibilities began to open up. And the moments and experiences which followed that one simple decision were nothing short of miraculous.

Within only two weeks, I felt better, which was quite a fast time frame for anyone after getting their heart broken. If that's not enough, within three months, I was in a happier and WAY healthier relationship with someone new who helped me balance my priorities. For the first time in my entire life, I was actually renting movies with my girlfriend (I still remember the smell of candy at the local Blockbuster™). I stopped spending all my Saturdays stuck in front of a computer screen and started enjoying them with her outside in nature. We were smiling and laughing every day. The happiness I experienced with her every day was something completely new, and it truly took my breath away.

Less than a month after that, money was finally flowing to me consistently and was no longer a problem. Now when I pulled my wallet out to buy something, there wasn't that sinking feeling that I "couldn't afford it."

Before I knew it, EVERYthing else in my life had positively changed as well, including my health, my fitness, my attitude, my gratitude, and every way in which I approached my life. Everyone knew my name at my new dojo. Friends who hadn't seen me in months were dying to know how I'd gotten in such great shape so quickly. I was waking up each and every day with this incredible sense of ease and joy.

But here's the key to this whole "Ignite Moment" of mine: The true "moment" was in that first decision to simply begin. After all, the results I ended up actually experiencing and enjoying didn't happen overnight. Nor did they happen all at once. It was all incremental. It was something that improved more and more as I simply kept up with my daily 'manifestation method' routine.

Again, I didn't actually feel better until after those first two weeks of doing this. But considering how low I was at the time, to feel any improvement in only 14 days was absolutely amazing — to say nothing of getting over my ex, getting my finances sorted out, and getting healthier than ever before in only a few short months.

Even though I was taking action through all of this, it was INSPIRED action. The workouts I did were fun. The diet changes I made were easy. Every choice I made felt like the next sensible step. It all just clicked.

After all those years struggling with my business and constantly feeling like there was something wrong with me, I finally understood that the only thing 'wrong' in all that time was my *attitude* and my *approach*.

The rocket fuel behind all of this — from that simple realization that nothing was actually wrong with me… to just 'knowing' when to take action and when to let things happen — was a simple five-minute routine of visualizing and feeling gratitude each and every day. This was the foundation of it all. It flawlessly set my mentality up for automatic success.

All I had to do was take five minutes and devote them to feeling grateful for my life. I could be grateful for things from my past. I could appreciate things in my present. I could even visualize things about my future and thank the Universe for them ahead of time, as if they were already there.

There was nothing complicated about any of this. The only difference from when I used to fail was that I wasn't trying to 'force' any specific result. And again, thanks to losing my company and my relationship within only a few days of one another, I was JUST motivated enough to stick with it JUST long enough to get results and finally see through my own life experience that this works when you actually do it!

Within those few short months, I was a completely new man, and I understood the simplicity of all of this on a level that no book could have ever taught me, no mentor could have ever told me, and no one could have ever shown me.

In the years that have followed, my life has continued to have its ebbs and flows, with some major wins and even a few setbacks. But through all of it, I am complete. I am fulfilled in all of my relationships. I feel wonderful in my body. I've even given myself permission to make everything I do in my business all about value, and I've never been more satisfied in every part of my life.

I waited 10 years before releasing my book and sharing the techniques that helped me get here. But in all that time, the most important lesson I learned has always been the same: This thing — this Law of Attraction — whatever it actually is — *it works*. It works IF you work it. It works if you try it. It works if you check your fears and doubts at the door, open your mind to endless possibilities, and commit to experiencing joy in SOME way — ANY way — for just five minutes a day… WITHOUT worrying about 'how' or 'when' your results will come. Simply do any method for manifesting that feels good to you. Do it for the sake of enjoying it. Don't force it. Just enjoy your life as much as you can and watch what happens.

Try it. You'll be absolutely floored by the possibilities. And you'll never look back.

Ignite Action Steps

Do the improvements I experienced in just a few short months seem too good to be true? There was a time when I would have thought the same thing. But there's only one way for you to really know if what I'm saying is true, and that's if you try this yourself. With that in mind, here's just ONE option (of many) to easily make gratitude a fun part of your day, so that you can invite improvements into your life that will blow your mind.

Step 1 — Before bed, set an alarm labeled "90 Seconds of Gratitude – RIGHT NOW."

Step 2 — When your alarm goes off the next morning, immediately devote 90 seconds to thinking of things you're grateful for. It can be the same things every day, or you can mix it up; there's no wrong way to do this as long as it feels good.

Step 3 — Begin your day knowing that even if something puts you in a bad mood, you've already done all the gratitude 'work' you need for the next 24 hours. As you continue this every day, you'll have more 'happy' moments and fewer 'unhappy' ones.

Step 4 — Before long, you'll notice that 90 seconds is WAY too easy, and you'll naturally stretch things longer and longer until you're up to five minutes a day. That's all you need from that point on. Things will just… start to happen after that.

That's the entire process! But if the above doesn't resonate with you for any reason, there's nothing stopping you from experimenting with other methods instead until you find one that you like (plenty can be found in books like mine or videos on YouTube™).

Remember, this is simply about taking a couple of minutes to feel good while thinking about what you have or what you want or both. Enjoy these moments every day, and watch the magic unfold.

Andrew Kap – United States of America
Author of "The Last Law of Attraction Book You'll Ever Need To Read"
http://www.lastlawofattractionbook.com

Dr. Gerald D. Curry

"Imagination elevates your dreams by connecting you to your unknown potential."

My hope is you discover the power of your imagination by determining your future reality. There is nothing more critical in identifying your boundless potential than fully understanding imagination. I encourage you to spend time with yourself and closely explore your imagination, and then watch your tremendous growth.

Optimizing Your Imagination

When I was a young child, I spent a large amount of my time reading, and those first books introduced new concepts, allowing me to travel back and forth in time. I was fascinated by antiquity, Egyptian and Roman architecture, and biographies of historical icons. Those readings became the foundation of my thoughts and beliefs and helped shape me into the person I am today.

I can recall one beautiful spring day, when I was about 7 or 8 years old, laying across my bed reading a book, and my mother came into the room and asked, "Gerald, don't you want to go outside and play with your brothers?"

I quickly responded, "No Ma'am. I just want to read my book!"

About 20 minutes went by, and my mother came back, and no longer kindly suggested that I go outside, but instead directed me to take my book and go play. As an obedient child, I complied and finished my book on the back steps of our house, and later played with my brothers. I learned several lessons that day. The first was that you can read anywhere, and that is exactly what I did. The second was to never allow anyone to stand between you and your dreams. I would revisit that second lesson multiple times in my life as I encountered life-changing events.

I grew up poor, in a community where my father was a minister (and worked additional jobs because preaching did not pay much), and my mother was a school teacher. We always had the basics, but never enough to live comfortably. Life for us, and everyone in our neighborhood, was a struggle. Almost everyone in our community was a low-level 'blue-collar' worker. The only 'professionals' living in our neighborhood were school teachers and preachers. My early exposure to professionals was limited. There were no lawyers, engineers, or medical doctors in our community. It was exceedingly difficult to imagine myself doing anything of importance other than what I saw around me. It became increasingly important for me to live vicariously through my books and imagination.

At the age of 10, I started taking karate lessons. About that time, Bruce Lee was starring in *The Green Hornet*. He instantly became my biggest on-screen hero! I read everything I could get my hands on pertaining to martial arts and dreamt of becoming a professional fighter and owning my own dojo. Those dreams became my deepest desires, and I would spend all day, every day practicing my karate techniques. Most nights I would lay in bed mentally punching, kicking, and rehearsing sparring sessions I had participated in earlier in the day. I was hooked!

My parents thought I would grow out of this fascination for martial arts, but when I started attending tournaments, I won, and won big! I placed in every karate tournament I participated in, and quickly developed a strong reputation as one of the best martial artists in the state of Florida within a short period of time.

During my college freshman year's spring break, I returned home to visit my parents and my sensei informed me of a tournament happening that weekend. He asked if I wanted to go. Naturally, I said yes. That evening, the promoter was hosting full-contact kickboxing bouts, and the Florida State Heavyweight Champion was defending his title. I had never personally attended a professional fight before. I was super excited!

Since I had not been seriously training for months, I did not want to participate in the tournament, but did assist by judging several bouts and helping other students. That evening, my sensei came running up asking if I wanted to fight in the full-contact bouts. Initially I said no, because I had not prepared, but he explained the opponent scheduled to fight the State Heavyweight Champ had hurt himself and was forced to forfeit. The event's promoter was in a pickle and searching for a replacement because he had a sold-out arena and did not want to disappoint the crowd. Other promoters had traveled from all over the country to witness this event and would be extremely disappointed to have missed out capitalizing on this championship fight.

The fight was billed as a nine-round championship bout. ESPN™ was filming coverage of the event. It was a big deal and this felt like a chance to put everything on the line and prove my skills. At the last minute, feeling nervous, I reluctantly decided to fill in. Fortunately, I always traveled with my uniform and belt, so I was prepared. I climbed into the ring, touched gloves with my opponent, and the fight was on!

The Champ won the first two rounds, but I was undaunted because I knew I could take my time to understand his strengths and see his weaknesses. In the third round I knocked him out with a powerful roundhouse kick to his temple; with that, I was the new Florida Heavyweight Champion! Instantly my dreams had become a reality!

Naturally, I was on cloud nine! The major martial art magazines started calling requesting interviews. Promoters wanted to know if I had professional representation, and if I would travel to their events. I went from being totally unknown to the State Champion, and listed by Professional Karate Association (PKA) as a top competitor. I would go on to be PKA's #3 Heavyweight Kickboxer in the world, and in 2010 inducted into the Black Belt Hall of Fame.

After a few days I found a quiet place to reflect on my new stardom. Though success had felt sudden at the time, I realized this event did not magically occur but was actually a continuation and expansion of previous dreams and the imagination I nurtured.

It was not long before I started teaching my own martial arts classes. I was a student at Tennessee State University and started the TSU Martial Arts Club. I posted signs all over campus and surprisingly I had over 50 students show up on the first night. I charged $5 per month; figuring most college students could afford $5, and this would give me some much-needed spending money. I soon realized the philosophies I was teaching in class were having a tremendous impact on changing the hearts and minds of both me and my students.

One of my favorite quotes came from author Napoleon Hill: "Whatever the mind of man can conceive and believe, it can achieve." This lesson made me realize the power of imagination and leveraging my mind for the good of everyone within my circle and community. It was during this time I began to believe that when we think about our deepest desires, and fuel these thoughts with encouraging support grounded in knowledge and proven wisdom, we cannot help but win!

While attending college, and reaching my third year of schooling, I fell madly in love with a young lady. We spent hours sitting at a nearby lake planning our life together. We talked about the number of children we wanted, the type of house we desired, and places we wanted to travel. Everything seemed so right, and we felt like this time would never end. After dating for about a year, the big day came, and we were married by my father. I was 21.

My wife became pregnant three months later. She was a small-framed lady, and being pregnant with twins, she was immediately placed on bedrest. The twins were born three months prematurely with their lungs severely undeveloped. One of my daughters would die just 14 days after birth. This anchored me in my values and caused me to focus on family.

Approximately six months would pass before we could take our new daughter home. She had to have tracheostomy surgery, where a small tube was inserted in her neck so she could breathe. When my child finally left the hospital, the doctor handed me my daughter and a $280,000 medical bill. Eleven surgeries later, our daughter died just two weeks before her third birthday. My wife and I were devastated.

During that period, I was a senior in college and would graduate with an Air Force Officer's commission as a Second Lieutenant. I entered into the military and still had to work multiple part-time jobs to pay off the outstanding medical debt. It would take me approximately 14 years to pay off that bill, all while keeping a pristine record to maintain Top Secret security clearance. Six months after paying off the medical debt, my wife was diagnosed with ovarian cancer, and she died after two years of chemotherapy treatments.

I was overwhelmed with grief and completely lost my way. Mentally, I was a lifetime away from that professional fighter living on cloud nine. When the love of my life died, a big part of me died as well. I immersed myself in deep thought, reflecting on the good times in my life, thinking about my original hopes and dreams and eventually remembering my goals of owning my own business and being able to financially help my family crawl out from economic insecurity.

I knew if I could just transfer my earlier success in the ring to the rest of my life, I would succeed. I started reading more and seeking knowledge with a newfound vengeance. I had to get my fighting spirit back because I still had a promising military career and a family to care for. My goal was to turn the world upside down with my desire for helping people by using my imagination, but I had to work on myself first.

After being in the Air Force for four years, I was promoted to the rank of Captain. That inspired me to go into the Military Clothing Store and purchase a Colonel's rank insignia (three ranks above my own) to serve as my aspiration. I pinned the rank inside my notebook. This was the future goal I was now aiming for.

One day while attending the Wing Commander's staff meeting, I was seated against the wall. Most of the important people and higher-ranking individuals sat at the conference room table. The sun just happened to reflect on the Colonel's rank in my notebook, casting a blinding glare across the room. After the meeting, a superior officer pulled me aside and inquired what was in my notebook that had created such a glare. I enthusiastically showed him the Colonel's insignia. Before I had a chance to explain, he rudely interrupted, and demanded I get rid of it! He went on to say, "You will never make Colonel, and you don't deserve to have it!"

As military protocol dictates, I quickly jumped to attention, and respectfully said, "Yes Sir!"

That evening, I moved the Colonel's insignia from the front of my notebook to the back. I knew better than to allow this officer or anyone else to deter me from my dreams. Everyday I looked at that rank, and I was determined to make Colonel. My commitment to my family and everything I believed in knew this was possible for me.

While on deployments, when my peers wanted to visit the bars and strip clubs, I would look at my notebook and be quickly reminded of my goals. When I felt low and did not have all the answers, I would look at the Colonel's insignia and it would feed my soul by reminding me of where I was trying to go.

Remarried, with three beautiful daughters and almost 15 years to the exact date of my berating, I was promoted to Colonel. I knew where I was going; what I was going to do with my life. I did not allow the significant ups and horrific downs of life to interfere with my vision for myself.

Fortunately, over the past 27 years of active duty and a total of 38 years in federal service, I have had a very successful career. I recognize my obligation to give back and invest in others. While serving as Commander of a military unit as a young Colonel, there was a Sergeant who exhibited superior achievement and excelled in all he did. I summoned him to my office and asked if he considered attending officer candidate's school. He said yes but did not know how to go about applying. I explained the process and he took advantage of the opportunity and is now 20 years later serving as Lieutenant Colonel. Throughout my career I have helped a dozen young military members become officers and elevate their achievement by embracing excellence. I now have over 150 plus mentees across the nation. My current mission is developing young leaders to use their imagination and create their best lives.

Your imagination gives you the ability to improve yourself and others. Sometimes, all you have is your imagination and thoughts. It is your beliefs, thoughts, and imagination that guides your life and shapes your future possibilities. Imagination elevates your dreams by connecting you to your unknown potential. There is nothing you cannot do when you imagine it so. Take the first steps, by creating the vision, writing it down, and then putting your plan into action.

There is nothing more powerful than a simple thought. Thoughts are things and pave the way to creating the unimaginable. When you dig a little deeper, trying to better understand the power of thoughts and thinking, you find it elevates creativity, innovativeness, and discovery. It is in this undiscovered space where the future lies. This level of thinking and creativity causes a unique uncomfortability and unsureness that presumes chaos. But just the opposite is created, because when this unknown is pursued by leveraging your innermost thoughts, and your passionate desire excels toward progress, a new reality is born.

Future success lies in our imagination. Solving the world's problems is currently sleeping inside your imagination. The end of global poverty, homelessness, and water shortages all reside in our imagination. When we dare to dream and make our dreams our new reality, we summon our deepest desire and untapped imagination by challenging ourselves to a whole new level.

There is power in your imagination. Look deep inside. Rediscover what your earliest thoughts and dreams of achievements were. Whatever that was, bring it to the surface and let it become your new reality. Thoughts are real things. The Universe will support your innermost desires and make it so. Dream big, dream bold, be a fighter, and knock out every obstacle to reach your personal mission.

Ignite Action Steps

- **Read more books.** Acquiring new knowledge can only come four ways: your life experiences, exposure to new ideas, having exciting and engaging conversations, and reading books. Reading offers the foundation of knowledge, and if you plan on being successful you must read from a variety of genres. Reading feeds the soul and allows the mind to traverse into experiences you have never encountered.

- **Carve out time for reflection.** Reflection allows a deliberate revisiting of life lessons and with practice can create a new learned behavior that solidifies your understanding. Spend time reflecting and thinking back on your past by immersing yourself in your thoughts and intentionally seeking ideas of improvement and elevation.

- **See the Bigger Picture.** Our imagination allows us to see bigger, deeper, and more introspectively than the superficial. Roots create our fruits. Leveraging internal growth will manifest into something bigger than what we visibly see.

- **Never underestimate the magnitude of change.** When change occurs, the whole world rallies in support of your journey. Even your smallest actions can reap big dividends. Work hard and know you are making a tremendous difference by impacting everyone in your circle.

- **Think and act differently.** Our imagination causes us to think and act differently than others. When you are driven by your beliefs, not your heart, you perform differently. Pursue your passion and always embrace your dreams.

Dr. Gerald Curry – United States of America
Director for the Air Force Review Boards Agency, Chief Operating Officer
for Curry Brothers Publishing, LLC, Entrepreneur.
geralddcurry@yahoo.com

DIANA LOCKETT, M.SC., R-EYT

*"When all else fails, turn toward your breath and trust
it to transform your experience of your life."*

**My longing is that you remember to find your breath when life takes you
on its unpredictable and uncomfortable journeys, especially the ones that
take you to your knees. And, when you find yourself gasping, remember
that the next grace-filled breath will find you.**

BREATHE AND EVERYTHING CHANGES

It was a cold and dreary Sunday morning in December as I paced back
and forth in the muddy field. The gray sky hung heavy on my shoulders
and I shivered, my tears beginning to freeze on my cheeks. "Breathe," I
kept repeating. "Breathe and everything changes." But nothing changed. I
couldn't find my breath. I was gasping for air. We had lost four businesses,
our investment properties, our cars, and our home. We lost our friends, our
dignity, our hope, and I paced back and forth, engulfed in deep and dark
shame. We were living in a little mouse-infested, mold contaminated, and
leaky "cottage" that we couldn't afford to fix, and we were now at risk of
losing that home having received a notification from the sheriff that we were
in default of our mortgage payments, again. They could repossess our home
at any time, making us homeless. My husband and I found ourselves out of

work, a million dollars in debt, and we had two children and nowhere to go should we fail to find the money to pay back the house — a house that barely deserved the name of a safe place to call home. I was so gripped by fear that I couldn't even speak clearly.

I called my friend, the wife of our 'financial collaborator,' and I begged her. "We need money. I am desperate. I feel hopeless. I don't know what to do. We have been friends for so many years and we gave you a job when you needed one. Please, talk to your partner and tell him he has to give us some money. I'm begging you. No money is coming in. We're stuck and have nowhere to go!" My shaky sobs turned to terror-filled shouts. I had spent my life building my investments, a retirement income, and a beautiful and safe home for my children. And now it was all gone. I told my friend, "I trusted you. I trusted your partner. You both betrayed me." I was so angry at her partner. I was so angry at her for introducing us to him.

It all seemed exciting and possible when I began this journey of entrepreneurship. I transitioned from a 23-year career as a Speech and Language Pathologist with the school board and, after experiencing the healing qualities of yoga, I decided that I wanted to spend the next 23 years teaching yoga. I yearned to open my own studio and make this my life purpose. My husband and I decided to build out two new studios, in local communities where our dreams would have the most impact.

In the beginning, I got caught up in design, marketing, sales systems, and schedules. It was exciting. I resigned from my job and transferred my entire pension to a Locked in Retirement Account (LIRA) which was self-directed meaning I could invest it anywhere I chose. I was encouraged to invest it in the business of our 'financial collaborator.'

When I recall that day, I know that my body was telling me something was not right. It was not a clear "yes" for me. I felt nauseous. Still, I signed the paperwork and transferred most of my retirement income to his business. I didn't really understand the transaction, nor did I ask the right questions. I trusted my 'friend' and her partner. I didn't trust myself or my body telling me that something was not right.

Our yoga studio was called Inspire Yoga. On the first day of operations, we had a ribbon-cutting ceremony with media coverage and a lineup out the door. I kept hearing: "If you build it, they will come." We made $40,000 that first day and witnessed an amazing loving community begin to form. It was magical. I knew my dharma was to build heart-centered communities and it took little effort to do so. I lived in a beautiful cul-de-sac, had investment properties, and was driving a luxury car. I worked around my kids' schedules, taught a few classes a week, and loved the flexibility of running my own service-driven business. Within a few months, I launched a Yoga Teacher Training Academy and was honored to witness my students transform before my eyes through this deep dive personal development journey disguised as yoga, watching them fall in love with themselves. Through it all, I was fortunate to practice yoga, meditation, and breathwork daily. I felt privileged and extremely grateful to have created my dream life.

Soon, two studios turned to three, and eventually four. We were building an Inspire Yoga empire and I taught classes of over 100 people at times and, with each class, weaved coaching into the asanas (postures) to help empower people. My students loved that perspective. It was always authentic as each day I taught what I needed to learn. At home with my children, life was good and breath was easy and plentiful for all of us.

The last studio we opened began the demise of our studio empire. We bought it from a reputable and wealthy woman in the community. We managed it for a few months while waiting for the transaction to be finalized, raising enough money to keep it profitable for at least half a year. Those funds raised were deposited into the woman's bank account. Once the ownership transfer was complete, it took weeks to access the bank account. When we were finally given access, the studio's account was empty... legally empty. We were horrified. We had no money and our lawyer told us to walk away, feeling he could not go up against the seller's powerful lawyer. We courageously tried to make it work. We went into hustle mode. We failed.

Within six months, the sacred doors of each studio slammed closed, one by one. I could feel my dreams shrinking away, a portal in my heart closing each time we lost another studio space. I dove into a deep pool of fight/flight. I could barely stay afloat. I forgot to breathe. I forgot to meditate. I forgot to practice yoga. I had let down all my students, my staff, and the contract teachers who had been my friends. And I was letting down my children, too. The studios were attached to our personal assets and it was only a matter of weeks before I would have to walk away from everything we owned, including our lovely family home.

We moved our personal belongings ourselves, one truckload at a time, to a decrepit little cottage I was embarrassed to be seen in. Worse, I didn't know how I would pay any of my house bills. I had little funds to buy food. And, there was this massive debt that I tried to ignore. From this day forward, my children's lives would be forever changed. I had to remind myself to keep breathing each minute.

We did our best to transform that awful dump of a house from a small one-bedroom to what felt like an even tinier three-bedroom house. We built walls using recycled boards taken off an old set of skids left behind an empty home-building supply store. During that time, my son, husband, and I shared a mattress on the floor of one room.

Living there challenged me in ways I had not expected. I can remember being awoken by our daughter one night soon after we had moved in, the roof having leaked a literal rainstorm onto her beloved books as she slept. Every single day brought more such discoveries, and I waffled back and forth between having gratitude for the roof above us and explosive frustration at the disastrous state of it.

Those were dark days and even darker nights. I went in and out of depression. After several months of not being able to pay the mortgage, I received the sheriff's order to vacate our home (I didn't even know we had sheriffs in my community). Desperate for money to pay for a house I didn't even want to admit I lived in, I applied to access my LIRA due to 'Financial Hardship.' With shame, grief, and through anguished tears, I begged for this approval. When I finally received the agreement in the mail to access my LIRA, I took a big exhale. It was a big win. I would get my money, pay back some of my debt and my overdue mortgage, and have some money left to finish the renovations on the home and get some food.

Unfortunately, I found out my 'financial collaborator' was banned from doing financial business in my province due to previous illegal activity and had registered his business in a different province. The order to release my funds was not recognized and they could not honor this request. No matter who I called, cried on, and pleaded to, there was nothing that anyone could do to release my funds, so, on that Sunday morning, in total despair and gasping for breath, I did the only thing that I could do… I pleaded with my friend on the phone, "Please, please talk to him. I need a roof over my babies' heads." I truly feared we would be out on the streets.

Within two days, they transferred me $10,000. It was just enough to keep us from being evicted. I felt a deep, shuddering inhalation fill my lungs and I realized how little I had been breathing until that moment.

I returned to my daily practice of yoga, meditation, and breathwork. I began to teach a few yoga classes in gyms, schools, and parks. Within a few weeks, I received a phone call from my previous school board asking if I would consider coming back to work there. I immediately said yes.

I returned to my gratitude practice waking up each morning saying: "Thank you." Thank you for being able to do my work. Thank you for giving me the opportunity to teach yoga. Thank you for being able to put food on the table. Thank you for the health and well-being of my children and myself. I could not yet express gratitude for this broken down cottage that I was forced to live in. I prayed for a miracle.

I made it through that dark winter and as I welcomed spring, I realized what a gem of a property I was sitting on. Although it was a tiny cottage in the city, it was on a conservation lot with a river in the backyard. I took long walks and pauses by the river. I found myself healing in that space as I did what I could to beautify the gardens, a symbol of hope with each new perennial. If only the cottage itself matched its surroundings.

By summer's end, I took inventory of our cottage. I was exquisitely aware that this house — this *home* — was the place that was going to be my children's childhood memories. And I wished for them all that we had once upon a time. My husband had tried his best to fix the house but little was finished because of his own overwhelm. The roof was repaired and no longer leaked; however, many of the ceilings and walls were missing drywall and were covered only with insulation and vapor barrier. There were tusks of spray foam hanging down from every seam of the walls. The stairs, lacking bannisters, were a fall risk. The kitchen counter was an unadorned piece of plywood and the rest of the kitchen was pieced together with whatever we could find at the time from a local secondhand store. There was a part of me that was proud that we reused EVERYTHING to build the house and part of me hungered to see it finished.

As my hope grew, so did my capacity to co-create my reality. I began to look at casting calls for various home renovation TV shows. There was one in particular that got my attention. It was called *I Wrecked My House*. I watched the pilot episode, which included four homes that were 'wrecked' by the home-owner. Halfway through the show, one home was chosen as the 'winning' home and received a $50,000 renovation. I hesitated only a minute before hitting the send button on my email application.

A few days later, the show asked me to submit a video. I now had to tell my husband that I had filled out a casting submission for the show and we would be required to admit we 'wrecked our house.' He was not impressed but played along. Hearing nothing after that request, I put it out of my mind until later in the fall. It was a cold and blustery day and the wind battered at windows and made my car rock. I was later than usual driving home from work and stopped to pick up a tea to sip while navigating traffic. As I waited for my tea, my phone rang with a call from an unknown number. The person at the other end introduced himself as the producer of the show and announced that our family — our home — had been selected. My breath caught in my chest. I was pleased that they had chosen us but told myself not to get too excited as I only had a 25 percent chance of receiving the renovation.

As he continued to talk, I heard him say that I would have to sign a non-disclosure, vacate the premises for a week, and meet with production staff within a few weeks. I stopped him and asked, "What are you telling me?" He replied, "You are getting the $50,000 renovation." I felt my tears falling as I laughed out loud and jumped up and down in the coffee shop. We won. My breath rushed in and out with joy.

We met with the production staff and designers and then moved out for one full week. We recorded some video footage and 'B' roll at a local hotel and waited in anticipation for the 'reveal' day. Finally, one week later, we were getting miked up in the trailer and filmed walking down the street. I contained my physical excitement and walked as if I was going on a stroll in the park. Inside, I felt my breath quickening while my body shook both from the cold and impatient anticipation. I approached the door. I slowly turned the handle. I unhurriedly stepped inside. I paused. I gasped. And then, I exhaled. For the first time in years, I exhaled. I relaxed my shoulders and felt gentle and grateful tears forming.

It was perfect.

The drywall was all finished. The ceilings edged in beautiful crown molding. The kitchen was simple and elegantly complete. And they used our own reclaimed wood for feature walls and mantels. They had turned my shabby little cottage into a beautiful, warm, and loving home. In that moment, I welcomed the recursive presence of my breath. The gentle inhale all the way to the peaceful exhale.

Even though I had a full season of forgetfulness, there is a part of me that always knew the Universe was benevolent. I know that my resilience, my gratitude, my determination, and my willingness to maintain a relationship to my breath were tools that allowed me to realign through this difficult time and opened me up to the possibilities of transforming a tattered and tired broken house into my loving home. In truth, the transformation of my home was symbolic for my life. For my family. For me.

Today, I know myself to be the version of me that is open, trusting, patient, and saying YES to all the possibilities in my life and my business. You can say yes, too, not in spite of what you've *been* through but because of what you have *come* through. You hold the key to transform your life and co-create your reality.

Through it all, I invite you to remember now and always… breathe and everything changes.

IGNITE ACTION STEPS

Re-Align To Thrive™

Start with a deep breath, then become **REAL** to welcome the possibilities of your life:

R = remember you are a divine miracle, even when you are losing everything.
E = explore your bodily sensations
A = acknowledge and label your sensations (using the language of sensations)
L = let it be. That is, there is no need to actively change anything.

Once you can tune into your body and its **REAL** state, you can begin to REAL**IGN** and notice the subtle messages from your body:

I = Intuitive pop ups — What does your body/heart/mind want you to know from this relaxed state?
G = gratitude — What are you grateful for in this moment?
N = needs — What do you need in this moment to feel nourished and keep on with life?

Diana Lockett, M.Sc., R-EYT — Canada
Canada's only Re-Alignment Coach
Founder of Re-Align To Thrive™
Dianalockett.com

TRACY STONE

"The only permission you need to tap into your
limitless potential is your own."

**My wholehearted wish is for you to let go of the limiting beliefs that are
holding you back from taking action and realizing the truth about you;
that you are already enough in every way. You matter. You are important.
All you will ever need is already baked into your DNA. A life of infinite
possibilities is available to you.**

BORROWING TRACTORS

I am the luckiest person I know. Seriously. Unreservedly. Absolutely, toe-tin-
glingly, lip-smackingly, shamrock tiara wearingly, blissed-out lucky.

That said, there have been times when I haven't always felt quite so lucky.
Times like the many spectacularly failed relationships and the ex who tried to
secretly remortgage my house and forged my signature so effectively that he
left me in debt up to my eyelashes. Not to mention, a whole series of close-
shave vehicular near-death experiences, including the car crash that very nearly
snuffed out my short and unlived life, which an optimistic person would say are
a testament to my instincts and razor-sharp reactions. In fact, I like to believe
that the Grim Reaper has gotten so accustomed to me being in his peripheral
vision that I have blended into the scenery and he actually ignores me now!
Lucky? Yes! My glass is way more than half full.

I truly thought that I had been through the emotional wringer so many times that I was primed and ready for what was to come. But, on October 16th, 2020 at 12:25 PM, I had the wind knocked out of me in a way I had never experienced. My dad broke my heart by dying.

To say it had been a heart-wrenching passing would be to understate the stark reality my family found ourselves wading through.

It was a greedy yet invisible quicksand swamp fraught with a Pandora's box of emotions; running the gamut from absolute and consuming bone-deep and unconditional love, all the way to tortured helplessness and terror via the unfightable undercurrent of acceptance that Dad could not fight the brave fight any longer. He had actually gone.

I was left exhausted and numb as if I had been pushed into a swirling, bottomless, darkly congealed pool of anaesthetic. Every part of my body felt like it was wading through treacle, and the sounds that reached my ears were at best distorted and distant.

Somehow, at the same time, I was also feeling everything, and all those conflicting emotions were pouring out of my eyes. I was in sensory overload; a hungry sponge greedily swallowing up every ounce of the pain, turmoil, sadness, abandonment, confusion, denial, and grief that was surrounding me.

Tears were switched to the 'ON' position as if that tap could only be turned off by the immediate return of my adored father. Surely there was something that could reset this? A teeny tiny 'do-over.' I mean, only a moment ago he was alive! But the ebb and flow of life doesn't work that way; he was gone and our lives had been forever altered.

HGLD (Handsome God-Like Dad), as I have called him ever since a flash of hero-worshipping inspiration decades ago, had been through an unceasing gladiatorial marathon of health issues over the years, any one of which could cut many to their knees either physically or mentally. Not HGLD. No Sirree. He was quite simply special.

If you weren't lucky enough to know him, let me paint you a masterpiece. Six-feet tall in his heyday and always standing upright with the tangible and infectious charisma of a true leader. Physically large from a lifetime of enjoying solid Irish man-sized meals (no low-carb, green juice nonsense for him!) but carrying it in a way that only added to his indomitable presence. A full head of professorial hair à la Kirk Douglas, the salt to pepper blend having long ago gracefully given way to salt, much like his diet. Topaz eyes that sparkled end-lessly with mischief and a ready smile which echoed and amplified his boyish joie de vivre. Intelligence rolled off and around him like waves eagerly danc-ing a symphony across an ocean; uncontainable, voracious, probing, bending, advancing, receding, gleefully expanding. Never without a book. Always smartly attired, so much so that he even cut the grass in a crisp white shirt and carefully chosen tie. He was blessed with a fifth appendage, a walking stick which multitasked as an extended finger pointing to anything up high or down low that tickled his fancy and caused many a passerby to duck. When he entered a room, the energy surrounding you changed in the most wonderful, palpable, effervescent way. Close your eyes and you can see him.

Above all, this was a man who was the very essence of the belief that ANYTHING IS POSSIBLE. In fact, if you look up 'Possibilities' in the encyclopedia, you will find a picture of him there, positively fizzing with his infectious energy and indefatigable drive.

Dad began his jam-packed life in Wexford, Ireland, the second son of three boys. He lost his mother at the tender age of 2 and was brought up lovingly by his gentle and cultured father, Bill, their devoted housekeeper, Mary Butler, and his Aunty Nellie, the family matriarch who lived next door. Aunty Nellie, a career school teacher who was revered throughout and beyond the town, was a perfect, dignified overseer for the family of three young boys. It was Aunty Nellie who would referee the antics of the boys which would regularly reach fever pitch, and on occasion blood spilt, generally because of Dad's mischievous nature. As a girl, I loved plying him for stories, listening raptly as he proudly regaled us with many typical boyish scenes, like taking a bite out of the only apple growing on his younger brother's apple tree while it was still on the branch and leaving it to be found by his brother on his daily pilgrimage down the garden with the indisputable evidence of Dad's teeth marks. With glee he would chortle his way through a compendium of memories of youth such as cheating at cards and marbles by distracting his friend's and brother's attention. The latter escapade resulted in him being thrown down the stairs by his rightfully disgruntled siblings! The punishment did nothing to curtail his spark for life and adventure, and I like to imagine that he laughed as he hit every step on his way to the bottom. The resulting broken arm was merely a badge of pride serving to bake in the gleeful memory. Yes, he was indeed special.

How did this boy with a twinkle in his eye turn out? Fast-forward with me to when he first asked my mother out on a date. Another colleague at their office had wanted to court her but was afraid to. So, brazen HGLD asked, originally wishing to inspire his friend by saying, "Ask her or I will." She said no which seemed to only increase the value of the prize and did nothing to dissuade his course. Eventually she agreed on the condition that he would stop asking.

Within two years, they were married; a union of devotion like no other which lasted 54 years and to his final breath. Anything is possible!

Dad was a truly loving father to my sister and me. When we were little, he would arrive home in the evening from work and come straight to our rooms to tuck us in for the night where he would quietly retrieve a secretly stashed sweet from his pocket with a conspiratorial wink, instructing us not to tell Mum (sorry Mum!). On Saturday mornings, he would often bring my sister and me to the factory he was General Manager of at the time and would whizz us around the enchanted spaces on an adventure, sweeping through mighty Perspex™ flapped doors on a forklift truck to our squeals of delight. He told us wildly colorful stories, took us on endless magical mystery tours, built forts out of the carpet sweeper, chairs, and a blanket, and made us 'egg in a cup' with far more butter than was good for us, but it was so good! He even helped us make daisy crowns and proceeded to majestically crown my sister the Queen of Tullyhogue Fairy Fort and me the Princess showing us anything is possible!

This was a man of vision, self-belief, and action who built a hugely successful food processing business based on unused by-products quite literally thrown away by others working in the same market. He was a man who became a much-valued consultant who turned businesses around with his personal blend of grit, vigor, inspiration, philosophy, psychology, and 20:20 vision for how to turn any problem into a successful solution. He was quite simply unshakeable.

HGLD was a man who could bend reality, long before bending reality became a trendy buzz phrase. What others saw as *im-possible* he would charge with his sword of limitless *possibility*.

Always one to make his own luck, he taught me to neither hang back or hope for luck, nor to admit defeat at life's many inevitable hurdles, but rather to seize the moment and take action. Dad's words still echo in my head, "Just make a plan and follow it through." He made mountainous tasks seem like simple 'no-brainers' and to him, the impossible just took a little more planning. His light had burned bright; a strong, vital, stimulating, nourishing, hypnotic, inspiring life force. His gravitational pull was so omnipresent that it had never realistically crossed my mind that he could be eclipsed. Yet somehow, he was actually gone. That brilliant light had been quenched and I found myself shrouded in shadow — dented, bleeding love and suddenly doubting my ability to move forward.

I silently sat watching over him early on the morning of his funeral, eagerly taking my turn to keep him company before he was forever removed from our lives. It hit me then, like the proverbial brick. Perhaps more like a ton of them. HE WAS NOT GONE. He had GONE nowhere. Yes, his body had valiantly fought its last battle and, as all knights eventually do, he had lowered his sword to finally rest. God knows he deserved to rest. Stationed there, enveloped by the easy chair and held up by invisible marionette strings, savoring this precious time with my HGLD, I picked up my laptop, balancing it on my knees, and started writing. The words, inspired by the life and times of this titan before me, flowed like a crystal brook, gambolling over the pebbles, navigating their course, freely and abundantly, bubbling over each other onto the page.

It was then I heard his voice as clear in my head as if he was truly speaking out loud, not lying there silently, unsettlingly and unyieldingly cold to the touch in a box. I realized all his many life lessons and profound yet simple insights were embroidered in the most colorful rainbow of silks into the tapestry of my heart and mind. A waterfall of his brain drops that comforted and advised were stitched into the very fiber of my being.

Sitting there in his still powerful presence, it struck me that I was his legacy. He had not only woven in his pearls of wisdom but had fearlessly walked the talk of 'make your own luck.' He had gallantly opened that same door to me and to all who were blessed to have known him. I was not alone. Neither was I unequipped. His appetite to embrace life was his unwavering gift to me. Mine to keep, grow, adapt, share, enjoy, and take comfort from indefinitely.

Draped in a veil of memories, my mind was full of his zest for living, his stories, and his vast passion for life. One story in particular came bubbling up. It's a story he has told so often that it is tattooed indelibly on my soul. It's an inspirational and unexpected tale about borrowing tractors. After all, we Irish are a nation of farmers.

The story goes something like this… There was a farmer, let's call him Joe, whose tractor had broken down so he decided to ask his good friend, who lived up the road on the next farm, if he could borrow his. So, it being a lovely day, off he sets out walking spritely up the road. However, Joe suddenly recalls that he had borrowed some money from his friend a few months ago and hadn't paid it back yet; "He'll never lend me his tractor." Still, Joe walks on. A few minutes later, he remembers that he borrowed his friend's fancy new tools and hadn't given them back; "If he remembers that, I have no chance of borrowing his tractor." Still, Joe pressed onward. As he turns and walks up the path to his friend's house, he sees the man's wife and is reminded of the recent party where he secretly stole a drunken kiss from her; "No damn way will he lend me his tractor." By now he is full of frustration and 'solid' reasons why he won't get what he wants. Joe knocks angrily on the door and stands waiting, getting more frustrated by the second. His friend opens the door, smiles in greeting at his neighbor, delighted with the visit, and extends his hand in friendship. Joe, enraged and full of negativity, yells at his confused friend, "You can keep your damn tractor," and marches back home, tractorless.

All through my life, any time Dad suspected I was making excuses or chickening out of taking action, all he needed to do was ask me if I was borrowing tractors. This simple story stops me in my tracks to this very day and constantly challenges me to reevaluate what is possible. And it's a story that I've shared with hundreds of people since.

I may not have quite realized it, but I had always been Dad's avid student, drinking heartily from the overflowing font of his knowledge and experience. Watching, listening, learning, assimilating, and embracing all that made Dad so truly electric, so packed full of possibilities. Every lesson was imbibed, stored away, pulled out and used, repurposed, repackaged, fueling my own life, my decisions, my actions. His words, his lessons, his presence were there within me in a way that I just knew and understood with absolute certainty and clarity. His lessons and parables are stored away, and I can still hear his voice so clearly. I can hear the pure honesty and intention. He is with me.

In that moment, I realized it was time to get out of my own way, step out from the shadows of self-doubt and into the golden rays of infinite possibility. I closed the lid on my laptop and leaned back in my chair. I opened my heart, mind, and body to this empowering choice; I felt strong, resilient, focused, lucky. Suddenly, things that I had previously believed to be impossible pipe dreams became not only possible but completely achievable! Instead of borrowing tractors and saying, "I can't do that because…," I Ignite my greatest wishes simply by changing my words to "In order to do that, what I need to do is…." Changing my words leads to a truly transformational shift in my beliefs, actions, and feelings.

Since I kissed HGLD's forehead for the last time, I have given myself free rein to accept that I actually do have limitless potential and that anything I choose to achieve is possible. It might not be easy or quick but it IS possible. Accepting that fully has liberated me from countless swirling, wasted hours arguing myself out of realizing my dreams or taking action. That, in turn, has lifted my energy and shifted my inner dialogue with ninja-like stealth as I am no longer fighting my self-imposed limitations. I feel lighter. Happier. More me. The real me.

That mind-expanding, life-transforming, boundless potential… *is inside of all of us*. It's a birthright, bestowed in our genetic makeup. It's quietly there, fizzing and tingling like electricity, just waiting to be given permission to use its voice, to spring panther-like into action. The truth is, the only permission we ever need to unleash our limitless potential… *is our own.*

There are no ifs, buts, or can'ts. Now it's all about 'How.' It's a beautiful place to live! In fact, the view is quite simply breathtaking. Why don't you join me? I unreservedly encourage you to step out from any shadows or limiting beliefs holding you back. Know that you do not need anybody's permission but your own. Give it wholeheartedly and unconditionally. Choose to have the life you desire. Choose to know that you are already enough in every way. Bask in the shimmering glow of your very own infinite possibilities.

IGNITE ACTION STEPS

Life flows so much better when we get out of our own way and allow ourselves to succeed. I challenge you to think about a time when you 'borrowed a tractor.'

- Think about something you wanted or want to achieve but believe you can't.
- Write down (yes, actually write or type it down — this action of taking it from your head down onto paper is a game changer) all the reasons you have for not being able to achieve the thing you wanted. Let's call them 'Limitations.'
- Now, beside those Limitations, capture what needs to change in your approach in order to achieve what you want, let's call these the 'Requirements.' Check your Requirements from the perspective of someone who knows and supports you; would they agree that these are really necessary?
- Now, beside each of the Requirements, drill down a level to identify the specific Actions you must take to achieve each Requirement.
- Finally, realize the truth; if you CHOOSE it and really want it, you can make it happen.

Tracy Stone – United Kingdom
Clinical Hypnotherapist, Transformational Coach & Author, Cl.Hyp, CPPD,
ARTT, GHR (Reg.)
🅵 🅾 @tracylimitless
www.LimitlessPotential.co.uk

GUY A. FORTT

"Make the unseen visible and the unknown possible."

It is my intention that my story will inspire you to rise to your supreme self and believe that nothing will stop you from your success. Know that from any tribulation that you may face, you can come out stronger than you were before. What I want you to imagine for yourself is greatness, empowerment, and that all things are possible. Trust that you have unwavering strength that no one can ever take away from you, and with that strength, you can step forward into incredible possibilities.

CALLING OFF CHRISTMAS

I always loved Christmas. Christmas is a time when family and friends come together, sit around the Christmas tree, and laugh and joke with one another. As a child, I remember watching snowflakes fall outside, like magic cotton balls from the sky. I recall our family sitting in the living room; we would listen to the beautiful voice of Nat King Cole serenading us, while dreaming of roasting chestnuts and marshmallows by the fireplace and kissing under the mistletoe. Not only was Christmas a special time for my family, it was *extra* special for me, because I was born on Christmas Eve. I have actually been called 'Mr. Christmas." Throughout my life, despite any ups and downs, our family never let anything get in the way of this one special holiday.

I am one of six siblings. We grew up in an impoverished neighborhood in Stamford's West Side, a part of the New York metropolitan area, a concrete jungle in the southwestern section of Connecticut. My mother, Doshia, served as both mother and father, and she tried hard to give us the best education available. She made sure that we were involved in academic programs that would set our lives on the right course. Thus, my siblings and I were sent to private schools at St. Cecilia's and St. Gabriel's. These were predominantly white Catholic schools, where I was often called the 'N-word.' Then, when returning home from school, I would walk through my urban neighborhood in my ivory turtleneck and navy slacks and was often called 'White Boy' by neighborhood kids. That duality of influence led me to become somewhat of a loner... and an independent thinker.

Music was another influence in my life: it always captivated my ears, my heart, and my soul. My mother managed a local R&B group called The Soul Musicians, who rehearsed in the basement of our apartment, across the street from a graveyard at the bottom of a long, sloping hill. I was always fascinated by their pristine sound, and even more than that, they were a family. When the sessions were done, I would often grab the microphone, creating the first episodes of my future gigs as a singer. The stage was calling me. I always had dreams of singing and acting, but I didn't start out focused enough to achieve that goal. As a teen, I started getting involved with drugs and running around in the streets at night. I didn't have any guidance. But the one thing that was always true is that during the holidays I could depend on our family coming together to celebrate Christmas.

But in the early afternoon of December 24, 1983, everything changed. My 20th birthday marked the moment my life was turned upside down.

My girlfriend Christel and I were at a friend's house. I heard a knock and went to answer the door. I didn't recognize the man standing in front of me, so we shook hands and he introduced himself as Jared. It immediately clicked for me that he was my girlfriend's ex-boyfriend. I had never seen him before, but he seemed OKAY and the word on the street was that he was a 'nice guy,' but sometimes he could 'become jealous.' He said he had just stopped by to say hello so I let him in and gave him and Christel space to talk. He was very humble, precise with his words, and quite respectful to everyone in the home.

Although they were three feet apart, her voice was slightly elevated. But I could barely hear him. As their conversation continued, I started noticing Christel getting agitated, and I heard her say to him, "If I wanted to meet you at the train station, I would have been there." Although the scene was getting more intense, his demeanor was very serene; cool and calm like the movement of a whale in the ocean as it comes up for air.

Next thing I knew, it looked like Jared had punched her, as she suddenly staggered toward me. I quickly stood up to better understand the situation. I ran to her as she lurched toward me, and our eyes locked. I will never forget the look in her eyes. It was like time stood still. She grabbed her throat as she fell into my arms. I thought he had only punched her, but as I removed her hands from her throat I saw the full reality of what had happened: he'd had a knife. I tried to stop the immense blood loss, but it happened so quickly. Her face seemed to deflate, and I could see the fear in her eyes pleading for my help. The evidence of her trauma was pooling all around her, and it wasn't anything like the movies. It was as if I could feel the life being sucked out of her body. She died in my arms that Christmas Eve, and all I could think of is: "Is this really happening?!"

I laid her down and I watched bright red surround her lifeless body. I realized that the threat was still looming, and I sprung into action. I looked up and he was there in the shadows, standing in the corner of the room like an angel of death. As I approached him, watching the drama unfold, again, time stood still. He met my eyes with a frozen stare. Suddenly, he took the same knife that ended Christel's life and used it violently on his own throat.

I felt shocked, stunned, and utterly confused. "Was this real?" I asked myself, "What had just happened?" Once the immediate threat was removed, somehow I came back to my senses, and I noticed I had the knife in my hand. "How?" The question that lingered in the back of my mind, at that time, was did I commit a double homicide?

I ran out of the house to the hospital, located right next door, with blood all over me. I frantically explained to the security guard at the hospital what had happened to the best of my ability. When the ambulance and police arrived, I was lucky there were other witnesses who could tell the story, because I couldn't. I became hysterical and punched the wall — falling to my knees and asking my Higher Power *why* had this happened. Christmas is a time for love and joy, but this time of the year would never be the same for me. I lost my faith, I lost my joy, and my belief in everything — I was devastated.

Following this tragic murder, I was reeling for a long time and started questioning my life's purpose. I didn't attend my girlfriend's funeral, and to this day that haunts me. There was so much pain and displaced grief, and I wanted to respect all those involved, including her family. And, I wanted to create space for healing and grace. Despite how others might have judged my choice, I was truly choosing to put others before myself.

I felt lost and alone, thinking no one could understand what I was feeling.

I felt guilty just for opening the door that day; such a simple act that changed everything. I was sure there wasn't a person on Earth that I could lean on, and I didn't ask. I also didn't know how to feel my feelings and was overwhelmed. I shut down from everyone and everything. I completely left behind the life that I knew. I decided to call off Christmas and doubted if there would ever be Christmas again.

I moved from Stamford, Connecticut to Toronto, Canada. For a short period I became a vagabond. I was homeless, I had no belongings, and no food — though I was also free. I was in a constant state of depression and I just walked the streets in disbelief that this was now my life; angry at the feelings of injustice. My mind was in a state of confusion, and I didn't know how to trust people. Still to this day, depending on who it is and what the situation is, 'trust' is a tough idea for me to handle.

I could have stayed in that spiral, refusing to see goodness or trust anyone ever again. But there was one person for whom I could make an exception; one person I still could trust. My mother had supported me my whole life, and I couldn't keep doing this to her.

I thought of my mother and knew that she needed me. I looked down at my dirty clothes, my unwashed skin, and my tangled beard felt heavy. I knew I had to change, to cleanse myself of the vagabond state I was in. I realized I was losing myself and I couldn't bear losing anything else. Not another day would go wasted. I had to pull myself together. I recognized that there was a resilience within me that was passed down from generations, and I needed to tap into that. I finally understood I had to become a deeper listener to my own intuition, and this became transformative to my well-being.

My mother was in Stamford, so Stamford was where I had to go.

Once I returned back home, I never sought help from anyone because I still couldn't trust that those who heard my story wouldn't judge me. I began to read slowly about mindfulness and Buddhist and Islamic practices. I learned breathing techniques that would heal my inner thoughts, and it had a calming effect on my outward appearance. I started to approach life from a holistic point of view — integrating mind, body, and soul. I was working out, eating correctly, studying, and becoming self-actualized. No longer choosing to be weighed down by it. I wanted to know how to help people do the same and that was what inspired me to turn the most tragic event in my life into a catalyst for living a more positive lifestyle.

Returning to the United States allowed me to reestablish my confidence and reclaim my strength, and I made a promise to myself that if a life-or-death situation ever happened to me again, I would know how to handle it. I decided that I wanted to become a professional firefighter and Emergency Medical Technician (EMT), and I did. I have since learned that being a firefighter *IS* the greatest job in the world. It saved my life, and I now have the tools to save a life… and to change a life.

Being a firefighter has not only enabled me to open up and to trust people, but to also show love to people during some of the most stressful and traumatic events in their lives. Being a firefighter also renewed my faith in Christmas; our yearly Toys-for-Tots charity campaign was a joyous time to share love with families in need. I knew Christmas would never be cancelled again.

Although I was afraid after the tragedy to ever trust in love again, I met a beautiful woman named Tabitha, and we fell madly in love. She was studying to be a doctor, and we eventually got married. I put my goals and my dreams of working in the entertainment field on hold so that my bride could finish medical school. She went to Georgetown University School of Medicine, and while she was in school, we had our first child together. Tabitha and I decided I would be the main caretaker, so for the next two years we lived five hours apart and came together on weekends as a family.

In Connecticut, I was helped by two babysitters. We had one for the night shift at the fire department, and one for the fire department's day shift. It was challenging to juggle work and what seemed to be my role as a 'semi-single father,' because I have never raised children by myself. It gave me a tiny taste of what my mother endured raising me and my five other siblings; alone. Despite the challenges, Tabitha inspired me to go back to school. I earned both my bachelor's degree and a master's degree from Columbia University in Sports and Entertainment Management. Not only had life returned back to what I had envisioned and dreamed of, I was having the best Christmases of my life.

Of all possible places and times, my fortunes took another unexpected turn in the rubble of America's most defining modern tragedy. I experienced this tragedy for myself and the entire country while volunteering at Ground Zero in the immediate aftermath of 9/11. Over 3,000 people died during that attack, including over 350 firefighters. Despite the trauma and the extreme loss, it could have been so much worse. The rescue and recovery efforts that day saved thousands of lives. Being a firefighter really is the most rewarding job that I could have ever dreamed of. I was destined for this role, and it allowed me to face my deepest fears and to overcome my greatest tragedy with confidence and resilience.

The reciprocity of the Universe continues to amaze me. My service at Ground Zero led to me being presented with an opportunity to fulfill my lifelong dreams of becoming an entertainer. While serving on 9/11, a CNN™ reporter asked me to describe what I saw. I compared the fallen twin towers, called 'The Pile,' to Moses parting the Red Sea of metal and wood. Bizarrely, the interview caught the eye of a casting director who got me a job in a Johnson & Johnson™ commercial, which led to a part in several movies including, *The Devil Wears Prada, The Sopranos,* and, eventually, to my Broadway debut in *The Color Purple.* My singing and acting dreams had become a reality.

My path to Broadway was mind-blowing. It certainly was not the logical and predictable one, but I have always believed in the law of attraction and Igniting the possibilities of success. So much has happened and now I am experiencing the life of my dreams with overwhelming abundance. I am in the process of coproducing several projects with TV and film production companies, and I am an actor in TV and film. I have had the honor of working for one of my heros, former President Barack Obama, on his *My Brother's Keeper* initiative. Through this program I have mentored several men to success.

To go from walking the streets to walking future leaders through life's challenges let me feel such amazement and fulfillment. Even after retiring from the Greenwich Fire Department, I continue to lead a life of service. I currently serve as President of the Stamford NAACP (National Association Advancement of Colored People) and we created a successful COVID-19 Mask Project which impacted over 28,000 lives. My upbeat personality belies the traumas I have endured. That's where the happy ending comes in. (That's how I would define a happy ending.)

My life story reaffirms the belief that once you put your dreams into the Universe, transformation begins. I had lost the ability to believe that anything was possible, but I will never doubt my own greatness again, nor should you doubt yours! I know that attaining your goals may mean that you have to clear the obstructions in front of you, but you should know that not only is it *possible*, but it is Done… if only you believe.

Even though my life story plays out like a vintage radio drama with its tragedy, despair, and epic backdrops, it's all in the theater of the mind. Much of my story demonstrates my resilience, my belief, and my trust that *all* things are possible. I am now living the life of my dreams, confident that it will only keep getting better and better. Each day is a gift, and that means Christmas is back on for good.

Ignite Action Steps

- Trust, Believe, and Be Resilient. Know you can withstand and grow from the tests that will confront you.
- Be Still. When you are silent and present in yourself, it's transformative.
- Remember you can't open the door (or your heart, or your mind) to everyone. Use discernment, instinct, and intuition to stay aligned with your purpose and determine who is worthy of your trust.
- Recognize that H.O.P.E. means Helping One Person Everyday.

Guy A. Fortt – United States of America
Speaker, Author, Entrepreneur,
CEO of "BuildingFortt's," SAG-AFTRA Actor
www.guyfortt.com
  guyafortt
  fearlessat50guy

Lisa Lynn Eveleth

*"Be an overcomer. Don't let obstacles destroy you
or define you; let them develop you."*

**I want to inspire others to overcome their own obstacles. I want to give
you hope when you're in a dark place. There *is* hope. There *are* answers.
They may not be easy to find sometimes, but they are there. Have hope
that you will find your way and *live*. Don't just exist; LIVE FULLY in
this journey of life.**

Fighter's Spirit

Lying on white sheets in an unfamiliar bed, surrounded by colorful balloons
and beautiful fresh flowers smelling like spring air, I was feeling hopeless. The
room was so dark and lonely. My sweet cousin was sitting on the side of my
hospital bed and, half comatose, I was watching both of us from above. She
began to speak in a soft voice telling me that I had so much more to do and
that many people needed me in this world. I could feel the pleading behind her
words… words that resonated inside of me. Was she reading my mind? Did she
know that I was giving up? Praying to God to PLEASE take me? How was it
that she understood how tired I was of the pain and suffering?

Growing up, I was healthy and extremely active. In the summertime, my
family lived at the softball fields. Mom coached my sister's team and Dad
coached my team. I can remember pitching several games in a row in the
southwest heat without getting tired. People would always comment about me
being the 'energizer bunny' and having a fighter's spirit.

When I was in my early teens, that spirit got tested. My immune system began attacking the platelets in my blood, preventing it from clotting. My diagnosis was ITP (*Idiopathic Thrombocytopenic Purpura*). My doctor was so worried about my bleeding that he would not even allow me to shave my legs or use knives in the kitchen. After long periods of high doses of medications and a massive list of side effects, he finally recommended a splenectomy and exploratory surgery. For a short while, my symptoms calmed, but it was only the calm before the storm hit. It was the beginning of my personal journey of living with chronic illness.

As I began to get involved teaching fitness classes in college, it became a struggle for me just to get out of bed. I developed severe swollen joints, weight loss, numbness in my hands and feet, achiness all over my body, pain in my chest, migraine headaches, constant low-grade fevers, anxiety, and my hair was falling out by the handfuls. I had deep mouth ulcers that made eating a challenge and a scaly inflamed rash over my nose and cheeks which was tough to disguise. I tried to push through all these symptoms, but sometimes the pain was so unbearable that the smallest tasks seemed to be impossible, like turning the handle on the water faucet to take a bath, raising my arms above my head to wash my hair in the shower, let alone simply standing in the shower. Everything became a challenge and I couldn't manage on my own.

After brushing my teeth one morning and looking down to see a sink covered in blood, like a murder scene that I had created with my toothbrush, I decided to go to the health center at school. The nurse reluctantly diagnosed me with *mononucleosis*, the tenth student she'd seen that day with the virus. She gave me antibiotics and sent me on my way. Despite taking my treatment as directed, I continued to decline and I knew I had to go home to Mom. I will never forget that visit. Climbing up the few steps to the front door was agony and I had to walk on the outsides of my feet because it was too painful to walk on the soles. Just turning the door handle took so much effort. As I walked in, Mom took one look at me and burst into tears. I saw the terror in her face and, seeing myself through her eyes for the first time since this had begun, I burst into tears myself. I guess when you live it, you don't realize how sick you look.

She took me to the emergency room and I was admitted immediately. It was becoming obvious to me that this was definitely not *mono*. The ER doctor did a full CT scan and physical check. My current symptoms, plus the low-grade fevers, thinning hair, butterfly rash on my face, and bleeding gums and lips were all too much to ignore. When he told me he thought I had *systemic lupus erythematosus*, I felt relief wash through me. Even though I did not have a clue as to what he was talking about, having a name for my condition gave me HOPE. Now that they suspected what the problem is, they should be able to fix me, right? They started me on medication and referred me to a rheumatologist that next day.

When I walked into the rheumatologist's office for the first time, he was compassionate and empathetic. He looked at me with his warm green eyes and told me I had LUPUS and it was a CHRONIC condition with NO CURE. Hearing those words, I felt this tightness crank down on me until I couldn't breathe. My stomach ached and my head pounded. Although my doctor was thorough with his explanations, walking out of his office, it felt like I had been hit by a 100-foot-tall ocean wave and knocked off my feet. I was so young and I had so many plans for my future. This diagnosis was not part of it.

Rather than give up, I began educating myself about my disease. This was not very promising at first. One book I read said the life expectancy after diagnosis was an average of five to 10 years. I was absolutely devastated, but even though my future seemed grim, I became fascinated with what was happening in my body and dedicated myself to doing whatever it would take to reclaim my health. Each time I would begin to heal, I would have another setback and end up back in the hospital with renewed activity from my disease. It was hard to remain hopeful.

Life was tough and I was beginning to give up. Dealing with pain and inflammation in the lining around my lungs as I took a deep breath was exhausting. Every time I moved was excruciating. I was living with my mother, still weak and sickly. One morning, I was writing in my journal and I could not even remember how to spell the word 'BROCCOLI.' For someone who had been in spelling bees growing up, it was obvious something was wrong! Later that day, I remember talking to my cousin on the phone and struggling with my words. The next thing I remember was seeing my cousin come through the door, the ambulance was there, and I was being carried out by a young paramedic. I began biting my tongue and blood started dripping out of my mouth.

Lying in the hospital, each day grew longer than the last. Each morning, the team of doctors would come in to check on me and 'learn' from me, hovering over me. The doctor would ask me to name three different items, like an orange, a pencil, and a book. I had trouble reciting any of them back to him. The puzzled look on his face and the way his brows rose troubled me. My brain was so inflamed that I acted very differently, pulling out IVs from my arms and biting nurses as they tried to hold me down. I was told I was very strong for being a small individual. With the lupus attacking my brain, it felt like everything that made me who I am was GONE. Eventually, I was transferred to the Medical Psychiatric wing where they had special staff to care for me and protect me from my own harm.

Meanwhile, my immune system not only attacked my brain, it also began attacking my kidneys. I was diagnosed with *cerebritis* and *nephritis*. I began *chemotherapy* to try to reboot my immune system. With chemo, my weight dropped to 72 pounds and my hair was gone. You could see my bone structure through my skin. As I would look down at my legs, they did not look like my own. I was unrecognizable even to myself, and when visitors would see me lying in my sterile hospital bed, they could not hide the shock on their faces. Dealing with *their* emotions was overwhelming. I finally asked my mother for no more visitors.

I thought I would never be able to take a walk again, let alone drive a car, and that I was destined to be pushed in a wheelchair for the rest of my life. Even worse, I had no sense of control over my own life. I began to wonder if life would ever be tolerable or if I would ever feel like a whole person again? I could not begin to make plans. I had a hard time imagining a future that wasn't completely dictated by my disease. I had no goals beyond surviving, and that was taking everything I had!

Lying in that hospital bed, smothered in the white sheets, I was falling prey to the darkness around me, and definitely ready to throw in the towel. My emotions were all over the place and just opening my eyes had become a struggle. My injured brain needed dark and quiet, but the dark and quiet was leeching out every ounce of my energy. My cousin came to visit me, sitting on my bed. Listening to her soft voice urging me to fight on, somehow, my thought process drifted. The darkness slowly became light. I knew that I needed to reclaim my fighting spirit despite not knowing why or what my purpose was at that specific moment. All I knew is that I *had* a purpose. And now, with the help of her words, I had a plan — and my plan was to survive!

We all have a purpose. Sometimes you fall into it. Most of the time, YOUR PASSION guides you to it. I was guided that day, and I do believe that our inside energy and positive reinforcement can move us into our next chapter of life. I knew I was more than ready for mine.

As I was released from the hospital, my grandmother came over to stay and help me recover. I cherish the memories of our short walks. At first, we would walk indoors only a few feet, but gradually we moved outdoors with the smell of fresh spring air and green leaves sprouting from the trees. Sometimes we would walk a block and then two, and each day we would add a few more steps. The simple things in life became just too precious to be ignored.

I learned to not take things for granted. I remember vividly one particular gratifying experience, after many months of physical therapy and recovering from seizures, getting in my car and DRIVING, by MYSELF to the grocery store! For the first time since my diagnosis, I *felt* what it was like to be independent again. I sat there, with my hands on the steering wheel, and my throat tightening from my sobbing as I began to shift the gear from 'park' into 'drive.'

After permission from my doctor, I slowly got back into working out and even began to teach fitness classes again. I met my future husband and things seemed slightly normal, although, I still continued to struggle with symptoms on and off for years. When my husband and I were planning our wedding, I became ill with *lupus nephritis* again, had to start chemo BEFORE the wedding, and my hair fell out. But, my amazing sister's church donated a spectacular wig for my big day and it all worked out magically!

That first year of marriage was tough with chemotherapy for 18 months, experiencing three family deaths, and dealing with the stress of it all. The stress takes a toll on everyone, especially someone with a compromised immune system that does not have an on/off switch. Days and months ran together as my body tried to recover, with trials of different medicines and various complications. Finally, when my immune system seemed to calm down a bit, we decided to see about getting pregnant. We saw a specialist at Iowa City Hospital to be monitored as, with Lupus, I was classified as a high-risk pregnancy.

One day shopping, while looking for a new dress, I fainted. I was hopeful I was possibly pregnant, but instead I tested positive for West Nile. Our dog, Rudee, at the time had terrible breath and we could not figure out why. We finally found a bone lodged in his mouth from a dead bird we found in the yard — the source of the West Nile virus. But West Nile threw me into another lupus flare and the doctors put me on high doses of IV steroids to calm things down.

What a year that was full of 105-degree fevers, ice baths, seizures, and Emergency Room visits. It seemed that life would never be normal again. I kept asking myself when would I get a break? Will life ever be full of roses? I know what doesn't kill you makes you stronger, but how much stronger did I need to be? What lessons was I learning from all the suffering? Where was the light at the end of the tunnel? Yet, somehow I kept my faith and felt blessed by all the good things I had in my life.

My lupus symptoms were a drag on my energy and a daily reminder of the power the illness had over my body. At times I felt I was not reaching my full potential. I knew there had to be more to life than living with a 'condition' and that inspired me to start researching how food could be used as medicine to heal. I wanted to find out how I could LIVE in this world and not just EXIST! The process of wanting a quality of life, and to feel like a whole person, made me excited to start living... *really* living!

I have worked hard to manage my disease. I eat a nutritious, balanced diet, exercise regularly, and remind myself to get enough rest. There was a point when I did not believe it was possible for me to get to where I am today, but by embracing that fighting spirit and setting my goals high, I have been able to accomplish everything I ever imagined possible for myself! Today, I am no longer reminded with every moment (or even every glance in the mirror) of my disease. The disease that seemed like it would rob me of my goals has given me a sense of purpose and determination. I have started a foundation called 'LIVEFIT WITH LUPUS' to help promote healthier lives for those living with an autoimmune illness. My foundation offers many programs for patients including nutritional guidance, exercise education, beauty wellness, specialty medical resources, and psychological and emotional support.

Holding on to that fighting spirit despite the challenges of everyday life with an autoimmune disease was the key. As strange as it may sound, I have been blessed by my experiences. I would never change anything I have gone through — not the pain, nor the suffering. It has built my character, strengthened my faith, and developed me into the person I am meant to be.

You have three choices when you are faced with an obstacle. You can let it DESTROY YOU, DEFINE YOU, or DEVELOP YOU. I invite you to embrace your fighting spirit. Take hope when you're in a dark place. There *is* hope. There *are* answers. Have hope that you will find your way and live. Don't just exist; LIVE FULLY in this journey of life. I do, and it's amazing!

IGNITE ACTION STEPS

Eat clean and limit sugar. I have taken the initiative to eat clean with low sugar, high micronutrient foods that can heal the body. We get our minerals from veggies and our vitamins from fruit. Sugar can cause inflammation in the body, so try to avoid this evil substance. It is best to eat whole foods with minimum ingredients.

Check your vitamin D levels. Supplement with vitamin D3 if your doctor recommends it. When vitamin D levels are high, you'll feel overall wellness and able to handle stress.

Take a probiotic. Another important key element in supplementation is a quality probiotic. Gut health is extremely important in getting your health back. We need to have a good balance of '80 percent good bacteria to 20 percent bad bacteria' in our gut.

Alkaline your body. Lemon water helps keep your body's PH level at a good alkaline level. Many stores carry water with a higher PH level. Try using a superfood product daily with organic ingredients and greens to help maintain alkalinity.

Exercise. Exercise is the key to long-term mobility. I always think of 'motion as lotion.' I exercise regularly and *love* to teach my group exercise classes. You are always welcome to join me.

Words of Affirmation. I recite daily 'words of affirmation' that help me believe I am healed and strong. I invite you to write your own words and recite them daily until you *BELIEVE it is true.*

Lisa Lynn Eveleth – United States of America
CEO & Founder of LIVEFIT WITH LUPUS (501c3)
Owner of Body Design Fitness & Wellness, Group Fitness Instructor, Personal Trainer, Nutritionist, Counselor, Wellness Coach, Fitness Model
www.livefitwithlupus.org, www.lisalynnfit.com

RENEE DUTTON

"Your greatest struggles may lead you to your greatest life."

My wish for you is that my story comforts you during difficult times, brings you hope when you have lost it, and gives you courage when you need it most. I hope my message uplifts, empowers, and leads you to the realization that YOU have the power to bring positive change to your life. Your painful past, present, and future moments all can guide you to an extraordinary life, overflowing with your deepest desires and infinite possibilities.

UNSILENCING

My friend and I jogged beside the gentle, crashing waves on a beach near our homes in Southern California. Palm trees swayed under the warm shimmering summer sun while Amy ran effortlessly, her strawberry blonde hair bouncing in its ponytail. I tried to match her pace, but my lungs were straining, unable to catch enough air. "I hear you wheezing and gasping," Amy exclaimed. "You are fit and should not be struggling to breathe," she continued." I let her words evaporate.

I was a master of denial, routinely suppressing my physical and emotional needs in order to avoid conflict, escape drama, and keep the peace. It was a self-preservation skill I learned during childhood, and perfected during my 24-year marriage. I had endured countless agonizing episodes of rejection, judgment, defensiveness, and emotional abandonment after pouring my heart out, in an effort to be heard and understood. I eventually gave up speaking my mind, concluding that it was better to stay silent, hide my pain, and play small.

After the encounter with Amy, I set out on a private mission to expand my lung capacity through intense cardiovascular exercise. I believed this would be the solution to fixing my shortness of breath. I jogged daily, while listening to "Run like the Wind," and songs which encouraged me to run faster and push harder. It soon became obvious that my plan wasn't working. I was forced to accept the reality of a breathing problem that I couldn't fix on my own. Avoiding doctors whenever possible, I reluctantly scheduled an appointment for the following week.

I nervously pulled into the parking lot at the doctor's office. Exiting my soccer-mom sedan, my hearing was overloaded by loud, shrill sirens from ambulances racing to a nearby hospital, and my heart raced in sympathy. My rational mind told me that my anxiety was unjustified, but my subconscious seemed keenly aware that I was directing myself down what was to become the most dark and unpredictable path I had yet faced. Something buried deep inside of me knew I was about to lose a very valuable treasure at a time when I would need it most.

The walls of the pulmonologist's waiting room were tranquil mint green, but that was little solace for my frazzled nerves. The stone-faced receptionist greeted me with a high-pitched, "Insurance card please." Next, the doctor put me through a series of inconclusive tests. At the end of all the poking and prodding, my fears were confirmed. "You will need to have surgery," he stated without a hint of emotion. "It will be done at the hospital and involves inserting a tiny camera down your throat," he said matter-of-factly. I gasped, asking if I would be unconscious. He nodded his head while my stomach knotted. I rocked my body from leg to leg in an effort to comfort myself. I hated the thought of being knocked out by anesthesia.

The next several months were a blur. I felt like a science project, bouncing from doctor to doctor, while each looked at my situation with curiosity, but not one provided answers. During my third surgery, the sedation was ineffective, rendering me able to hear everything, but unable to speak or move. No one knew I was alert and listening to their every word. The surgeon suddenly gasped, "Oh wow," he said. "Come look. There is nothing we can do about this!" The medical team was fascinated by a large mass positioned inside my trachea, obstructing my breathing. I was terrified. I had so many questions, but was unable to move or speak. While in the recovery room, I was informed that I was being referred to a specialist surgeon at a big city hospital. Uncontrollable tears streamed down my face.

The day of my fourth surgery, I was exhausted, disillusioned, and unable to think clearly. Energy vanished from my body, making it difficult to get out of bed. My legs trembled and my mind raced while the nurse wheeled me into the operating room. The surgeon sensed my fear and tried to comfort me, explaining that the procedure he was performing was a safe and simple way to remove the mass. Awakening from anesthesia, my throat was raw and I could barely whisper. Multiple doctors assured me this was temporary and my voice would return in a few days. They were wrong.

The aggressive lasering removed the mass, but caused scar tissue to grow and attach to my vocal cord, leaving me unable to speak. The valuable treasure I had buried for safekeeping could not be dug up now. I was completely silenced!

Home alone, I sunk into my down-filled, white denim couch trying to process the reality of my dire situation. Peaceful sounds of the fountain trickling in my backyard had brought me serenity and joy in the past, but those positive feelings were no longer accessible. I was exhausted, overwhelmed, and depressed. In an effort to bury my pain, I forced myself to get out of the house and run errands.

I temporarily forgot my problems while taking in the sights, sounds, and smells of downtown Santa Barbara. The fresh, crisp air was a welcome change to the sterile hospitals where I had been spending much of my time. The smell of warm croissants brought me pleasure as I walked toward an open-air bakery. I stopped to breathe it in. My peaceful moment abruptly halted when a well-dressed woman walked by and said, "Hi!" and when she didn't hear my response… quickly followed it with "Bitch!" I felt the blood rushing to my face in rage, knowing that I tried to say hi but couldn't. That one little word was like a dagger, penetrating directly into my heart, causing a deep, invisible wound. I felt like a bullied 5-year-old, helpless and small. Again!

Days later, my oldest daughter called from her study-abroad program in Florence, Italy. She was crying hysterically and pleading to hear her mother's reassuring voice. "Mom! Mom!" she cried. "Mom! Are you there?" I desperately wanted to respond and comfort her. Temporarily forgetting the excruciating pain, I strained so she could hear my faint whispers. Not being able to speak to her was heart-wrenching. That night, I cried myself to sleep with a pillow over my head, so that no one would hear me. I was depleted — physically, emotionally, and spiritually.

A month later, I underwent my fifth surgery. Groggy, but regaining consciousness, I heard a muffled, "Hello." My heart sank, seeing my surgeon with a dissatisfied look on his face, knowing that something had gone wrong. He paused to clear his throat before telling me, "The surgery was aborted. After closer examination, we decided it was too risky." My head was spinning and my world was spiraling out of control.

"NO! NO! NO!" My mouth formed the words, but no sound came out. I felt outrage and betrayal. I desperately wished I had the iPad™ I used to communicate with, but it had been taken away before the surgery. Now I could only convey my thoughts and feelings with gestures. The surgeon quickly left me to wallow alone. I felt invisible and abandoned. I feared the voice I had buried long ago might be gone for good.

I was irritable and hungover from multiple medical cocktails of anesthesia, steroids, and other drugs required for surgeries. I felt like giving up; yet something deep inside was telling me to persist, to keep going. I knew I wasn't a quitter! Surgery number six was scheduled with a new hospital, a new doctor, and another unsuccessful result. The doctor had been unable to get the laser positioned where it was needed, in the tiny area directly behind the vocal cord. It all felt surreal. And I was still voiceless.

The following day, I reluctantly agreed to attend a birthday party. I was handed a glass of chardonnay, although warm water with honey and lemon is what I desired. Hiding my intense physical and emotional pain, I pasted on my best fake smile and listened to my then-husband explain that my vocal cord was tethered and it wasn't possible for me to talk.

"That's awesome," blurted one of the 50-year-old men. "How do I get my wife to lose her voice?"

"Mine too," said another. They all cackled with delight, while my soul screamed in helpless outrage. I felt defenseless and small, but at the same time, I could feel the voice inside of me starting to step up and assert itself.

At the six-week surgical follow-up appointment, my doctor began advocating yet another surgery.

"ENOUGH!" I heard with surprising clarity, roaring from deep inside my soul. My thoughts interrupted his voice. It was as if I pushed the mute button and could no longer hear him. At that moment, it became clear to me that I would regain my voice and would make it happen without additional surgeries. I was no longer going to be a voiceless victim, at the mercy of surgeons and doctors. I was taking charge of my health, asserting my power, and was certain I would find a way to reclaim the treasure I had buried long ago. I knew I was being guided by God.

I quickly typed on my iPad, "Are there any non-surgical possibilities?" His eyes rolled toward the ceiling, while he thought in silence. I held my breath, waiting for a response. "We could try injecting the paralyzed side of your vocal cord with filler, but this would only be a temporary solution with no guarantees that it will work," he said. Hastily, I scribbled an instant "Yes, let's try that," on my iPad, begging him to do it now. He sighed before nodding and instructing the nurse to set up for the injection. I gasped in disbelief when he grabbed the longest needle I've ever seen. After several painful attempts, he got it properly positioned and injected my vocal cord with filler.

In the upcoming days, I was very careful not to strain and create additional scar tissue. Determined to regain my voice on my terms, I learned everything I could about my condition. I scheduled sessions with a speech therapist and an acupuncturist, learned meditation, spent time in nature, practiced yoga and Pilates, refined my diet, and calmed my frazzled nervous system through slow, deep breathing, mindfulness, and focusing on my blessings. My voice slowly returned, whispering a few faint words at first, then strengthened and remained strong, even after the filling wore off.

As of this writing, my voice has been back for eight years and counting. I will never bury my treasure again!

I know how it feels to be **knocked unconscious**, **out of control**, **undervalued**, and **in need of kindness**. I now seek out daily opportunities to help others in difficult situations. It appears that this intention has caused amazing synchronicities to unfold, putting me in the right place, at the right time, ready and willing to help.

KNOCKED UNCONSCIOUS... On a warm summer's night following my divorce, a friend was driving me home from a birthday party in downtown Los Angeles. I heard honking horns as I noticed pedestrians gathering on a sidewalk next to a very busy intersection with multi-lane, one-way streets. I spotted a tiny white Toyota™ going the wrong direction heading into oncoming traffic. Cars swerved to get out of the way and bystanders observed the chaos but offered no help. Rolling down my window, I saw a petite, female body slumped over the steering wheel. "It could be one of my daughters," I thought in horror. I knew I needed to take action to help her.

Adrenaline fueled me, as I leaped out of the passenger's seat in my cocktail dress and three-inch patent leather heels, rushing to the moving car. I pulled frantically at the door handles, but they were locked. The car was inching closer to oncoming traffic. My heart pounded as I yelled and pleaded for assistance while positioning my 120-pound body in front of the car in a desperate attempt to halt it. "Can someone please help?" I screamed. A young man appeared. I instructed him to take my position in front of the car. I tried to squeeze my fingers in between the glass and rubber window seal, without success. Another good Samaritan appeared and quickly broke into the passenger's door. Together, we brought the car to a stop. I gently shook the unconscious girl, but got no response. Her pink cell phone lay on the floor. Discovering it unlocked, I blurted out a loud, "Thank you God." I called her Mom, put the phone on speaker, and exited the scene as ambulances and police cars arrived. I felt great peace knowing she was in good hands and my treasure was back.

UNDERVALUED... Exiting the parking lot on a spring afternoon, smooth jazz filled the air. I followed the mesmerizing sound and was surprised to discover a boy in his mid-20s playing solo saxophone on the street corner. His tattered case, open for tips, was overflowing with $1 bills. Recognizing his talent, my inner voice told me to invite him to play at a small fundraiser in my backyard. The event introduced him to people who helped launch his career. Two years later, he was making a seven-figure annual income touring internationally with a well-known band. During a recent call, my heart swelled with gratitude as he humbly thanked me for helping him when he was losing hope. He attributed his success to performing at the event in my backyard, which opened so many doors for him. My inner voice had known he could be a superstar with limitless possibilities. It was a voice I was learning to listen to.

OUT OF CONTROL... Another opportunity appeared on a fall morning while driving my little, white convertible alongside scenic coastal horse trails. Yellow, orange, and red leaves captured my attention until it was diverted by a woman leaping off her horse to assist a rider sprawled out on the dusty trail. In the distance, I spotted two large horses galloping out of control. Speeding up to get closer, I witnessed the rider being bucked off, flying through the air and landing on a soft patch of green grass. The woman was shaken up, but okay. I boldly asked if she wanted to get into my car so we could catch up with the horses, and she happily agreed. We drove alongside them for a while, not knowing how we would capture them. Then, oncoming traffic blocked the horses, creating the opportunity to maneuver my car in front of them forcing them into a confined, gated area which opened at the perfect time as a car exited the complex and closed as soon as the horses entered; safely securing them. The sheriff appeared and I continued home with another feeling of elation and satisfaction.

IN NEED OF KINDNESS... My personal mission is now focused on creating opportunities for worldwide kindness, compassion, altruism, and upliftment. ThePositiveReport.com was established with this in mind. We are creating new possibilities for everyone on the planet to participate in uplifting one another through small, loving actions or words. We are hopeful that thoughtful gestures will become a normal part of life and are facilitating this opportunity through The Positive Report's weekly "Kindness Challenges." Over 275,000 challenges have currently been accepted in over 40 countries… touching people and positively impacting the world.

You too have the power to create any possibility in your life. I hope my story has inspired you and perhaps brought you the comfort and hope you have been needing. Find your inner strength. Use the struggles and lessons of your past and present to guide your life toward one overflowing with passion, purpose, and joy. Use that superpower to transform your current existence to a life beyond your wildest dreams.

IGNITE ACTION STEPS

Keep an open mind — Make the decision that you are ultimately in charge of your health and destiny. Never accept anyone's limitations for your life. Do your own research and try to stay open to all possibilities. Focus on personal empowerment and optimal health through exercise, nutrition, ongoing learning, and spiritual practices.

Visualize your problem disappearing — Your body has an amazing capacity to heal under the right physical and emotional circumstances. You don't have to figure out how the problem will go away in order to visualize it gone.

Help someone — A fast way to lighten your pain and increase happiness is by focusing on others. Participate in random acts of kindness and create enjoyable moments for yourself and others. Making someone laugh will benefit both of you.

Find the silver lining — Your situation may feel negative when you are going through it, but chances are, you will eventually look back and realize that something bigger than you was at work. As they say, God works in mysterious ways. Your struggles may be part of the necessary process that leads you to your best life.

Renee Dutton - United States of America
Cofounder of The Positive Report, Author, Kindness Creator
thepositivereport.com

Amy Hackett-Jones

"By facing our fears, even with a whisper, the unimaginable soon becomes imaginable; the unthinkable becomes thinkable; the impossible becomes possible."

You are not lost, and neither is your voice. Your true, authentic voice is right there, buried under cultural conditioning, other people's opinions, and inaccurate conclusions you drew that became your beliefs about who you are, why you are here, and what you are capable of. Finding your voice is about returning home to yourself. An unlearning, an excavation, a remembering who you were before the world got its hands on you; then being empowered to embrace it, transmute it into love, and use it to powerfully contribute to the world.

Shouting Down Fear with a Wild Whisper

I forget to breathe as I witness the room filling up and the people around me buzzing with excitement and anticipation. It is Panama's first TEDx™ event, I am last in the lineup to speak, and this is my first time speaking in public. As I sit in the front row of the audience, awaiting my turn, I feel the energy of the room rise and fall as each new speaker delivers their story. My mind darts all over the place, will I remember what I have to say? What if I lose my voice? What if I speak too fast? I feel the pressure compounding as the minutes tick by.

I close my eyes, zone out for a while, and tune in to my inner world... focusing on all the things I've practiced over the last two weeks; moving about on stage, speaking slowly and eloquently, anchoring in certain points of the story, locking eyes with three key people — all the classic tricks of accomplished speakers. I look like an elegantly dressed woman, but inside I'm 6 years old.

Thirty years earlier; I was sitting in primary class, staring out the window, as I often did. From within the dimly lit classroom, I gazed out through the tall, Victorian windows, into the vibrant and enchanted garden, magnificent against the backdrop of the deep blue sky. The wisp of the weeping willow swayed gently in the breeze and the shimmering summer sun gleamed through the window.

I daydreamed for what seemed like hours, staring out those windows in awe and wonder at the big wide world beyond my reach. I was spellbound by it. I'd make up stories in my own imaginary world, with my own characters and my own adventures. It was far more intriguing than the dark, austere confines of the blackboard.

One morning just before recess, I was sitting in class, in my usual seat by the window. The sun was incandescent as it shone through the flickering of the willow tree's leaves outside. I was a million miles away, in my own expansive world. Tinkerbell™ was hanging out with me, being cheeky and making me laugh to myself as we were chasing bees and butterflies and singing 'My Favorite Things.'

"PAY ATTENTION!!!!!"

I felt his yell before I had a chance to hear the words. Mr. Bennett's gargantuan six-foot frame loomed over me, his deep baritone voice at full volume, a crossbow strike through my heart. The bright world of my playful, daydreaming curiosity burst just like a bubble and winked out of existence. Thunderstruck, my child's body, now empty… sat frozen.

From that moment on, my behavior in class changed. I stopped staring out the window and faced the ominous blackboard instead. I shrunk myself into invisibility. I kept my head down, stopped putting my hand up. Every time I was asked to read a passage or to answer a question out loud, I froze. I felt the heat of my blood rising up from my heart, pounding toward my head, at the sheer dread and embarrassment of speaking, my face flashing crimson, my mind blank.

Over the years, I found myself bending and twisting pretzel-style just so I'd fit into what everyone else expected of me and wanted for me; I lost any sense of belief in myself. I was very well aware of my limits, where I stopped short, knowing I desperately wanted to speak up and speak out, but the door was locked and the key to the lock had been unceremoniously thrown away.

Two decades later, I began traveling the world, interviewing the heads of state of Third World nations to attract foreign direct investment into those countries. Asking questions of these statesmen and women was easy for me, as the spotlight was on them. Any time the tables were turned however, and *I* was asked a question, I'd freeze again. My mind blank; I'd go bright red, and anything interesting I might have had to say vanished, like Tinkerbell.

In between interviews in Botswana, I went on safari in the Okavango Delta, where I met a team of the most incredible safari rangers. They worked in such inspiring synchronicity with, and respect for, the animals within the vast boundaries of their game reserves. They adopted me as one of their own while I was there, and taught me how to close my eyes, slow my breath, tune in to the world around me, be present to the sounds and the smells of the Delta in order to heighten my senses and know where the animals might be. In essence, I learned how to meditate from them.

In Panama, after interviewing the President about the Panama Canal expansion plan, I was invited to an event called Phenomenal Women in Business. The room of the decadent five-star boutique hotel was full to the brim with extraordinary women… and one man. He wasn't at the front of the room leading the event; instead, he was handing out name badges and leaflets and supporting his wife who was on stage. He was in his early 70s, a spitting image of Jack Nicholson, with a similar twinkle in his eye and a *very* cheeky smile. I found my seat next to a Swedish woman who I discovered was a former Olympic swimmer. I had just started triathlon training and she offered me some top tips on how to improve my swimming stroke.

As we were talking, the Jack Nicholson look-alike snuck up behind us and introduced himself, "The name's Hawk…" he said, his eyes sparkling with mischief. He'd overheard some of our conversation and leaned forward between the two of us and said, "I can help you too." I gave him one look up and down and thought, 'You?!' — he wasn't exactly athletic-looking. Then he pointed to his forehead, and said "Not from here… from here," moving his hand to his heart. That *really* had me intrigued.

After the event we met for a coffee and he told me about his incredible life journey to becoming a shaman. I felt honored and excited to have met him, he certainly was a most enigmatic character. I was hungry to know more. I had been searching for more knowledge, more wisdom, more life force since the Delta and its inhabitants began whispering to me. I knew there was more to life. I knew there was more to me. I just hadn't found the key to unlock the door. They say, when the student is ready, the teacher appears. *Possibility*, in that moment, came alive for me… a whole new world of possibility in fact.

I began to study shamanism with Hawk and we built a business together, coaching government officials, business leaders, and executive teams in the art of authentic leadership. He used to say to me, all the time: "Find your voice!" I had no idea really what he meant. *Yes*, speak up. *Yes*, say something. *Yes*, say anything at all. But I had no map for this. No compass. No cell memory. It just didn't compute.

Because I didn't say a lot, I'd spent my whole life profoundly listening to other people. And there I was, being profoundly listened to. Hawk was someone who truly, deeply listened. The experience of being deeply heard and truly seen for who I was as well as the possibility of who I could become, was the greatest gift I have ever been given. Whether we were walking in the Panamanian jungle or sitting around a fire, the way he gave me his time, his presence, and his attention triggered a metamorphosis in me from caterpillar to butterfly, without me even realizing I was coming out of my chrysalis.

Hawk taught me self-respect. He taught me the power of discernment and of authentic choice — not from ego, but from spirit — and how to recognize the difference between the two. Ego is always fear-driven, spirit is always love-driven. It's that simple; yet when in ego, we always overcomplicate matters; we'd always rather be right, than happy.

The more self-aware I became, the more I could choose to respond consciously and proactively. The organizer of Panama's first TEDx event wanted Hawk to speak. Hawk wasn't interested. I begged and pleaded with Hawk to do it, as it would have been great PR and marketing for our business; but again, he said no.

It dawned on me: if Hawk wasn't going to do it… I could! My annoyance with Hawk's refusal morphed into an increasing determination as my focus shifted from my inability to speak to my desire to give our business exposure. My choice to take on the spotlight pushed me beyond my chrysalis. It was no longer about me but about our business and making a difference. The moment I committed, providence moved too.

Hawk's refusal had been no accident; with a cheeky combination of encouragement, support, and challenge, he stepped back so that I could step up. No matter how far I had come, the demons that haunted me vehemently insisted I had nothing interesting to say; the fear of not being good enough blocked me every step of the way. Frustrated tears took up residence on my cheeks. Exasperated butterflies trapped in my stomach flapped their wings harder and faster, desperate to be set free.

I walked around my room putting Post-It™ notes on each wall, trying to anchor my speech in the physical act of moving across the room, each wall a different chapter of my story. I practiced in front of friends and mirrors alike, day and night, for two weeks. I paced up and down in my brain fog, and I almost reneged on the 'Yes!" desperately yearning for the cocoon to welcome me back into its warm and cosy embrace. How much easier it would have been, to say no; to pull back from the light, from this new opportunity to break through. That was no longer an option.

I emerged from the blur and my moment of truth arrived. I found myself there in the front row trying to calm my fears. Five minutes before I was due to go on, the fear escalated; I felt claustrophobic in my own skin, I had to leave the auditorium in order to breathe. I called Hawk, as I welled up, leaving mascara-stained tear marks trickling down my cheeks. He reminded me to take one deep breath after another… after another.

As I walked on stage, the organizer miked me up and said they were having some technical difficulties so I'd have to stand in one spot and not move at all. I nodded, barely registering what he'd said. I delivered my opening phrase on autopilot, I was so nervous… wondering what they'd think, if they'd understand me, if I'd freeze and go blank, or if the crowd would even follow me. I took one long, slow, deep breath in and out and reminded myself of what Hawk had said moments before, that the audience is just a reflection of me; if I was nervous, they'd be nervous for me.

My story started awkwardly, as if I were apologizing for actually being there. In truth, I was. I had my notes, verbatim written out on paper, resting on a lectern beside me, just in case, because I didn't trust my brain to remember anything. Having them there, I felt like such a fraud. I tried my hardest not to give that away, as the imposter in me raised its ugly head, reminding me constantly why I wasn't qualified to be there. After all, who was I to have anything interesting to say anyway…?

As I warmed up, I relaxed into it with each word I spoke. I could palpably feel the audience relax with me. When they joined me in meditation halfway through, putting their hands on their hearts as I asked them to, I knew the impact of my message had been received. A deep sense of inner peace rippled through my body and set those butterflies free.

Four months later, life took me on another roller coaster. I was told that Mum had collapsed and had 48 hours to live. Her cancer had metastasized. I drove straight to the airport, got on a flight home to Britain. Travel had taken 24 hours. She now had 24 hours left. I clung to her hand, searching her eyes, and told her I loved her; that I wasn't going anywhere. As those 24 hours expired, I chose to stay home and care for her. Twenty-four hours blossomed into two and a half years. She defied every prognosis the doctors gave her; a walking, talking miracle until the day she died. I studied various forms of energy healing and began to understand the biology of our belief systems and how they cause dis-ease in the body. I made it my mission to show up every day for my mother with my heart at peace, no matter what state I'd find her in each morning, because I understood that my own fears of losing her weren't going to support her in her journey, whatever the outcome might be.

Eighteen months after she passed, I was asked to speak at the Cancer Patient Symposium. This was the second time I was to speak in public. I'd have an hour to fill, so I prepared myself thoroughly. Again, I was the last person in the lineup. As I was being miked up, the organizer told me we were running over time and my slot had been cut in half. *Deep breath,* I thought. *Deep breath.* I knew I'd never get through all my material. *Deep breath.* I felt the 'what ifs' reemerging. *Deep breath.* I put my notes and slide clicker down. *Deep breath.* I began to tell my story instead.

I told the story of my mother's journey through cancer and my daily commitment to inner peace as I journeyed with her. I shared the underlying emotions of cancer (anger and bitterness) and the limiting beliefs that are often conjoined. I had no other option but to trust the story that I was instinctively telling; trust that it would be received by the people in the room, and that it was, in fact, what they needed to hear. I spoke from the heart, and as they found themselves in the emotions and beliefs I was describing, there was not a dry eye in the house… they felt so profoundly listened to, heard, seen… as I had been with Hawk. It was as if the story I was sharing so gently and in such a raw, authentic, real way, gave them permission to reveal and acknowledge their deepest emotions for the very first time, and they felt safe and held in doing so.

After this second talk, I realized the power of presence, of stillness, of profoundly listening, in a world that is so infrequently quiet. The space I held for those people was transformational. I learned to trust my voice and the simple yet powerful message that came through me. If I put my fears to one side, I can hear the message I must speak.

I understood then that being quiet is okay. Not wrong. It is in fact perfect. Because it is what is. I understood that I didn't need a big booming voice like Mr Bennett's. I understood that my power is both in my speaking and also in my whispering. Being the Peace Whisperer, as I became known, is my unique way of using my voice and is the soft, gentle power with which I speak. When you whisper, you invite people to silence their inner noise, to get closer and pay attention. A *wild* whisper can have more impact than the loudest of voices; one that is *Wise, Inspired, Loving,* and *Divine.*

We are free to choose how we see the world around us and respond with life-affirming love, or crippling fear. I learned that nothing has any meaning apart from the meaning we give it. I made that "PAY ATTENTION!" mean that I had no voice; that I was fundamentally flawed and was utterly not good enough. I held on to that conditioned belief for 30 years. Only in the unlearning, the remembering of who I was before the world got its hands on me, did I rediscover my authentic voice, embrace it, and transmute it into love.

Those daydreams you had as a child are a critical piece of your life's puzzle, as are the events in your life that you reacted to, and gave meaning to, by shutting yourself down. You are not lost, and neither is your voice. The twists and turns in the path of your very own hero's journey that conditioned your beliefs about yourself are only a layer of dust obscuring what you already know. Return home to yourself, use your voice in a *wild* way, and contribute powerfully to the world. You are the one we've been waiting for.

IGNITE ACTION STEPS

- Revisit those daydreams, those sparks from deep within. Lean in, listen to them, no matter how faint that WILD whisper! Be your very own daydream believer.
- Know that choice is one of the most powerful words in the English language and you have the choice which story you wish to feed; the ego story of fear and smallness, or the spirit story of love and expansion.
- What are you still holding on to that no longer serves you? I invite you to step out of your chrysalis, to commit wholeheartedly, and let providence move for you too.

Amy Hackett-Jones – United Kingdom
Peace Whisperer, Coach, Healer, Speaker, Author
www.amyhackettjones.com
 @amyhackettjones
 @amyhackettjones

JIMMY HAYS NELSON

"Your significance and impact are only one well-crafted story away."

Your personal story is the most powerful thing you have to create a life of impact, fulfillment, and freedom. Everyone's story, where it is TODAY, can have an impact on another person. You are already relatable and don't need any extra metrics. As long as you're two steps in front of someone, you can teach them something valuable. We can serve people where we are today; this is where our true fulfillment lies.

BECOMING WILLING TO BE WILLING

That irritating buzz of the alarm jars me from an intoxicating deep sleep. As I try to find the source of the irritation, I notice it's still dark. "What is going on? What time is it?" and "Where is that noise coming from so I can smash it!" … Then I remember: I set the alarm. It's 5 AM on a chilly winter morning in New York City, and this Texas boy is not a fan of the cold nor of waking up early. However, this particular morning in New York City, I had to leave my little apartment in Queens, bundled up in multiple layers, and walk a few blocks down to the subway station to take a short little ride into Manhattan. Magical Manhattan. More specifically Times Square which was the center of my universe at the time. Yet, this morning I was not excited for this visit.

The whole reason I was in New York City was because way back in the first grade, I found my first addiction — probably the strongest addiction I've ever experienced in my entire life! In the first grade, my west Texas elementary school put on a Christmas play. My first grade class was picked to do a musical number called *Too Fat for the Chimney*. It was a gripping story of how Santa Claus wasn't going to be able to deliver presents for Christmas because he was too fat to get down the chimney. I was *the only* fat kid in my class, so I assumed I'd play the role of Santa Claus. Finally my big break! But it wasn't to be, because my best friend, Justin Martin (who happened to be the skinniest kid in class) was chosen to be Saint Nick. They tied pillows around his middle to fill him out. All my friends were dressed up in 1980s aerobic gear with the leg warmers and headbands, and they were all upstage safe and together doing a workout routine to help Santa lose some weight. As for me, I was front and center. Terrified and insecure little chubby Jimmy. I shuffled my way down to the isolated edge of the stage, the red toes of my footed pajamas hanging over the lip, longing to be hidden in the safety of the group behind me. The pajamas were ridiculous — long johns with a drop bottom and a stocking cap that my granny made. I stood there in the spotlight, staring into a sea of my peers. The butterflies in my stomach started to feel more like ravenous dragons. It took everything in me to calm my nerves enough to open my mouth and start to sing: "*He's too fat for the chimney, too fat for the chimney…*"

Then — right then — that's where the addiction started. They weren't pointing or laughing. As I got into the song, I saw a nod. And then a smile. It was the first time I got a positive response from a peer group … and it dawned on me: This is what I'm meant to do the rest of my life! I'm made for getting an emotional response from an audience that causes *real* change!

Do you know the worst part about knowing what you're supposed to do the rest of your life when you are only 6 years old? The immediate lists that you come up with of why you'll never be able to achieve it. For me, being an overweight kid from a broken home with no confidence was just the beginning of what became a very long list of 'reasons' I'd never fulfill my potential. I just didn't feel like I belonged anywhere. I didn't know who I was. I was always trying to morph into something to make people love me, but I just want to be accepted. Except for when I was on stage. That was home. There, they liked me.

They liked me just because I was being myself, not because I was playing a *version* of myself. I was just doing something I love doing, and it started me on a journey of knowing that I was meant for something more. But I still had my list of all the reasons I'd never be able to do this and it planted a seed of resentment in me.

That seed grew into an overweight preteen and then a solidly round and bitter teenager as I continued to get bigger and put on more weight right through high school. I wanted to go to acting school, but my mom said, "Jimmy, we can't even afford to put you on a plane to let you audition." It felt so frustrating! I just kept seeing other people do the things I wanted to do and I had to settle for so much less. I wanted to get the best training and have the acting life I felt I was created for, but it was so impossibly hard. It seemed so easy for everyone else whose parents were paying for school and they didn't have to work. My thoughts were an endless bitter cycle of, "But of course they're going to have success. Look, they have a scholarship, their parents are paying for their schooling. They're not working two jobs like me, trying to be in the theater department and audition and be in shows. Of course *they're* successful."

How often is it that we look at somebody else and discredit their success because we think, *"Oh, it came easy to them. They don't understand my situation."* We have no idea what that person's story is. What we see is their 'highlight reel,' never realizing that they probably have their own challenges and struggles as well.

I continued to try and fail and try and fail until, in my early 20s, I found myself a hundred pounds overweight, a three-time college dropout, living back at home with my parents, and working waiting tables. No audiences to impact. I wasn't making a difference. I wasn't living my purpose. Plan A didn't work. I went from pursuing a dream to surviving day to day. I woke up every morning already thinking, "How am I going to make it to the end of the day?" My life was like a bad rerun and there was nothing to look forward to day after day.

On that particular weekday, I don't recall what day as they all blurred together, my alarm clock went off with its familiar annoying buzz, rousing me from sleep at the 'god-awful' early time of 11 AM as I had a lunch shift that day. I was waiting tables and bartending at night, and as I got out of the shower and wrapped a towel around me, I stopped in front of the mirror. That was a place that a guy 100 pounds overweight doesn't like to spend a lot of time in, but that particular morning, I just stopped and looked at myself.

I didn't respect the person looking back at me.

As I looked myself up and down from head to toe, I felt numb. It was as if I was looking at a stranger. I never thought this was where I was going to end up. All I remember thinking was, "Who is going to love this?"

My chest felt tight with the force of that sobering moment. There had been so much hope in that first-grade kid at the thought of how many people I could impact, and now here I was, standing in front of an audience of one — a reflected audience, at that — and I said to myself, "Jimmy, if you don't change, you're going to be alone the rest of your life."

Now, there was no lightning and thunder. My life didn't change at that moment. But for the first time ever, I was *willing to be willing* to try something else.

I started to take baby steps every day using the resources that I had, instead of focusing on the resources I didn't. Those small consistent steps over time helped me lose 100 pounds and reignited my dream of being on stage, ultimately taking me to New York City where I was turning off the annoying buzz of my alarm clock at 5 AM on that chilly winter morning.

I bundled up and got on the subway. It was cold, but I wasn't heading into Manhattan for a rehearsal for a Broadway production or to be on a TV show or in a movie. I was doing promotions. 'Promotions' just means doing any little side hustle job that you can use to string things together to barely make rent and eat. I had done coffee demonstrations in Macy's™, I literally had been a filler at a party, just walking around pretending I was supposed to be there. I had no clue what job was in store for me that morning, but regardless of my apprehension, I was on my way.

When I got there, I thought, "This one must be the worst. This *is* the worst. The worst, the worst, the worst." A, it's early. B, it's cold. C, as soon as I got there, they handed me a costume that looked like something a newsboy might have worn in the 1930s, complete with a stupid hat and messenger bag hanging across my chest. I'm damn near 30 years old by this point, and this felt beyond ridiculous. I wanted to walk away, but I needed the gig to pay the rent. I struggled into the costume and then they handed me boxes of chocolates to hand out to the 'friendly New Yorkers' as they bitterly hurried to work at 6 AM.

Just like that moment in the mirror… it sucked. Not being able to go to the colleges I wanted to… also sucked. Doing coffee demonstrations in Macy's… you guessed it, it sucked. But nothing was as awful as that morning, awkwardly trying to hand chocolates to busy New Yorkers while dressed like an idiot. The chocolates were free. I wasn't trying to get them to pay me anything. But they still refused to acknowledge that I was even standing there; that I even existed. I was so humiliated, and I found myself looking up — literally looking up at all the billboards in Times Square thinking my name should be up there.

On one side, the billboard was advertising the newest Broadway show. Another, a hit talk show. Then a blockbuster movie and a hot new series. I felt behind in life. I was supposed to have had it all figured out by now. Most of my friends had their careers or families or some kind of purpose, and there I was staring at the fact that mine was never going to happen. That was supposed to be me on those billboards. It was supposed to be the little kid from Texas whose name was in those lights! In that moment, a small voice inside me whispered, "Quit waiting for somebody else to give you your stage and go create your own."

For the past 13 years, that is exactly what I've done. I've stood on stage and shared my story all over the world and watched it light up the hearts, minds, and passions of the people in my audiences. I use my stories to spark change. To inspire people to believe in themselves and take action for the life they want. There's nothing better than telling your story and watching someone actually start doing the work to change their life because of the story you shared with them!

I've not only created stages for myself, I've also worked with people from all sorts of backgrounds as I help them craft their own personal stories in order to feel that sense of significance from the impact they have on their audiences!

I'd love to tell you that in that moment in Times Square, it just all clicked; that I was super clear on exactly what I needed to do and how I was going to do it... but that was far from the case. I had no clue where to begin. Anything I thought I could help someone with, there were already other people teaching the same thing who I thought were far more qualified than I was. Who was going to listen to me? Wasn't everyone going to flock to someone who had lost more weight, had more success, had gathered a bigger following, had made more money, etc.? For months, I tried to chase certain made-up metrics silently until I considered my story 'good enough' for the public. What I've learned over the past 13 years is that wherever we are in our story is more than 'good enough' to have an impact. I believe everyone has a seven-figure story if it's well-crafted. Why seven figures? The marketplace rewards whoever serves them most. The 'seven figures' just represents the amount of lives and the significance of the impact you have had. To someone who is two steps behind you, your story is not only inspiring, it's relatable and attainable.

One of my clients wanted to be an all-star online health and fitness coach. She told me, "Jimmy I can't wait to help so many people get healthy. I just need to lose 40 more pounds, then I will launch my business because I've only lost 30 so far and I haven't started exercising as regularly as I would like." HIT THE BRAKES!!! What? I pointed out to her that the 30 pounds she had already lost made her a rock star to the millions of people who had only been thinking about getting started. We only have to be a few steps ahead of someone else in order to guide and help them. Where our stories are today is many times more relatable to an audience than that 'big expert' you're constantly chasing.

We will always be chasing the next goal or metric, but let's not let that keep us from sharing our stories even as we are busy writing the next chapters. I'm here to tell you that your story is powerful where it is today, even if you have other things you want to improve and accomplish. Tell your 'today story' while you are working on crafting the one for tomorrow. You have value! Your story is powerful! Tell a story — change the world.

Ignite Action Steps

The three things I had to do to get started were:

- **Be Willing to Be Willing.** I had to be open and willing to look at, try, and do things differently than I had been up to that point in my life. In order to have something different, we have to be willing to try something different on a consistent basis. We can have our ego or we can have results. This mental shift is key.

- **Be Bad Before Being Good.** Somewhere along the way, we as a society start believing if we aren't already good at something, we aren't meant to do it. We think we are supposed to magically stumble upon something that we are an expert at from the beginning. It doesn't work that way! Everyone you've ever looked up to because of their accomplishments or stories was willing to be really bad at something before getting to great. The faster we are willing to barrel into the 'being bad' phase, the faster we can move through it to being good and having the impact we desire.

- **Vulnerability is Powerful!** As I work with clients to determine which story we want to craft, I have found it's usually the story we *don't* want to tell that is the one we *should* be telling. When we are willing to be vulnerable and share more than just our highlights, our audience trusts us. They see someone who has struggled just like them. It is the fastest way to create a true know, like, and trust bond! That connection is your greatest marketing tool!

Jimmy Hays Nelson – United States of America
International Speaker & Storytelling Coach
www.TheCoachJimmy.com
IG: @TheCoachJimmy

Kirusha Kulcar

"When we unlearn the things that are keeping us small, we free ourselves to grow into our infinite potential."

What if Earth is a playground, not a school? Imagine the exhilarating heights of the swings, challenging climbs, or simple pleasures like playing with grains of sand. You choose your experience. Each experience delivers an opportunity to learn through play; an outlet for your sparks of inspiration and expansion. I am inviting you to see life on Earth as playing in a playground. How would your reality look if you started playing big?

What Choice Do I Have?

It was a hot summer day and the kitchen was sweltering. My daughter, a year old, sat in a high chair swinging her chubby legs while her siblings were dancing around like entertaining clowns. The electric clippers in her father's hand started buzzing. I looked on silently as each of her chocolate-colored curls fell to the ground. Occasionally I would scoop up a perfectly formed lock, letting it encircle the contours of my finger, before putting it into a little bag for her memory box.

My husband was shaving off all the hair on my child's head, just as he had done with our first two children. This rite of passage, as contained in ancient Sanskrit texts, was a tradition in my family of origin. According to writings about karma, sins and karmic debt accumulated in past lives are represented by hair which grows in the womb.

As I tucked each lock of hair into the bag, I grieved the loss of the only mop of curls in our home, as deep down I knew they would not grow back with such tenacious spring. My own hair has never been curly so I resorted to curling contraptions in my youth. Now, watching my husband shaving her at my request, a scream begins to rise up in my body: "STOP!"

The intention behind shaving my daughter's head was to give her a clean slate for this lifetime. Admittedly, my understanding of karma was quite basic, you reap what you sow — cause and effect. Then, once you have learned all the lessons, you graduate and don't need to be reborn. As much as I believed in karma, part of me also refused to believe everything was a foregone conclusion.

Earlier in my life, when my future seemed mapped out, I was living in a nice, leafy suburb with a friend from university, in my fifth year of law school, when it hit me: "I don't want to be a lawyer." This was an extremely uncomfortable realization after years of study and accumulating student debt. I went to a prestigious law firm to do the required work experience, and I remember being struck by how all the lawyers looked so stressed and miserable.

In that moment, I could see before me two distinct paths: one where I could pivot and explore more creative pursuits and the other where I stay the course and do what is expected and sensible.

The sensible path looked bright, lit up by a five-star level of success and a smooth, sealed road laid out for me to travel over the next 40 years. The other path was dimly lit and fraught with danger, twists and turns of the unknown, and the overgrowth I would need to cut through, reeking of the nauseating smell of fear and failure.

It was my first experience with the enticing lure of the comfort zone.

I had already been programmed to buy the lie that survival is good enough, that thriving was something people only dream of. Somehow I exiled the prospect of change to a secret fantasy world where it was unlikely to happen because I didn't believe it could. By this stage in my life, I was well versed in the guidebook to being a human and used to giving up my flow, freedom, and choice to buy love, respect, and acceptance.

I dutifully graduated and started work. Afterall, it was the logical next step for a perfectionist suffering from an insatiable need to overachieve. I enjoyed the feeling of being a winner, however fleeting. I loved the look of pride in my parents' eyes. I had willingly bought the meaning of life sold by the society I live in, because I dared not lead a life outside the box for fear of being an outcast. I accepted without question what I had to be and do in order to be a 'successful' member of society. And that somehow, that success would buy me choices and freedom.

I put on my suits, which felt stiff as straitjackets, stifling my movement and squashing my wings. When the elevator door opened to my office, an invisible filter programmed my words like a script and the corporate mask felt as if it were now welded onto my face, like a protective layer of armor.

Over the next eight years, I changed jobs five times, trying everything my degrees qualified me for as if they were chocolates in a sampler box. I was looking for something that I could stomach even though these job changes were leaving black marks on my resume. I was worried about spending the next 40 years at a workplace where my soul song would be insidiously silenced as my life force seeped out.

With stolen moments of downtime and crystals tucked inside my bra, I turned to the things that helped me survive my work day; energy healing and metaphysical connections. In those moments I found myself in a flow state, batteries recharged, and glimpsing an existence beyond the limits. The little sneaky licks I allowed myself of soul expression and sovereignty made my survival mode, hamster on the wheel day-to-day existence, by contrast, more and more unbearable. A chasm started to develop between who I *am* and what I *do*. I was leading a secret double life.

I became aware that some colleagues, the ones who were also just surviving lawyering, couldn't see any other options. It was as if they had made their choice a long time ago, to study law, and were now irrevocably locked into the consequences of their quicksand karma. When I asked one such friend, who was visibly suffering physically and emotionally, "What lights you up and makes you feel alive? What if you tried something new?" She stared at me blankly with a zombie-like expression. Her eye roll told me she thought I was crazy.

Her gaze dropped to the floor as she said, "I don't remember the last time I felt anything like that, if ever. I am lucky to have a great job, I am on my way up the ladder to partner, it's as good as it gets. If I take a break to detour now it will all have been for nothing. What choice do I have?"

The rhetorical question landed with a deafening thud. The vision in my mind was of her unable to get off the spinning equipment at the playground, spinning so fast her eyesight blurred and she couldn't see the rest of the playground or what was on offer. Not even ovarian cancer and the miscarriage of her only child could disrupt the autopilot nature of her life. Feeling like she had no other option, she went straight back to work and kept climbing the corporate ladder.

In contrast to her devastating tunnel vision, I embraced a greater vision of what could be possible for my life by remembering that I have choices outside the cage I had agreed to live in. I had to become aware, challenge all the assumptions I had accepted as truth, and rewire my subconscious mind out of autopilot. Then came the freedom to choose.

Three years into my marriage and pregnant with my first child, I chose to give up law once and for all. Mothering made me feel alive and excited to learn and grow.

Life held up a mirror for me to check my commitment to my choices. Based on my reputation as a high-achieving alumni, my high school offered to interview me. Would I still qualify as a "success story"? Under the title of 'Rekindling the Spirit,' I decided to share my message: *Don't limit yourself, you can be academic, intuitive, and anything else you choose.* I wanted to empower the students so they wouldn't let themselves be pigeonholed. When it was published, someone I had known since childhood questioned why I would publicize the fact that I had left my corporate career and was therefore now a failure. But my response confirmed that I was no longer helplessly subject to the projections of others and slave to assumptions that were not truth in my reality. For the first time, I felt who I am and what I do were aligned. The article was still being shared at the school a decade later.

For me, that initial fork in the road was now opening up a myriad of options, paths, and possibilities. My question was "What choices do I have?" I felt like a kid in a candy shop, surveying the delicious bounty, one more delectable than the next.

Then, there was that voice, like a little devil on my shoulder, whispering in my ear, "You better make the right choice." This was it, my existential crisis. *Who am I? What is my mission?* In breaking free from my cage and stripping away everything I thought I was to date, all the labels, projections, and limiting beliefs fell away. My soul led me to knowing that *I am an immortal being with access to infinite possibilities*, and I felt a superhero-like empowerment, unavailable to those who believe they are mere mortals.

As a young girl I used to love being on stage. I acted in a school play with a girl who is now a star in Hollywood and still managed to get my own standing ovation. I often wondered, what if I hadn't been pegged as a nerdy academic at school? What if I didn't believe the doom and gloom narrative and explored a creative path to see where it led? Many years after that play, I decided to apply for a role on a TV series. The little devil whispered again, "You are too old and fat now, corporate success will be closed to you forever more. You will be an embarrassment to your family and anyway, they will never choose you." I was one of 10 people chosen out of nearly 5,000. It felt like the impossible had become possible in my life all because I decided to give it a go. I ignored the devil's whisper and got to play on one of the unique sets of my life. When one of my children heard about it and exclaimed, "Mum! You were on TV?" a smile lit up and spread across my face as I remembered all the fun I had let myself have.

I reflected on my toddler's recent experiences on the spinning roundabout equipment at the playground. The first time she tried it she was alone, she pushed and pulled it so that it would spin at her pace. She was choosing her experience and as I looked on, her joy sounded out in an uplifting "Wheeeee!" Then an older child got on. My little one clung on at the mercy of the bigger and stronger child who spun the ride as fast as he could. Her joy turned to nauseating terror, as I watched the ride complete a single rotation. She was too busy trying to survive to scream for help or pull on the brake herself, and was too afraid to jump off for fear of getting hurt. By the time I stepped in, she had shut her eyes tight, held her breath, white knuckles squeezing the metal, and was going along for the ride.

Now, standing in my kitchen in a situation of my own making, I was the one holding my breath and considering the jump off the merry-go-round I was on. I needed to step in for myself. The beliefs which had caused me to cut my daughter's hair were falling away like her locks. That scream to stop, which rose up in my body, almost escaped but was suddenly halted by a download dropping into my consciousness. I stood frozen, thrown into a tornado of questions:

Do traditions and routines place us in a state of autopilot?

Do our current habits have any relevance to the present moment?

Do our actions align with our intention?

Do we assign false meaning to events?

Is the purpose of our life to keep learning lessons until we graduate to a higher plane of existence?

Why do we get stuck in cycles and how do we break free?

How do we liberate ourselves from fate and choose the life we want?

The surge of subliminal information spirals around and through my body with a vibration, and I feel a million different things at once, without any chaos or overwhelm. In my mind's eye, the spiral shape lights up, and I see it is the loops within the Akashic records, connecting events across various moments in time, space, and dimensions. The loops exist but are not meant to be the ball and chain I have made them into.

The fireworks of questions dissolve into an awareness that *life is not about learning our lessons so we can become a higher consciousness; we are already a higher consciousness choosing our experience.*

When the tornado dissipated, it felt like time had stood still. No one even noticed. The burning hot summer sun was still beating down and my little one's giggles bubbled over, like a water fountain, as her sweaty head was unveiled.

I pushed aside my Earth school desk and chair as I realized that I no longer believed in fate as a prison of consequences we get locked into. Nor that karma had me strapped helplessly in the passenger seat. I attuned instead to the true meaning of karma. I felt empowered, like a God of my own destiny, to remember that I am the creator and chooser of my thoughts, words, and actions, and the journey I take with them. I know I didn't choose to come here only to live this life like a wild animal tranquilized in a cage. What a waste to be trapped by the invisible bondage of subconscious beliefs, societal constructs, and cycles which serve no purpose.

My journey has invited me to free myself of life-defeating cycles, and now I have become the invitation to others to do the same. So many people are scared of change, but change is often the doorway to life-changing transformation. Staying in the comfort zone past the expiry date is anything but comfortable, in fact it's often more damaging than change could ever be.

There is a common phrase *giving away your power,* but we give away our power and so much more, we give away the infinite potential of a fully self-expressed life. I invite you to remember who you truly are, what you are capable of, and that you have the right and ability to choose.

Break free from the idea that Earth is a school where we come to learn our lessons over and over again and build resilience. Instead, be as curious as a young child, viewing the world for the first time with awe and wonder. Earth *is* a playground… what will you choose to play with?

IGNITE ACTION STEPS

What are you storing in your "one day" basket? Write down all those things that seem so far away and unreachable that they are currently unlikely to happen. Then pick your favorite one.

For example, I always knew that one day I would become an author. A number of people had expressed interest in reading the "book I have in me," although I never openly stated I would write one. There were so many excuses and reasons why writing should stay on the back burner, like a lack of time and a fear of putting my thoughts and feelings out in public.

To get from A to B, the future you who has achieved the goal and is living the dream holds the clues. What are the **thoughts, beliefs,** and **actions** of this future version of you? See him/her in front of you and ask questions, be curious. Also see how it feels to be that future you and align the present version of you with that frequency.

The future version of me, the author, thinks that by holding on to what I have to share, I am holding back not only myself but also others who resonate with my message. My author self believes that there is nothing in her way and that in the present moment, everything is available to her. Her first action was to choose writing as a priority, then setting out other aligned actions, like allocating uninterrupted writing time.

You can do the same. Start experiencing the things that are in *your* basket, one step at a time. Seize the present moment and remember to have fun along the way. Earth is *your* playground, enjoy it!

Kirusha Kulcar – Australia
LLB, BAsianSt, Reiki II, C.Hyp, Rapid Transformational Therapist
Multidimensional Mentor, Author, Speaker
www.kirusha.com
🔲 *@Free Your Flow*
🔲 *@flow_with_kirusha*

PAT LABEZ

"A joyful heart is the beat of life."

This chapter in my bumpy road of life shares the beautiful reminder of valuable lessons in every adversity. Hand in hand, my sister and I vowed to fight for life with grit and grace, to live and love, bless and be blessed, till the end. I was never afraid to die and now I am not afraid to live. I've learned to make a joyful noise, no matter what, with love and light. Many have called me The Joy Boomer, a baby boomer helping others tap and amplify their joy, rekindle dreams, and even reinvent themselves regardless of age. I hope we can all dare to reach out and boldly live. It's never too late.

FIND JOY IN THE JOURNEY

"Anytime you're ready," the gentleman said. I shook, took a deep breath, and with a flick of a switch, I could hear the motor activate behind me. I turned around and saw my Joy — my beloved sister and best friend — getting rolled into the chamber. At a distance, I could see a light. It was the end of a journey. Just like that. Cremation. As she had wished.

She was the planner in the family. She had the plots and funeral arrangements done years beforehand. But flicking that switch was never an option given before. I was conflicted, feeling like I, myself, was setting her on fire. But I decided to embrace the moment as a gift, traveling right with her from start to finish. I found strength with the handful of loving friends watching from behind the glass window, and her *Kumu*, her *hula* teacher, right beside me. "She's up in the big *luau,* celebrating with the others!" he said, smiling. He opened his jacket to reveal a white *aloha* shirt made of the same material as the white *muumuu* on Joy. An unexpected video showing a tropical beach ran behind us, bringing us back to our roots in Hawaii. Coincidence?

Just two years earlier, Joy was told, "You're doing good!" I thought, "Whew! Thank God!" She survived the odds. I survived caregiving. You see, at the age of 58, she had been diagnosed with stage IV pancreatic cancer plus stage II breast cancer that was deemed unusual and unrelated. She was given three months maximum to live. Together, we embarked upon her journey, scrambling for options in the middle of a busy holiday season with bitter cold winter temperatures. Against all odds, she knocked down her buzzing pancreatic C-Fairy, as she called it, not wanting to say the (cancer) word. It was enough for doctors to recommend a mastectomy for the other C-Fairy. After those treatments, Joy was on her way to recovery. At her 30-day checkup, I was relieved with a successful post-op evaluation. I could exhale a bit. Or so I thought.

As I opened my eyes — BAM! This time it was ME! I couldn't move. The pain was so intense. Questions overtook my mind. "What happened? What's going on? Am I dreaming?" I struggled to get out of bed, but finally found my way through the fog. The doctor's shocking news: six degenerative discs on my neck and a pea-sized brain tumor on my right temple. "Meningioma is 70 percent benign but we highly recommend surgery," she said. Of course, our family history was in the forefront of concern. Our brother died at age 18 from brain cancer; our oldest sister had a touch of skin cancer; Joy was battling pancreatic and breast cancer; and now, a brain tumor for me. The darn cancer cells seem to just love us. We had also already lost three other siblings, two in their 50s, one in his 60s. Joy and I teased each other about just trying to make it into our 60s. My concerns this time were Joy, husband Dave, and daughter Amanda, all of whom had health challenges. I was the primary caregiver and could not take any chances of a surgery gone awry, something that I, unfortunately, have witnessed. Major painkillers were prescribed.

We moved on as best we could. I did my regular quarterly MRIs, knowing the best case I could hope for was keeping the tumor from growing. Doctors insisted I really needed to have surgery in anticipation of the tumor's continued growth, which would put pressure on my brain. "I'll take my risks," I said, taking a leap of faith. "I'm not afraid of dying. When it's my time, it's my time," I said. But, of course, I was hopeful that the 'pea' could somehow just behave and leave me alone, at least long enough so I could help those relying on me.

The insanity of life continued with the day-to-day struggles of survival. Every time I'd get a headache, I wondered if that was 'the pea' acting up. Somehow, I managed to function. I conducted even more research on cellular health and the supplement that I was giving Joy, then opted to get on it, feeling that it was my only remedy in avoiding prescriptions and their side effects. Focusing on others was really my chosen therapy, along with lifestyle adjustments, gratitude, and prayer. I figured Joy was already beating the odds and wondered, "Could any of that have made a difference?"

Bewildering even to her oncology team, Joy was called the miracle girl with her inner light glowing. Infusion trips became 'going to the spa.' Chemo was her cocktail. I decided I'd follow that mindset.

Joy and I were always close, despite being so different. I was in awe of her many achievements and how she had such a solid plan for everything including our retirement years. With "why not?" as my motto, I was the go with the flow explorer. Joy was the only one who ever saw every single place I've ever lived in, from Hawaii to California through Virginia, with many stops in between. Through all of life's many struggles, we always reminded ourselves to breathe and keep looking up.

Things seemed to be under control. In anticipation of Amanda's college transition and being an empty nester, I returned to volunteering, along with my health advocacy initiatives. It's a good way to serve, expand a purpose, and meet new people. After years in long-term care, I needed a change from the emotional drain of caregiving and loss, so I opted for something more creative, going back to my earlier roots as a performer. I chose a film lab to escape the big unknown of my future. I was asked for a talent directory headshot. I resisted, but ultimately agreed. Why not? Next thing I knew, I had a short film. The role: a mom dying of cancer. Coincidence? After 25 years of absence from the industry, I never really expected to be returning to it as I approached 60 and with an illness to boot. I was about to decline as I was uncomfortable leaving Joy for the three-day filming in New York, but she said, "You need to do this, Pat. Follow your destiny. Go, I'll be fine."

In the summer of Amanda's graduation, Joy encouraged us to spend some family time exploring Europe to open the world for our young lady. Joy opted to stay behind and just asked for photographs throughout the adventure. One day, I got the call with her faint voice whispering, "I'm not well." It was Independence Day. I flew right back. I found her on the couch, curled up in the dark. We hugged, sat side by side, and held each other. No words. Just being together, sensing each other's thoughts. It was the roughest part of the journey, witnessing firsthand the pain and agony of the body succumbing to a disease while the spirit fought on through Christmas and into the New Year. No matter what, through the tears, she managed to smile, joke, and bring joy to whomever was there. In solitude, she loved her Hawaiian and gospel music playing.

On January 22, 2017, as a favorite song played, "Let Me Walk Through Paradise With You, Lord," her beautiful, tender *hula* hands lay lifeless. "Take my hand and lead the way," floated across the room as Joy took her last breath. Coincidence? With friends and family by her side, love and light permeated the room. Feeling numb, I kept quiet, focusing on the tasks at hand. Perhaps it was denial, fear, or disbelief, but we were convinced she could beat this to the end, somehow. But next thing I knew, she was placed in a body bag. Down the elevator. Loaded up in the trunk of a station wagon. That was it.

Five days later, I was asked to identify her. Clinging on to each other, my friend, Joann, and I walked into the mortuary, not quite knowing what to expect. A few yards away, we could see a body in a plain gray cardboard casket at the front of the room. For a moment we stayed back, unsure if we were intruding in someone else's ID viewing. The funeral aide nodded. "That's her?" I asked. Joann and I just looked at each other, quietly dumbfounded. Ever so slowly, we walked up. Other than her pink top, nothing else seemed recognizable. I looked her over, shaking, confused, and shocked, asking myself, "This is Joy?" Looking hard, I guess I could see some resemblance of the family features? But she seemed empty, like a somewhat deflated balloon. It was then that I knew and understood. That was not Joy. It was merely a shell to house her beautiful spirit that's now soaring, pain-free, celebrating life again without the confines of her earthly body.

Relief and a sense of peace washed over me, easing the heaviness in my heart since her passing. As I accepted this spiritual awareness and connection, the freedom of our souls beyond this life, my perception of living changed. The *manini*, trivial little things, lost their importance. What mattered was staying healthy, in spirit, body, and relationships; so, I moved on. Aware and cognizant of the importance of stress management for my own health and wellness, I went about life, taking care of whatever was necessary for final arrangements. Joy was so loved, we had a Celebration of Life in Washington, D.C., to honor her with the many friends she had made throughout her 26-year residency in the area. Then, as she wished, her final Celebration of Life followed a month later in Hawaii, overlooking the panoramic *Ko'olau* mountain range and the Pacific ocean, resting in the same vault as our beloved brother, Zach. To everyone, he was her dance partner. To Joy, he was her soul mate and she'd always say,

"I miss him." As I danced the same *hula* she taught me to the song that was playing as she took her last breath, a beautiful white dove mysteriously flew behind me across the indoor stage. Coincidence?

The path to healing was still a long road to walk. I had *my* life to live and to attend to family needs. To stay motivated, I went on, adopting the mantra, "Find Joy in the Journey." It seemed to help me cope and focus on the goodness in things, people, situations… rather than the imperfections and ongoing challenges of life. It renewed my appreciation of everything, especially health. I tried to imagine how Joy might've lived. *Carpe Diem!* was another sentiment I used to live by, but had forgotten. I brought it back. Yes, "Seize the Day!" It was back to living in the moment with my signature *go with the flow, come what may* mindset. "Bring it on!" I'd say, whenever another crisis came up. Through it all, I'd find humor in everything; found a silver lining through every adversity.

Reconnecting with myself brought me back to showbiz. Not intentionally, but the path seemingly could not be denied. Once I let it be, doors opened, even with my occasional resistance. Part of my Joy therapy was enjoying shows on Broadway. While watching *Hello, Dolly*! I formed an immediate connection with an acquaintance, Marya, who invited me to her home. I resisted. But nine months later, there she was at the screening of the short film Joy insisted I do. By summer, her friend and talent manager, Bob, was asking if I'd be interested in acting again. I resisted, again, but finally said, "Why not?" Then I was asked if I'd like to join pianist Bobby and their singing sessions. Sure enough, I resisted. Other than a short stint with a church choir chorus, I'd never sung in public past my high school musicals. I was 60, for cryin' out loud. Then a voice said, "Why not?!" By the following summer, I was performing with six other artists in *The Green Room 42* at Times Square. Two months later, a second New York City performance at the Triad Theater. It was also Amanda's 21st birthday so she took on my "Why not?!" mantra and sang! The show was a hit and such a special experience. By the way, we later discovered that Marya and I are actually related. Coincidence?

"Is this for real?" I'd often ask. Besides all the surprise singing, I felt compelled to produce a short film, *Howard*, inspired by two amazing friends I met through Joy. At its screening, I was asked if this was something Joy and I had discussed. It wasn't. Apparently, Joy had been wanting to share the story many years earlier. And on the day of screening, wishing she was there to witness its unveiling, I opened my computer to search for *Beautiful Kauai*, a dance we learned together in our teens, and there I stumbled on her last *hula* performance at the Smithsonian National Museum of the American Indian in D.C., dancing to the words, "Tonight, I am here with you; tonight, I have returned... " Coincidence? The film received the Audience Choice Award at the Asian Pacific American Film Festival and a feature film is in the works. Did Joy have a hand at this too?

Later that year, another family loss in Hawaii took place with the passing of my brother-in-law, Harold. I spent over a month there, helping my sister, Alma. Upon my return, I realized I hadn't had my regular MRIs! With no symptoms whatsoever and sheer busyness, I'd forgotten about my little 'pea!' When I finally scheduled a scan, the doctor said, "Pat, check your MRI. We could not find the tumor. It's all good!"

What?! How?! When?! I was perplexed. But no matter. I accept — the gift of health, the gift of life — with deep gratitude.

Perhaps it was that news, baffling as it was, that gave me even more courage — or reason — to sing, dance, act, and live to the fullest! I landed television spots on *Blue Bloods* and *New Amsterdam,* and at 62, my friends seemed amused at this "late bloomer" coming back to life. I was blooming and thriving amid adversity, doing virtual benefit concerts, and creating more projects to support others. At 63, I was inspired yet again… this time, writing! "When the student is ready, the teacher will appear," they say. And so it is. Our friend, Tom, who was on this 'knocking down the C-Fairy' bandwagon with Joy and me, reached out with the gift of encouragement on my next creative project. Then another angel on earth, Kate, popped into my life sharing *Ignite Possibilities.* So here I am! Coincidence?

I've always said, "I'm not afraid to die." Yet, I now realize that perhaps "I was afraid to live" also held true. I find it ironic that I've come full circle as my journey of introspective understanding at 63 is what I started on at 23, thwarted by, but enriched with, life lessons. As a young adult, I heard the phrase, "Life is not a dress rehearsal." It may have taken a lifetime, but I finally see it. I believe there are no coincidences and things happen for a reason.

Embarking on your fight for life, believe that it's truly about living in the moment, as the future is promised to no one. Like a flick of a switch, life changes. And the body is merely a costume for our spirit. We're all performers on the stage of life, improvising along the way until the journey ends with your final curtain call. Make the most of it. Do good. Be good. Blessings are everywhere; often simply disguised. Even so-called disappointments can later uncover opportunity and joy beyond imagination. Yes, through all the ups and downs, zigzags, and detours of life, we can each find joy in the journey!

IGNITE ACTION STEPS

Read the inspirational poem, *Desiderata,* by Max Ehrmann, filled with virtues and ideals on life… "Keep peace in your soul. With all its sham, drudgery and broken dreams, it is still a beautiful world. Be cheerful. Strive to be happy."

Allow these words to remind you...

- Be open to possibilities. Ask, "Why not?!"
- H.O.P.E. — Help One Person Everyday. Volunteer. You can make a difference.
- Keep looking up. Believe. Take action.
- Be grateful and strive to live in JOY.

Pat Labez – United States of America
Performing Arts, Health & Senior Advocate, Writer
www.PatLabez.com

BARBARA DRTINA

"You are not the pain you have known,
you are the possibilities you choose to live into."

I want to inspire people to rise above their pain and live into their possibilities. Everyone needs to know that you are allowed to have joy and happiness after a traumatic experience. You may even feel more joy because you have felt such pain. I wish everyone to know how much they matter to this world just as my daughter, Erin, mattered to me. I want to be an Ambassador of her life story to open conversations surrounding Parental Alienation (PA) and Suicide, both of which are on the rise. I hope my story will make an impact on parents and the choices they make for their families.

PLEASE REMEMBER ME, MOM

I'm in my car heading to Winter Park, and I am drawn to the thought of "The Bench." Not just any bench, but a public bench overlooking a small tranquil pond. It's my bench, my memory bench. A beautiful setting under Florida's ancient oaks overlooking the stately cypress trees in the water. I wondered how many people walking by took notice of the plaque that carries my daughter's name.

No one wants their child to be remembered by a bench, in a park, on the shore of a pond. But that is all that I have and I am eternally grateful to my dear friend Karen and our neighbors who made it happen. This is such a special pond in our neighborhood; a center for connection and community. At Christmas we all come down to decorate a Christmas tree that will float in the middle of it. We play games and exchange cookies. It was where my daughter loved to play with her friends.

My daughter and I would often walk our dog around the pond and would stop at a bench that was put there in honor of a boy named Jimmy. Jimmy's parents had a large home facing the pond. I never knew Jimmy, but I knew *of* him and his battle with cancer as a young adult. I always felt a sense of reverence when I walked by and a feeling of gratitude that his parents could look out and be reminded of their beautiful son. I hope that people walking by Erin's bench will have that same feeling.

As I park my car, I am so grateful to have a place to come to sit and to feel Erin's energy. I have often wanted to just sleep there overnight so I could be close to my child. I don't live in Winter Park anymore, but when I visit, I always stop at my bench.

I wish this wasn't my story, but it is. I never could have imagined that my life would end up this way. As time has gone by, I have a new perspective about Erin, her sister, and life itself. You see, I was ready to leave my marriage before I had Erin. I was miserable. As I gathered up my courage to separate, Erin chose to come into our family and I chose to put my divorce on hold. Looking back, I wish that I hadn't.

Erin was a character, and it took all my energy, stamina, and parenting prowess to try to figure her out. She was like no other child I had ever known. I had been a teacher and had taught a lot of young children over the years, yet not one was like Erin.

Being unique was both a blessing and a challenge for her in school. You either got Erin or you didn't, and it sure made life tough for us with some of her teachers. She was a free thinker and no way was she going to be your average run-of-the-mill student. Watching her challenge the status quo, reading her creative stories, and listening to her insights about life, I knew without a doubt that Erin was gifted. And, like many gifted students, she had nuances that needed to be understood.

I was so excited when Erin was accepted into the gifted program at school, but Erin wasn't. My hope was that she would have a teacher that could better understand her, and she would be happier, but Erin wasn't happy in this world. She was brilliant and beautiful, but a conflicted child.

I couldn't wait for Erin to be an adult and for her to fly. Erin loved to write and dreamed of being a journalist with National Geographic™. She documented her life on the calendar I would give her each Christmas. She was always writing and journaling. I marvelled at what she wrote.

Erin's sensitivity gave her the ability to care about others. She surprised me when she asked for my support on a project she was organizing. She was gathering a group of her friends together to put on a Halloween party for the children at an abused women's shelter. She and her best friend did all the work, I was just the designated driver as she and her friends put on a fabulous event that made the children feel special.

As incredible a blessing as Erin was, when you have a conflicted child, it puts even more strain on your other children, and ultimately your marriage. And as I mentioned earlier, my marriage was already unhappy. I saw the handwriting on the wall and knew I had done everything in my power to try to make this work. When my 40th birthday rolled around, I took the opportunity to go away and spend time by myself.

I looked at my future and knew that it wasn't going to change. I didn't want a life like this. I felt lost and I needed to find "me" again. I wanted to be happy. I wanted time to reflect, to renew, and to catch my breath, so I went to my Happy Place, the beach.

I remember early one morning as I walked along the shore, I could feel my despair leaving me. I began to feel excited, I felt hope and joy and the possibility of a life filled with opportunity. I wanted to grow into the person that I was meant to be, instead of withering away in an emotionally abusive marriage. I remember the playful feeling I had chasing the sandpipers by the water's edge. I found myself singing these words: "I'm going to be free, I am going to be free, I can't wait to be free!" I knew my life would be different once I was on my own.

When I got back, I didn't wait to bring up the subject of divorce, because I knew I couldn't wait or I would lose my nerve. Conflict has always been hard for me. I grew up in a family where you weren't allowed to have an opinion. This was my moment and I was going to seize it. I realized that I had married the same person I was trying to escape. I thought of Mel Robbins' 'five second rule.' You have five seconds to act or you will lose the moment.

I brought it up and to my surprise, my husband agreed to separate. I felt so empowered. When we sat down to tell the girls, I remember Erin despondently sighing, "I knew this was going to happen," as she stomped off to her room.

Little did I know just how painful this journey of separation would be. The girls' father refused to communicate on any level. His words were, "I will never go where you go or talk to anyone you talk to." Yet we had two girls to raise together. If we couldn't communicate in a marriage, how would we communicate separated? At that time, there were no cell phones or internet, so you had to talk; but we didn't.

Although I wanted a peaceful separation for the sake of our children, that was not to be. The following years were filled with conflict. The girl's father would send me letters which I dreaded opening or he would fax me at my workplace. You can't imagine the obstacles this created in my job and in my life. Even my attorneys and orders issued by the courts could not make him stop this abuse.

In the meantime, Erin began acting out in various ways at school and at home. This is not unusual for children put in this position. The courts ordered us to attend a program created especially for high-conflict divorces called, *Focus on the Children*. It was held at the courthouse under the presence of armed guards. Three of the most professional mediators were teaching us how to negotiate. As we role-played family scenarios with different partners, I once again had hope that things would get better.

Since both girls were staying with their father, I was shocked when one night I saw my daughter walking around the school yard, at nine o'clock at night. She spotted me and ran up to my car to tell me that Erin was missing! Despite the fact she was eventually found, I realized that it was only by divine grace that I discovered she was even missing. I wasn't told by my ex-husband and only *formally* notified a few days later via a letter that came in the mail.

There is something called Parental Alienation (PA). It is a slow, insidious process that brainwashes our children against the other parent. Right now it is a global epidemic and our children are the ones paying the price. I had become the "Alienated Parent," and this is an unwanted label I still carry today.

The only communication I received from my ex was through antagonistic letters. I would be so emotionally affected by these letters that I resorted to opening them with my therapist. I remember him helping me compose my responses. He told me that you have to anticipate how a Narcissist thinks. After a few sessions, he commented on how exhausting this process was. I certainly knew. Not only was it draining, it was expensive using my sessions for letter writing.

We had all just finished our six-week *Focus on the Children'* program and my birthday was fast approaching. I knew that I had to do something fun; it had been so long. I needed something entertaining, where I didn't have to think. I decided to book tickets for Cirque du Soleil in Orlando. Erin was unable to come, but my parents and my other daughter joined me. It felt so good to be out with family.

I will never forget the conversation that we had in the car on the way there. My daughter told her grandparents that Erin wanted to go to a boarding school, at the suggestion of one of the top Adolescent Psychologists in our area. Erin was so excited to get away from our tense situation. She had even picked out a school in Santa Barbara and was applying for a scholarship. My parents and my daughter were saying how Erin needed to be punished for her rebellious behavior and not rewarded with going to a boarding school. I remember my words clearly to this day, "This is not about punishing Erin, this is about saving Erin's life."

The next Saturday night, I was heading to a movie with a friend when my ex-husband called to tell me to come over right away. Something was wrong. My friend asked me to drop her off at home first. On the way to her house we were stopped to let ambulances, a firetruck, and several police cruisers go by. As their sirens wailed we wondered what could have happened in our little town. I soon found out.

When I got to my ex's house, all the emergency vehicles were parked out front with yellow tape surrounding the house for a crime scene. My heart stopped and I could barely walk up the drive. The cop said there was an accident. When I entered the house, they told me Erin had tried to take her life and they were working on her. After what seemed like an eternity, they finally came out with her. I watched in shock with tears streaming down my face as a body bag was wheeled out. She had hung herself in her room while her father was home.

I couldn't save my daughter.

There are events and turning points in our lives that change the trajectory of our future and this was one for me. I knew that I did not want to waste my life in grief and sorrow, yet I felt paralyzed. I had never experienced such loss in my life. I learned that grief takes time and I had to feel it to move on. I gave myself the necessary time to heal. It was then that I noticed, a thought that kept coming up over and over. *I still had the gift of life and I had a responsibility to make the most of it.* I found that my grief was actually the catalyst that ultimately led me to this moment in time and new possibilities for my life. I can feel joy again and I am finding a new purpose for my future.

I soon discovered that when I shared my story, I felt better. Telling my story to help another helped me too, and I felt I was making a difference in the world. I was being called to use this for good. To make something empowering out of something traumatic.

I kept this in mind when I had to go back for the follow-up session for the *Focus on the Children* program. So much had happened since we had last met. As I drove there, I was filled with so much anxiety. How would all these couples respond? How do I tell my story while Erin's father was in the room? I was so relieved that he never showed up to face this group where he had so proudly professed to have learned nothing.

When it was my turn to share, I could barely get the words out, but I remembered that I had made a vow to myself to use Erin's life story to serve a purpose. I composed myself so I could tell her story in such a way that it would make an impact on these struggling couples. I can still see the anger, shock, and concern on their faces after my story was told. Could this happen to them too? I ended with these words: "Are you willing to play Russian roulette with your child's life? Is the anger you have toward the other parent worth your child's life?" It was then that I held up a picture of Erin — the Mass card from her funeral. I wanted all that had happened to be a teaching moment for everyone.

The impact my story — Erin's story — had on the group caused the program directors to invite me back to speak to other couples. Today, I teach workshops to women going through separation and divorce with children — the things I wished someone had told me so I could lessen the collateral damage and trauma on my own children. Maybe we could even save a child's life.

My desire is to bring awareness to Parental Alienation and help to eliminate it. Our children need both parents. And today, I believe that it was the root cause of not only my daughter's death but the estrangement of my other daughter and grandson.

No one talks about PA, yet it affects three times more children than autism. I want Erin's life and death to shine a light on this cultural epidemic of one parent overriding the other parent to *"win the children."* This is what it has become in our Family Courts today. Our children are an asset just like the house, the car, or the bank account. The realities of suicide, self-harm, unhealthy relationships, and violence often stem from family dysfunction. Let's start a conversation surrounding the traumatizing and alienation of our children during the divorce and separation process. This is life or death and I want parents to hear it LOUD AND CLEAR… We are hurting our children's future and it in turn hurts all of us.

I couldn't tell my story until now. First I had to grieve, forgive, and heal. I also had to consider the risk of telling my story. I didn't want to jeopardize my relationship with my other daughter. I feel compelled that this story needs to be told Right Now. I know there are other Erins, and other parents out there just like me.

We do not know where our lives will start or stop — that 'dash' between our birth date and the day we pass. But Erin did, she chose her dash. She used her gift of free will to make a powerful statement and I am the messenger. She passed me the baton.

Now I am in a co-creative partnership with Erin, for her courage to make her *dash* a meaningful message to others. I think she knew I would be her *voice* for change.

Thank you Erin for letting me be your mom and for taking me on a deep journey of knowingness about my mission here. I am a better person having lived through this pain. I now have endless Possibilities to be of service and to feel great joy. Like the famous quote says:

"Be the Change You Wish to See in the World."

May your journey through pain lead you to new possibilities in your life. I wish you great happiness along the way.

IGNITE ACTION STEPS

- Please love your children unconditionally. Please do not block the other parent from their children, they have the right of a loving relationship too.
- I encourage each of you to add mindfulness practices into your life. This could be Prayer, Yoga, Meditation, or Nature Baths. There are so many options.
- Grief has no instruction manual and it takes time. Honor your own personal journey of healing. We all grieve differently.
- Please become aware of Parental Alienation. I encourage you to watch the movie, *Erasing the Family.*

Barbara Drtina – United States of America
Founder & CEO of Wellness Matters, You Matter, LLC
Biohacker ~ Author ~ Speaker ~ Educator
www.WellnessMattersYouMatter.com
Info@wellnessmattersyoumatter.com
f *Wellness Matters You Matter*
© *WellnessMattersYouMatter*

DERRICK HILL

"To create the life you want, you must lead yourself to free yourself!"

It is my intention that reading this story touches, moves, and inspires your beautiful heart and soul into action. As you connect with my story, I desire that your experience is like a match Igniting the end of many firecrackers tied together, leading to a massive explosion within — an explosion of what's possible for you to awaken and heal from any traumatic wounding encountered over the course of your life. I want you to discover that super-natural, heroic power that propels you into taking a courageous stand to have and create the life that you desire — a fulfilling life that honors your passion and creativity to serve and impact humanity in a great way. The time to lead yourself and free yourself is now!

A BROKEN HUMAN BEING'S RISE · STAND · TRANSFORM OF SELF

From age 11 till 42, each day I imagined I was on the Golden Gate bridge in San Francisco. My own personal boat was waiting below in the water. I'd stare out at the Alcatraz prison, even on the foggy days of not being able to see it, knowing it was there. I would climb up onto the bridge rail and jump, my arms and legs spiraled out of control as I descended down toward the boat. I then landed on the deck with a thump and my heart racing. I'd stumble my way to the control room to take the role as Captain of my boat and start that trip across the water to the prison.

The ride was lonely, choppy, cold, and windy, mirroring what was going on inside me. The feeling of isolation, withdrawal, and intense raging anger in the midst of my silent voice. My silence held me back like someone had superglued my lips. For 31 years, I never spoke up or took a stand for myself, killing my heart and soul over time.

I'd finally arrived at the prison. It felt so cold and I shivered all the way from the prison door down the dull, dingy, dark hallway to my daily reserved prison cell. A 'Derrick Hill' etched nameplate on the door identified what life's experience was: a prison cell of intense pain and suffering. Every day, I'd walk in and make sure I was double bolted and locked in. Safe from...

My Ignite moment occurred in the spring of 2018 in Louisville, Kentucky, and I was 42 years old. As the severe storms and torrential rains ushered in a new climate season, I found myself in a waterfall of tears and a severe internal storm along with a family in crisis. Those compilation of life challenges, struggles, and devastating traumas led me right into a new season of hitting rock-bottom after torturing myself day in and out for the last 30-plus years since "it" happened.

What was that unfathomable, unexplainable 'it' moment? The 'it' was when another human being, a man, decided to lure and inject his sickness of pedophilia on a pure and innocent 11-year-old boy's heart and soul. I endured six months of lies, control, manipulation, and sexual abuse. That unwelcomed surgical incision of darkness into my heart and soul began my imprisonment.

Unfortunately, the only way back out of my prison was to self-abuse and numb the pain daily with the substance of choice: a strong will to win at anyone's demise; an egotistical, obnoxious energy and presence, all while pursuing bigger and better jobs, cars, a white picket fence house, or what they call 'The American Dream.' Then, at the end of each day, there was the evening bottle that would provide escape and make people and events going on around me more tolerable. I did all this to create and project a false image of wellness and happiness to everything and everyone around me.

Like the tree branch after an ice storm bearing too much weight, I reached my inevitable breaking point. I dug myself into a massive hole with my own shovel for years by making poor choices and not healing. One day, after the waterfall of tears, facing my life crisis and my most severe storm, I was laying facedown in the slimy pit of muddy muck and utter darkness. I had just come off a bottle and a half of wine and around three hours of sleep that night before having to be back at work. My drinking had intensified significantly over the last three months, as I faced a separation and divorce after 20 years of marriage. It was then I heard and felt something different.

After leaving a late morning work meeting, a confidante asked me a question that would forever change my life, "I've always known you to be a leader, so when are you going to be a leader for yourself in this crisis you are in?" Those words and syllables percolated around and around in my head like the making of a slow drip pot of coffee as I headed down the elevator and out the door to walk to the gym. It was like time turned into a slow-motion picture video as I headed down the street. Then, as I strolled under the 2nd Street bridge in downtown Louisville, I felt it: that burst of supernatural power like I just ate a whole package of my favorite sugary candy.

That was followed by the calm feeling from a still, small voice deep within calling out to me in my sickness and darkness. The rays of light from the sunshine beaming down into my brokenness deep within on that perfect warm, crystal clear, blue-sky spring day. A slight breeze whispered into my ear, "Derrick, Derrick, it is time to stop torturing and start nurturing yourself to heal and reclaim your great power." It felt like a crayon was coloring an empty picture and bringing radiance back into my entire being. Indeed, it was an epiphany moment and inner calling that unleashed a great power, freedom, and transcendence to transform *mySelf*.

I knew immediately that this was unlike any other experience I'd had in my life except for when I witnessed the birth of my two sons. It was a spiritual connection back to the supernatural power and presence of God. It was surreal and magical, like seeing Superman, my favorite all-time hero character, for the first time as a kid. However, this time I realized that *I'm* my favorite heroic character who has everything within to win.

To move forward, I acknowledged that I had to roll up my sleeves and get started. I had to pivot from an old negative way of thinking into a new healthy, positive way of *being*. After all, as a man thinketh, so is he! Taking a stand for myself with action required new disciplines in my life. It is like a pivot in basketball, one of my favorite sports, requiring you to plant one foot firmly on the floor without moving it and one foot to move around and away from a defender to gain an advantage. My defence was getting away from anyone or anything that no longer served me in leading myself to freedom.

Part of my pivoting consisted of taking a number of radical actions in the days ahead. I started listening to motivational videos that injected me daily with positivity and new ideas for rebuilding my life. I researched different meditation practices that calmed down the negative leech-sucking energies and received training to ground and center myself. I moved out of the house and back in with my parents at 42 years old: that is a humbling experience for certain. I prayed, reflected, and started pouring my heart out by writing all my thoughts, feelings, and emotions in a journal. Furthermore, I started to articulate on paper what I wanted to magnificently create for the rest of my life.

It felt amazing to start getting a daily injection of positivity, calmness, and authentic connection of love. However, there were still ongoing challenges and struggles, a lot of that due to breaking the strong willpower of my ego. I fell down a lot and resorted back to old patterns of thinking as I worked to climb up out of that muddy hole I had dug with my shovel for all those years. I remember one day listening to a motivational speech by one of the best of all time, Mr. Les Brown. It was like in that moment he spoke directly down into my heart. Mr. Brown said, "Make sure that when you fall down, you land on your back so you can look up to get up!" I chose to stop beating myself up for all the failures and realized this is now a lifelong journey of getting back up once you fall down. Life is a marathon and not a sprint.

There were radical shifts and transformations that took place in the next two years in all areas of my life. I started to cleanse and purge material possessions and people who no longer supported my best creative passions out of my life. I recall writing in my journal that, "If it is not real, then I no longer want it." A simple statement, yet so profound when I started putting that into practice. Practice does make perfect!

As time continued to pass by, I kept having new insights into what my focus needed to be going forward: a focus that consisted of not allowing all this pain, suffering, and failure to go to waste. I decided that I wanted to lead and serve humanity by offering my gifts, talents, and passion — a passion that became a consuming fire of compassion for all those who had experienced childhood wounding from abuse and dissolving a tenured marriage.

For a car to be built and drive off the assembly line to fulfill its purpose, it must go through a manufacturing process. That is exactly what it felt like for me over the course of the next year of healing and creating the next best version of myself to give out to the world. I signed up for Co-Active Training Institute to obtain my certification in life coaching. I branded and started my Transcend Coaching and Consulting business, and launched my speaking career. Additionally, I brought myself into a space of going where I had never gone before by telling my personal story through writing and self-publishing my book: *The Marble Effect*, giving myself the greatest gift of healing in the process.

One of the most impactful lessons I've learned is that I have to lead myself to free myself. From a larva at rest, to a crawling caterpillar, to a butterfly spreading its wings to fly, a metamorphosis process *is* necessary. A transformation of self doesn't take place without something to Ignite it. It is possible for you to heal and live a fulfilling life; rich with purpose. That will propel you into action to become what you never thought possible. Value yourself, and use your great power within to lead yourself forward.

I wrote this chapter to call *you* forth to Ignite something in yourself that you never thought possible. I never thought it was possible for me to heal from trauma and Ignite a new, outside-the-box social movement and mission called *#WeTogether*. We, together, can unite and RISE, STAND, and TRANSFORM ourselves to heal together. And, in finding that connection to my purpose, my mission is to spark healing within you. This mission, **HealU mission VII** is a miracle that consisted of myself coming into not just a refined belief system, but a *knowing* deep within of what my seven core truths are to create healing. They are...

HealU mission VII: Ignite Self with Action Now to Receive Miracle

I know everyone has a powerful story that offers inspiration to humanity. You are a miracle and deserve to have your voice heard!

I know about grass roots and not forgetting where you come from. You are a beautiful creation with a rich heritage and legacy to fulfill!

I know one is only at their best when authentic to their core. You must be who you truly are, and not what others label you!

I know there is a supernatural power, greatness, creativity, and destiny for one's life and purpose. These often get blocked by all the limits, cultural conditioning, and negativity from others' opinions and judgments, which robs you of living a fulfilling life. You are extraordinary — with special, unique gifts, talents, and passions!

I know true love only when true vulnerability is present. The essence of who you are is only love!

I know it takes courage to stand up and take action to create what you want for yourself in the midst of life's challenges. You are worthy and more than enough!

I know that one cannot give what they do not have within themselves first — like true love, peace, joy, happiness, contentment, and fulfillment — that only comes from an authentic connection with 'self'. You only attract what you are!

These are the seven things that I hope you will come to know that can guide you for the rest of your life. They empower us to become a product of true love.

After all, the essence of what you are is LOVE! A love that is **L**oyal, **O**ptimistic, **V**ulnerable, and **E**xtraordinary! The rich purity and cleansing light of authentic love heals all wounds and diminishes even the deepest scars over time.

As you connect back to the story line, your curiosity was likely piqued and thoughts were swirling around like a bumblebee nest being disrupted. You may be wondering what's behind this: **R**ISE · S**T**AND · TRANSF**O**R**M** with a bold callout to specific letters. It's a laser-focused approach for a magical roller coaster trip to self-healing and a true healing logical expression for one's heart and soul:

IS(IgniteSelf) + AN(ActionNow) = RM(ReceiveMiracle)

My favorite roller coaster, The Banshee, is a ride with many twists and turns, and so is this emotional journey; an Ignite moment of many twists and turns in this season of life that brought forth this spiritual awakening; a miraculous awakening from the slumber of intense darkness and being beyond broken mentally, physically, and spiritually. I think of healing this way: to launch a spaceship or explode a firework, the rockets and wick have to be Ignited with an intentional, sparking action to produce a miraculous result. Your miracle of healing life's traumas and childhood woundings is no different.

You may be beat down and find yourself at the bottom of the pit. Your darkness stems from life's traumas and woundings, cultural conditioning, and the negativity, devaluing, or disrespect from others. You may feel overwhelmed, anxious, depressed, or be experiencing Post Traumatic Stress Syndrome (PTSD). Despite all these conditions, I want to say something so important to you: *you are a beautiful miracle of creation with special gifts, talents, and passions.* It is time to connect back to Self and unleash the creative genius deep within yourself to fulfill your destiny and purpose. We all, from day one when the sperm hits the egg, have been ordained to make a difference and impact humanity. Throughout life's journey and amid your unique story, realize that you can move forward in life by connecting back to your infinite light.

Ignite Action Steps

The time is now for you to take the first step of your journey of healing and connecting to your light. You must lead yourself to free yourself. I want you to get up now from wherever you are to go seek and find a package of matches, a lighter, or a flame striker. Once you have this in hand, read on to what's next.

What you hold in your hands is your moment to initiate the processing of Igniting a fire. To get the fire, you must use your fingertip to initiate the spark and light the flame. You have to take action to create a flame of glowing light. Quite simply, *you have to lead yourself* to create this spark and flame. Consider this the start of your fire within and the freeing of yourself.

As you connect to the light and flame, I want you to realize you've now Ignited the courage and passion within yourself to take the next steps to heal yourself. Ignite yourself, act now, and receive the miracle.

Remember, blazing wildfires all start with a single spark! Be your own blazing wildfire today by Confronting the Darkness; Awakening the Spirit; Exploring and Discovering the Next Best Version of Self through Life Purpose, Values, and Leading From Within; and Creating from a Pure Heart and Soul.

Derrick Hill – United States of America
Author, Speaker, Life Coach
www.transcendwithtranscend.com
🐦 *@themarbleeffect*
📷 *transcendwithtranscend*
💼 *derrick-hill-83980511*

ASHLEY PATTERSON

"Do something you've never done to expose your vision within."

No matter where you are in your life, you have possibilities and potential. Sometimes, the only way to see the resources available to you is to do something that you have never done before. God has given you the imagination and the wherewithal to tap into your vision. Your greatness is aided by the resources that God has created for you. Your vision appears to you based on the gifts or special abilities that lie within you. My wish is that you realize your gift, show gratitude for it, explore it, refine it, and then expose it. This exposure is the gift that you give to the world. This is what makes your presence possible.

MAKING MYSELF POSSIBLE

I have had many losses within my family, but none hit me quite as hard as the loss of my cousin. She was a tall, thin, absolute firecracker who had inherited that fiery Puerto Rican energy and brought excitement to any room she walked into. She was also my best friend. We told each other all of our secrets, hopes, and dreams. We laughed together, cried together, argued with each other, and defended each other against the world. She was the first person I told after I signed the papers to launch my own business, and despite not knowing a single thing about my intentions, she was excited for me. I can even remember the pitch of her voice when I told her that I started the business and I called it Elite Acuity. She did not know what Elite Acuity was nor what the title meant, but she was the only one who made me feel that she believed in me unconditionally. Even if I was wrong, she stayed on my right. She was always there to support me without any judgment.

The world lost its color the day my best friend left it.

I will miss everything about her for the rest of my life. I will miss her unapologetic energy and the way she laughed. I will miss her flare. I will miss her spirit. To some, she was only a cousin, but for me, she was a piece of me that I adored and leaned on for unconditional support. She was the fire side of me. At times, she was who I wanted to be. I am so grateful for what she brought to my life and I will never grow up with another cousin quite like her. I miss her immensely, even as I write this right now.

Without her, there will be no food fights or family videos with Tamia's music playing in the background. No more drinking 'Pink Panties' all night and laughing about our failed relationships. No more phone conversations on my days off. No more dreams of "JamaicaMon." No more road trips singing Alicia Keys for an entire weekend. No more hot wing competitions. No more life with my beautiful best friend.

Her passing left me weakened, reduced, and diminished. I felt lost and alone. With those memories replaying in my head came severe anxiety, sadness, and hopelessness. It was like my whole world was dimming by the second. I never took time off when she died. Between my day job and my business, I felt that I had to keep going to avoid mourning her loss. I would wake up and cry, suffer through the day, then go back to sleep to repeat the same agony the next day. Denial pushed me to my breaking point. I had reached both rock-bottom and a brick wall with both my day job and my business. I wanted everything to just stop. There was nowhere else to go. There was nothing else to be. That was it. I had given up. I resigned from my job of 15 years and I lost hope.

Life felt impossible.

I could not predict how much damage the stress would do to my body, my mind, and my spirit. I did not realize that stress would cause me to gain weight, lose my hair, and contribute to an imbalance of hormones, which caused me to be severely deficient in vitamin absorption. I did not know that refusing to get out of bed would lead to me not even wanting to look at myself in the mirror. And, that refusing to look at myself in the mirror would decrease my self-worth. I did not love myself because the piece of me that felt loved passed away with my best friend. I even made sure not to take deep breaths because the exhale would guarantee uncontrollable tears. I kept myself dehydrated, malnourished, and isolated from the world around me while depriving myself from the basic benefits of everything, including the gift of deep breathing for healing.

We can all relate to trials and tribulations that caused us distress and/or harm, whether it be the loss of a loved one, or a job, or experiencing a rough childhood, abuse, divorce, or heartbreak. Some of us are still trying to navigate through the tunnel of pain, discouragement, or suffering. Yet through the pain, my journey focuses on the possibilities from making myself possible.

What do I mean by making myself possible?

Out of desperation, I began to take baby steps to attempt being happy again by doing little things around the house. I would start by playing music as loudly as possible from a YouTube™ stream while cleaning to get myself out of the funk. The thing about YouTube is that once you put a song on, if it is on AutoPlay, it will create a playlist that is similar to what you originally selected.

I recall one morning, six months into my isolation, I was standing at the sink rinsing the crumbs off a plate before putting it in the dishwasher. There was a hole in the fingertip of my rubber gloves and I could feel the water seeping in, cold and slimy with soap. I hated the sensation of it but did nothing. I had reached such a low that I didn't even care about making myself feel good while doing something so minute as washing dishes. I loved myself so little that I was willing to stay uncomfortable rather than just take the time to dry my hands and switch gloves.

You never know when your Ignite moment will happen.

The song I was listening to changed and, oddly enough, a Dr. Myles Munroe speech came on. When his voice began, I realized that the playlist that I had selected was no longer playing. I placed the plate in the dishwasher, took off the gloves, and attempted to dry my hands with a paper towel so that I could put the music back on. It was then that his voice captivated me. It was like his rhetoric had me stuck in a trance. He spoke about finding your purpose, maximizing your potential, and having a vision. Little did I know at the time, he was the bread crumb that would lead me out of the destructive mental state that I was in.

After I heard his speech, I rewound it a few times to capture everything he was saying. I even began to take notes. From his speech, I got the urge to read the Bible. Surely, there was something I needed to find in the Bible since I was so captivated by his references and lessons. After the replays ended, I ran to the guest room to look for my Bible. Oddly enough, it was in a chest with all my other degrees, awards, caps, and gowns. Why did I put the Bible with my accomplishments and not in the bookcase? I must have had that Bible for at least 10 years and never bothered to open it. You can always tell if someone reads their Bible by its appearance. Mine was pristine.

The most intriguing portion of the Bible was the introduction just before the Old Testament section. It was there that I discovered the philosophy and methodology of how the Bible is translated. Some areas are formal-equivalent, which is literal and *word-for-word*. However, and most importantly for me, there is also dynamic-equivalent, which is *thought-for-thought* theory. This would eventually give me enough intrigue to dig deep within my own self; within my own turmoil.

By the time I finished the introduction and got to Genesis, the first *book* in the Bible, I was floored. I had never understood until then that the world was made for me and that I was created in the image of something greater than myself and my best friend. I began to grow, learn, and expand on who I was and why I was here. I started to attract people of the same interest, and I was able to get different perspectives and breakdowns of the scripture and how it applied to my daily life. Over time, I continued to read the Bible and other books that were inspired by the Word. I formed a bible study to teach others how to read the Bible cover to cover in just one year, starting from the title page. That shifted my tears of pain to become tears of relief and hope.

I was no longer alone. I was becoming aware!

I learned that before we entered our physical body, we were spirits with God. When we entered into our physical form, some of us became disconnected from God and our own internal spirit. We began to advance physically, all the while participating in self-destruction and the limitation of our abilities. The word 'rehab' is short for rehabilitation and restoration. Giving God permission to *rehab* or operate in our lives will restore and strengthen our abilities by breaking the habit of self-destruction.

As time went on, my spirituality took on a new form. I was no longer carrying the burden of all my aches and pains, which meant that I gave myself permission to let go and let God. I gave myself permission to forgive. Permission to find happiness, joy, and enlightenment through the expression of gratitude. Through my journey, I was presented with opportunities and people that I could not have imagined were on my path.

In less than one year, I found a mentor that helped me to better understand the experiences of my spiritual growth. I was presented with an honorable coin, a unique award directly from an Air Force colonel, and I got a puppy. Most importantly, I started a short gratitude list to keep my momentum. Things took off, and in the span of four days, I spoke for the first time on stage about my company which forwarded the opportunity for more clients. I met my future publisher, found an accountability partner, and I prayed with the motivational leader, Les Brown. All this by making myself possible.

All this, and I was still having difficulty with self-love and self-worth. Someone once asked me what my financial goals were, and it was hard for me to answer. I really did not know. I did not think I was deserving of money or anything for that matter. I was just happy that God loved me enough to show me grace and mercy. Without a true answer, I began to deep dive into who I really was. I studied more about the conscience and subconscious mind, my vision, Dr. Munroe's teaching, along with the scriptures. The answer that I was missing was right in front of my face the entire time.

While I was grateful for the Earth that God created, which is a formal-equivalent (literal) theory, I had not tapped into the dynamic-equivalent (thought-for-thought) theory. He literally made the Earth for me to cultivate, but what else? He created everything I could ever need to accomplish the vision of Elite Acuity, and he placed it on my heart. Everything I could ever need, want, or desire was already created by Him.

When I grasped that concept, the world began to look colorful again.

Every plant, animal, thought, and person in my life began to take on a new form and meaning. Time was no longer a daunting factor. I began to appreciate my past rather than long for it to return. I choose to write with my non-dominant hand permanently. I decided to see the world from a different perspective; a possible perspective. When I was able to release the horrible thoughts about myself out of myself, I instantly felt light as a feather. I slept better than I had slept in years. My body began to heal itself from the destruction of anxiety and stress. I started to believe in my self-worth. I embraced my best friend's spirit rather than mourn her death. My gratitude list took a form of its own because I was no longer trying to find things to be happy about. Instead, I wrote from the heart.

I was revived.

Anyone who knows me knows that I am a very private person. I do not typically talk about my life, or my feelings. Instead, I put it on paper. I recently discovered that living a private life is not the same as holding myself back from my dreams and aspirations. Living a private life, as I would define it, would only hinder my growth and possibilities.

Enlightenment is the vibration that I strive for every day. Perhaps that is why I am finally ready to share the lessons of my life story. I did not wake up one random morning and write this message without careful consideration.

Instead, I used this story as a process to release my experience and my gift. I continue to address what I think are the essential things about spirituality and how to connect the dots on an accelerated level.

I now define Elite Acuity, my consulting company, as the most powerful keenness of perception. That keenness of perception is what I had to make possible. My new story is about making myself possible through a needed season of strength, courage, and faith.

We are all given unique gifts. Our only real job in life is to discover that gift and cultivate it to share with the world. Before we can talk about purpose and gifts, we must start from the beginning. In the Bible and many other readings, you will find that God created the heaven, the Earth, the seas, and everything in it. After the creation of everything, we were created and given the breath of life and dominion. With all of God's creations, everything has a seed. That is how we decipher what is *kosher* and what is not. In other words, was this fruit or vegetable a seed directly from God, or an item from God altered by man? Notice that anything created by God was created for advancement and cultivation. Mankind is included in that category. We were created to have dominion over the Earth and everything in it, we were also created to be fruitful and most importantly, advance. Opposition in our life is not meant for dwelling, regret, or resistance.

Opposition is how we advance toward cultivation.

Every obstacle that we go through is intended to enhance our advancement. Our only limitation is the areas that are deemed self-destructive. In other words, we are called to avoid acting, being, and participating in the things that separate us from the gifts given to us, and God.

I remind myself every day about this idea. We were made in the image of God. Therefore, if we believe God to be all, great, and mighty, then we were created for *all*, greatness, and might. When I say I made myself possible, I am actually recapping my story. I made myself push through opposition by submitting to God. Through submission, I received the clarity of my gifts to serve others to Ignite their belief and faith by letting go and letting God operate. By letting go and letting God, we are granted the ability to see the *elite acuity* — the most powerful keenness of perception.

No matter where you are in your life, you have possibilities. You have potential. We are all created for greatness. Imagine the places you would go if you sought to use the abundance that God has given to you. You have been given all the resources that you could ever need or even think of. They are right in front of you, though you may be oblivious to them. We will never be able to eat all the apples in the world, drink all the water, inherit all the money, or monopolize every industry. All of God's creations are resources that fall under our dominion, so why not thank God and then show gratitude by cherishing those resources. Make yourself possible for the ability and openness to receiving such blessings.

I wrote this message in hopes that my journey may help you along your journey. We all have different trials and tribulations that we must get through, but the overarching process is the same. Something that I once read and that I now live by, is a passage, *"I walk my journey, and if you choose to walk the journey with me, then we walk the journey together."*

IGNITE ACTION STEPS

The first and most important step to this process is awareness of your current position. Make a decision on the level of vibration that you strive to be. Once you reflect and decide, do something you have never done. It does not have to be major. For example, if you walk your dog every day, walk the opposite direction, if you usually wake up at 7 AM in the morning, try waking up at 6:45 to give yourself 15 minutes to meditate, pray, or write a gratitude list. If you do not have a gratitude list, start one! If you are not sure what to be thankful for, that is okay. It is neither a race nor competition, so start out slow and honest. Write down one or two things that you see as a blessing. Allow your list to grow as you see new blessings come into your life. Set your intentions to the vibration that you decided for yourself every day. If you want to be happy, tell yourself that you are happy. If you want to be joyful, then be joyful. Finally, repeat the cycle and do something you've never done to expose the vision within. Imagine if you did something new every day to get something you have never had every day of your life.

Ashley Patterson – United States of America
Elite Acuity Founder and CEO
www.eliteacuity.com

Tammy McCann

"Your courage to let go of the old is rewarded with the successes of the new."

My wish for you is that as you read my story, you begin to recognize your true power within. If you're finding yourself struggling with your challenges, those imposed on you or chosen by you, I invite you to go deeper. There you will discover the new version of YOU who is open to limitless possibilities.

Quantum Shift Your Paradigm

I flung open the glossy white doors on the top floor of the office building where I held my monthly evening event for business owners, *Quantum Reconnection.* High vibe music filled the ultra-modern penthouse marketing suite of my London-based office. I set up small trampolines, more commonly called 'rebounders,' for my business clients to bounce on and energize themselves after their long working week. I loved this intimate event as it was like no other: qi gong energy moves done to music followed by meditation and spiritual teaching. I was buzzing with excitement, eager to show my clients a video clip I had found of Tibetan monks performing an extraordinary feat.

Several months earlier, I had felt a strong urge to include this unique event as part of my clients' business Mastermind program, which over time, had fostered a close family-like community that went beyond being simply a business networking group. But my idea had initially come up against a little resistance from my fellow lead coach and business partner: my husband, Adam. Previously, as government-endorsed GrowthAccelerator™ coaches and trainers, we had the luxury of financial backing to help small business owners grow their teams, increase their sales, and improve their position in the market. But once the Department for Business dissolved this initiative in 2016 we, like thousands of other registered coaches, no longer had guaranteed, funded work.

During this new pivotal time it felt right to transition and further define our niche. However, much to my husband's confusion, I did this by flavoring our business coaching practices with my esoteric and spiritual philosophies. My Buddhist upbringing had taught me to follow my intuitive whispers; something which my logical, systems-minded husband often deemed to be a little 'out there.' Quantum Reconnection was one of those ideas, and it created tension between us.

In our business partnership, we had previously dovetailed our coaching sessions together. Our trainings included technical topics, such as creating a webpage or systems automation; areas in which Adam took the lead. We also ran courses such as personal branding or authentic selling. For these, I took the lead. I loved that we complemented each other. But as we repositioned the business, I started to sprinkle in 'breathing' and mindfulness work that aligned with my true sense of being. I just *knew* it was the right thing to do, and was rewarded with wonderful opportunities to introduce *Mindfulness* to teachers looking to support their stressed students. However, this meant Adam's and my core business focus was slowly changing. He was out of his depth and I could see him struggling to understand the significance of spiritual, quantum ideas in successful business practice. The strain between us mounted and it began to create a chink in our united force.

Despite the doubts that were ebbing and flowing within my partnership, I persisted in bringing Quantum Reconnection to fruition; listening to the inner voice that whispered I was on the right path. Out of that whisper, this evening of music and meditation came to be.

The first to arrive at Quantum Reconnection that evening was Theresa. Her confident strides echoed in the bright, oak-floored entrance. Breathless yet beaming, her dark eyes were fixed on me, sparkling with a secret ready to be shared. Smiling inwardly and out, I greeted her with arms outstretched ready to embrace her in our customary heart-to-heart hug.

We had been working together for a while. She was a private client who came for business insights, but what I unraveled were much deeper personal issues. Theresa had experienced a hard life which I recognized manifested in physical dis-ease and illness. She was jailed by a long-term disorder, chronic

Sarcoidosis, which debilitated her movements and kept her in unbearable pain, bedridden for years. While a combination of alternative therapies and a multitude of vitamins helped to provide a light relief, nothing truly alleviated her agony in a meaningful way. Despite this, Theresa was also trying to run a concierge business, which was failing miserably. She had come to me as a last resort recommended by a mutual friend, who I later discovered described me as the spiritual coach that helped transform all areas of life and business.

The energized Theresa who showed up to Quantum Reconnection that night was unrecognizable to the lady who hobbled into my home in excruciating pain earlier in the year. Within minutes all the group members, all consciously aware business owners and entrepreneurs, had arrived and were warmly greeting each other with hugs; enthusiastically bouncing on the rebounders while the music was pumping.

After a few minutes, I switched off the music and invited everyone to come ground themselves. Once we completed our grounding session to the sweet sound of the Tibetan singing bowl, I turned to Theresa, meeting her soulful gaze. I sensed she had something important to say and was working hard to keep herself centered. She took a deep breath, trying to keep her strong tenor voice steady as she began to share her story. She had just been given the results after the latest routine round of blood tests that checked for various markers for her numerous medical issues. She had come straight from the hospital and we were the first privileged few to hear her news. My group sat silent, eager to hear her share: ***"I no longer have the indicators for Sarcoidosis!"***

It took us a second to take in the significance of this information, and then came the ecstatic cheers, whooping, and shrieks of disbelief. In the recent months spent working with Theresa to heal the wounds of her difficult upbringing, we had all witnessed the extraordinary transformation in her. The channeling work we delved into was rewarded by Theresa discovering her sixth sense, a gift that enabled her to channel prophetic insight through intuitive poems. Woven in her words was often news of future events or a timely message for a specific individual, and the group had been enraptured by these poems each month. But in that moment, the extraordinary announcement of these test results was the medical confirmation of her powerful physical self-healing, and it was awe-inspiring.

For me, the news that evening was a confirmation that I truly needed to run with this Quantum energetic aspect and apply it to my work. Though I had trained as a reiki healer and clinical hypnotherapist, I had never before blurred the lines of business coaching and energy work. Celebrating with Theresa, I could feel something was brewing… somehow it was the start of something new.

As the night progressed and the mood of the room mellowed, I dimmed the lights. I wanted to show my students the extraordinary video of the Tibetan monks moving a massive boulder using sound frequency alone. My intention was to illustrate what is possible outside the normal laws of the physical world; a message that was especially fitting that evening.

As my eyes adjusted to the darkness, I felt a sense of stillness come over me. The voice of the narrator seemed to diminish as if broadcast from another worldly plane, the ethereal flickering light from the screen developed a lucid quality, and I seemed to disperse and blend into the room. I was embraced by a sense of clarity and calm, yet simultaneously I felt my inner self expanding exponentially into a heightened state. In that sacred moment, I could *feel* the lightness in the energy of my students as they were opening themselves up to the seemingly impossible. It struck me there and then, how much they trusted me to support them with their *lives*, not simply their businesses. Sitting in this space where time didn't exist, each and every victorious outcome they had so valiantly battled with themselves to achieve played out in my mind... I had witnessed the inner battle of their own egos and the external challenges of their personal situations. Time and time again through my inner eye, I witnessed the death of their victimhood and watched them choose to transcend into their authentic, true selves. Each person had their own story of transformation and each of them supported the others, creating a unified field of energy that was greater than the sum of its parts.

In that moment, I knew this is what I was truly here for. It washed over me from head to toe with a heat that felt both warm and uncomfortable. I could feel something inside of me shifting at a profound level. It was a knowing, body deep, and it was challenging me to change *everything* about my life. I felt a flicker of light and hope, and I knew that I had to listen. *My whole life had led me on a spiritual journey, gifting to me this very moment of knowing in which I deeply embodied my purpose.*

As I consciously jolted back into the room, a tsunami wave of emotion rushed over me, and I couldn't hold back the hot tears of humble pride. Re-witnessing my clients' journeys was testament to believing in my gift for energetic healing and spiritual guidance. In addition, I was determined to share it with these incredible individuals who had made it their mission to make a positive impact in their own way with their clients, their community, or for the greater good. I wanted to empower them, and create a safe space for them to grow and evolve.

As the video came to an end, I wiped my eyes, took a deep breath, and resolved from that moment on to focus my energy on creating new, more impactful programs to help my clients to make the quickest and most powerful energetic transformations. On the heels of this resolution, though, I realized my first challenge was to explain this to my husband.

The journey that followed was a bumpy one. As he rightly pointed out, our potential clients would come to us with the goal of growing their business upon reaching a glass ceiling of financial success. They measured success in terms of increasing sales, turnover, and profits. How was I to explain succinctly that breaking through the ceiling was not always a consequence of changing the marketing strategy or working on their sales technique? How was I to change their perception toward understanding that the real currency for creating success was *Universal energy*? Over the following days and weeks, I spent much of my own energy trying to explain this concept to my skeptical husband: describing how, within us, energy doesn't FLOW freely if we hold onto dense limiting beliefs that lead to ineffective action.

At first it was not easy to proclaim that no matter how hard our clients worked or whatever strategy was used, they would manifest outcomes that were still in alignment with their negative subconscious beliefs. The whole premise of Quantum energy goes against the grain of the traditional business coaching we had adopted for so many years, and I found myself butting up against my husband's logical reasoning time and time again.

It was extremely challenging to take on my husband's naysaying. While he no longer doubted my ability to help our clients using this new approach, it was our difference in values and beliefs that really got in the way. I knew inherently that when we fully utilized our different yet complementary skills and abilities, it enabled us to get into FLOW, so I truly wanted us to run with this new Quantum concept *together*. This desire of mine started to make rifts in so many facets of our business relationship. We needed every ounce of compassion, faith, and tuning into our love to prevent our marriage from souring.

After countless, repeated arguments, however, I slowly began to recognize it was part of my own conscious journey to simply move forward with my intuitive decision. Journaling and doing my own inner work allowed me to see my own fears of taking the helm, taking the perceived 'risk' of changing the course of our business and ultimately our lives. My *old* self wanted the safety of our Yin-Yang partnership, but my *new* self realized I was whole and complete on my own. My working with Theresa had been a gift within a gift. Her personal rebirth was my sign that my unique method, Quantum Transformation coaching, was my purpose. That what I do indeed reshapes lives. With all the courage I could muster, *I* took responsibility for my own internal change and surrendered to my chosen path.

I fell deeply in love with working with my clients in this way. The more I tuned into their energy, the more I was able to read *where* they were at, *what* they needed to do, and *why*. Through word of mouth, I became known for my Quantum transformations and 'knowings,' which took me by surprise as I never advertised to my normal business community. I strictly selected who I chose to work with. These were the visionaries who, like many small business owners, were stuck in the 'doing' of their lives but held a deep-rooted desire to be, do, and have more — to be more on purpose. Together we focused on rapidly breaking the paradigm of their 'old' life to create a new life of empowerment, mission, and purpose, while also having the wealth they so rightly deserved.

One such client was Caragh, a spiritually aware branding consultant. Caragh arrived with tens of thousands of pounds of debt and a lack of consistent income. Our first session sliced through Caragh's limiting beliefs. By the end of the first week, she had paid off her debt; within months, she had made twice what she owed. On one particular day, during a business Mastermind event, I strongly *intuited* that Caragh urgently had to address an area of her life that she had avoided looking at: her *health*. I shared this intuition with her, and a few days later she called to say she had found a lump in her breast and was going into hospital to get it biopsied. Caragh shared that while in the hospital reception room, she saw a clock on the wall and on it read the word 'QUANTUM.' She understood it was part of her spiritual journey, but it still didn't prepare her for receiving the news of having a particularly aggressive form of breast cancer. Our bodies are barometers for unresolved issues that have not yet been addressed. For Caragh, her cancer became the catalyst for deep spiritual inner work. Over the ensuing months we went deep into uncovering the layers of her life. All of it created a picture that was subtly awash with grief, distress, and hardship. Each aspect held a group of limiting beliefs like pieces of a jigsaw puzzle for a 'life' picture that no longer resonated with her. We slowly removed each part of the jigsaw that did not match her greater life vision, painstakingly working piece by piece until a whole new picture was created. This was deep spiritual work. As I energetically navigated Caragh on her journey to owning her *spiritual Sovereignty*, she uncovered a stronger, more purpose-aligned version of herself. Our Quantum coaching sessions prepared her to truly value her own worth and find her voice to ultimately speak her TRUTH. As Caragh's confidence grew so did her business, to multiple six figures within months, but more importantly, Caragh had stepped into the role of conscious changemaker.

By stepping into my gift and trusting my internal voice, my Quantum coaching business has grown and evolved in many ways and is now a true reflection of me. I now feel so honored and privileged to have worked with hundreds of amazing clients who were able to redesign their lives without getting stuck in the drama of whatever was going on with them. They showed courage in stripping back those layers and entrusting me to guide them through the miracle of their next level challenge, in life and business. The true gift of working with them has shown me that there are indeed no limits, only our perception of the world. My inner whispers continue to guide me to work with those that choose to play a bigger game; are on a mission to improve lives, with love, and to create a ripple in the world.

Perhaps you may think you have external challenges holding you back, but that's just a consequence. The real challenge is the inner challenge to change aspects of your own beliefs. By choosing to let go of your current perceived reality and step into the *'unknown,'* you will unleash your Quantum power and open Pandora's box of infinite possibilities.

Ignite Action Steps

If in your life right now you feel the need to break through your glass ceiling and reach that next level of business, wealth, intimacy, or health and wellness, notice what resistance comes up first and journal about it. Ask yourself the following questions:

How deep do I wish to dive into the unknown?
What am I choosing not to look at?
What am I prepared to let go of?
How far am I willing to go and WHY?

It takes courage to strip back those layers, so be honest with yourself and notice what shows up as your answers will form the foundations of the new version of YOU.

Tammy McCann – United Kingdom
Quantum Transformation Coach
https://tammy-mccann.com

SORANA PASCARIU

"Enduring is survival; strength is making a change so you can thrive."

It is my intention to wake you up to the fact that your potential is infinite. I want my story to reveal to you the limiting beliefs and paradigms that keep you stuck and help you transmute them into the infinite possibilities that are waiting to be brought into existence by your intention and commitment. Wherever you may be right now, life can become magical, rewarding, juicy, and worthwhile.

THE DAY I DECIDED

I am what they call a poor rich girl. Rich because I have had a lot of privilege in my life: enough money to pay for a great education, lovely homes, stylish clothes, and glamorous vacations. I had smart and educated parents who took me to museums and to ballet lessons and taught me to speak several languages. But, I am also poor because the clothes, vacations, homes, good universities, and French lessons came with a share of emotional pain that nearly killed me.

I was born in a family of Romanian intellectuals who became very successful bankers after the fall of communism in 1989. My father was one of the key individuals who rebuilt the Romanian banking system in postcommunist Romania. My mother was beautiful, brilliant, and my absolute role model in this world. She had a PhD in economics, spoke seven languages, and was deeply admired in the small elite community of Bucharest.

My world started to crumble when I was a teenager. My mother began showing signs of mental illness. She heard voices that told her strange and dark things. She believed she was being persecuted and followed. And at the same time, she believed she was chosen by God for some great purpose. This was back in the 90s, in postcommunist Romania, so there was very little information available about mental illness. As her child, I didn't know that she was displaying symptoms of the onset of paranoid schizophrenia.

As I entered college, my father left home as he could not cope with my mother's illness anymore. He would have sunk into darkness as well. I understood. I wanted him to have a shot at happiness. But I was not ready for him to leave me alone to deal with my mother.

I understand now that he simply did the best he could, but at the time I was incredibly angry at him for leaving me to manage her unraveling behavior. Mom was violent — not toward me, but toward herself — and I was overwhelmed. I went to him repeatedly, begging for help, and all he would say was, "She's your mother; she's your responsibility."

It was so difficult to not have his support and, enraged by it, I once went to his house in the middle of the night and broke every single piece of china he had. I wanted so desperately for him to hear me and know I was sinking. When my grandfather came down to the kitchen the next morning, the pile of broken pieces was knee-high. But neither my father nor my grandfather could see it as the desperate cry for help that it was. Dismissively, the only thing I got was, "You scared Grandpa."

The separation from my father pushed my mother over the edge. She descended into madness. Her particular form of mental illness, coupled with her beliefs and mindset, produced the most violently negative and suffering-prone person I have ever met. She victimized herself daily, with a level of negativity that led to catastrophizing; making sure that she sunk deeper every day. She tore apart everything that could have been good in her life and twisted it until it was a disaster. She refused to take care of herself and starved herself and at times self-harmed by cutting her wrists with a blunt knife — not to take her own life but to portray herself as a victim. She kept cats in her house and refused to neuter them or stop them from having babies, until there were 50 of them peeing on the walls, scratching furniture, and destroying everything she owned. She refused to fix things when they broke and soon everything around her was in ruin.

The next 10 years of my life were dedicated to trying to save my mother. I forgot about myself, sabotaged my relationships, did the bare minimum for my career, and I still couldn't move the needle on her well-being.

Despite that horrible situation, I struggled to hold it together, to stick to my goals. I managed to get into a good business school — Kellogg School of Management in Chicago — and to graduate. By no means did I get good grades, but it was honestly a miracle I could study at all. After graduation, I returned home to Romania and started a tech company, and then another. I worked hard to build my reputation both professionally and in my community, and was proud of holding my own in a society that knew me as my parents' daughter. I fell in love with a man who I thought loved me back, and for a while it seemed like things were getting better for me.

After two and a half years together, this man whom I loved deeply told me he no longer wanted to be with me. It felt like the ground disappeared from underneath me; a betrayal that seemed to mirror my father's. In an attempt to keep it together, I went to a party hoping that I would see him and get to talk to him. Instead, a friend shared the news that his photo was in the Romanian tabloids... with another girl... a girl who represented everything I despised: tacky plastic surgery, flashy, uneducated. There were articles about them and videos of them making out. My community was aflame with gossip about our breakup and it hit me hard. I was in shock. I descended into a level of suffering that was reminiscent of my mother.

The next year and a half, I hovered between life and death as pill bottles littered my bedside table. I had depression and PTSD and was put on heavy medication — benzodiazepines for my shock, Ambien to fight the insomnia, and antidepressants. I didn't eat and was underweight; so thin I was transparent. The medication kept my pain suppressed to the level where I could survive, but it could not cure me. I had to do that for myself.

I was a ghost. A ghost who wanted to die every single day.

The darkness felt overwhelming but there was a part of me, something deep inside of me, that had had enough of that feeling and wanted to live. I couldn't wake up every day contemplating suicide. I knew I needed help beyond what I was already getting, and I reached out to get it. About a year into my ordeal, I was introduced to a wonderful therapist called Dan and he helped me grieve.

It was in one of our sessions that Dan changed *everything* for me and helped save my life. I was telling him: "I don't understand how I got to this. I endured so much. I have always been strong. I managed to function through everything that happened with my mother. How did I collapse from this?"

"Well," he said, "there are two things here. First, there is a huge difference between enduring and being strong. We believe it's the same thing, but they are vastly different energies. Enduring is survival. Strength is making a change so you can thrive. When you endure, your nervous system takes in all that pressure. You think you're being strong, but what you're doing is making yourself weaker. When a hit comes that you would normally be able to handle, your system just collapses."

His words resonated through me and down to my core, especially the *enduring* versus *strength* part. I'd built an identity around my so-called strength: "I can endure and that makes me strong and special." I understand where this paradigm came from. There were times in history when people could not make a change in their lives. When they could not leave a marriage, change cities, or start a business. Their circumstances were fixed and all they could do was endure. That belief was lodged deep within my subconscious and affected how I perceived the world.

One day, about three months after my conversation with Dan, I made a decision... I decided I was going to get well. I was not going to be that person that hovers between life and death and lives without being alive. As soon as I made that decision, I suddenly had energy. I could feel it coursing through me, waves of life-force energy animating my body where previously it had felt numb and limp. *Energy was the answer.* Energy was the key to the healing I needed.

I decided I was going to master energy healing and heal myself. I had been dabbling in spirituality and energy healing for some time, and I knew how powerful it was. I turned to my most trusted coping mechanism — reading. Since I was a child, reading was a way to escape my problems and now reading was going to solve them. I decided I was going to read *everything* that had been written on the topic and teach myself how to heal. I knew it was possible, and I knew I was going to do it.

After devouring four or five of the most popular writings on the topic, the solution came from the 'recommendation engine' on my Kindle™. The book was *Becoming Supernatural* by Dr. Joe DiSpenza. As soon as I read the description, I just knew the answer lay within its pages. And it did.

The salvation I had been looking for consisted of a guided meditation crafted by Dr. Joe. I learned that meditation is a word that describes many things. This particular meditation was a three-part exercise that consisted of a breathing technique taken from Kundalini. I would start by focusing on tightening my pelvic muscles and then breathe from the bottom of my pelvis, up my spine, to the top of my head. Next, I focused on different parts of my body, alternating between a convergent (closed) and divergent (open) focus. Finally, I visualized how I would love my life to look. I envisioned all the beautiful things I wanted for my life. I visualized writing a book and speaking at TED X™, and brought up all the emotions those things would create. And there, in that meditation, I found happiness again. It was the first time I had felt happiness in a year and a half, and I knew that by meditating in this way, I'd have an hour of elevated emotions every day... guaranteed.

I committed to doing this meditation twice a day, no matter how hard it was to focus at times. Three weeks later, I was fully healed. The depression and PTSD disappeared as if by miracle. I just realized I was not sick anymore. My heart was not broken anymore. I would wake up feeling happiness, gratitude, and joy, just like I had practiced in my meditation.

Experiencing what amounts to a miraculous healing is a complete paradigm-changer. It made me question everything I had been taught about how we function as humans and about how the world functions. I thought to myself, "If this is possible, then what else is possible?"

The answer to that question is: ANYTHING. Anything you can dream of is possible. It will most likely not happen overnight. It can take time, but being committed to both visualizing and working toward it daily will bring it into existence. You can heal yourself and change your life in ways that seem impossible.

Does that mean that once I had my breakthrough moment, I never struggled or suffered again? Definitely not. My mother had modeled an addiction for suffering and I learned that lesson well. It might seem counterintuitive, but suffering is in fact very addictive. On a neurochemical level, your body gets used to the chemistry of suffering and feels at home in it. Happiness feels incredibly foreign and you subconsciously try to get back to what you know. When your belief system is built around suffering, you automatically recreate that again and again in your life. Suffering can make you feel special. Chosen. Strong. It can also be that you believe there is too much to lose when you are happy; suffering is safer. There is no height to tumble down from, you're already on the ground.

I never again got down as low as I did at that point in my life, but I did have more subconscious attempts to recreate suffering, loneliness, and misery. But, every time I created a victim situation for myself, I had the awareness of what was going on. There was a detached observer perspective that allowed me to witness what I was doing, then employ all the tools and healing methods I had acquired along the way.

Five years from that darkest point, I am now gloriously celebrating the anniversary of my healing in Tulum, a beach town in Mexico where I now live part time. It is an extraordinary place, a paradise of aquamarine waters and verdant jungle that is home to a community of incredible humans — spiritual, conscious, awakened, and free. The world I live in now is so different. It is a world of endless possibilities. I am living a level of happiness and fulfillment that I did not believe possible before. Being this happy brought up a lot of guilt for not being able to save my mother. For her being in hell and me in paradise. But instead of letting the guilt engulf me, instead of sinking into suffering so I could stay loyal to her, I grieved. I grieved, and then I let her go. In doing so, I allowed myself to feel all the happiness that I deserve.

Today, I'm living a life that I love, and this brings me happiness every day. I adore my work. I coach people on living an extraordinary life. Through my podcast, *Mindset For Mars*, I get to meet the most interesting people on the planet with whom I have fascinating conversations. I've spoken at TEDx about happiness, and I am in the final stages of writing and editing the book that I visualized in that very first meditation. I am surrounded by amazing people whom I love deeply and with whom I have conscious relationships. I have found my tribe and my soul family. The relationship with my father has also evolved and we share a level of connection that deepens every day. I am excited about life and about everything I am doing. My life is filled with magic.

I am here to tell you that I am not special. I am human, as are you. It is part of our potential to create anything we dream of. If I could do it, if I could heal myself from debilitating depression and PTSD, if I could shift my legacy of deep suffering, then so can you. Your life can be extraordinary. You can do work that feels like play. You can have conscious relationships in which you are loved exactly as you are and in which every day is an opportunity for growth. Your life can be absolute magic. You can dream of the impossible and make it all possible!

Ignite Action Steps

Decide that you will create the life you want on your own terms. This is a powerful psychological step; a promise that you make to yourself.

Heal the pain that is keeping you back. I do not say this lightly. I know healing can be difficult and take a long time, but once you really decide, you will find the courage to access that pain and heal it.

Envision what it is that you want. Write it out in detail, in the present tense. Picture it like a movie in your head every morning in your meditation, and evoke the emotions that it would prompt in you — gratitude, joy, euphoria; emotions that make living worthwhile.

Commit to bringing what you want into existence. Visualizing is only part of the equation; you have to also take daily action. Write the book, start the business, book the therapy appointment. Whatever it is that you need to do, go do it.

Sorana Pascariu – Romania & United Kingdom
Human Potential Expert & Transformational Coach
www.mindsetformars.com
Sorana Pascariu
@sorana.pascariu

DONNA LOCKETT, PhD

*"Wisdom is the quiet knowing in the midst of a challenging time
that tomorrow springs forth the promise of a new day."*

As you read this chapter, it is my hope that you will feel the power of possibilities, for yourself and for those around you. The possibility that you can heal. The possibility that trauma does not need to be a life sentence. The possibility that, with proper support, YOU can learn to not only release trauma but to live a more compassionate, authentic, embodied, heart, and spirit-centered life.

LEANING INTO BROKENNESS, AWAKENING TO GRACE

September 1, 1995 was a clear day. The sky was blue, the air was fresh. It was Friday before Labor Day weekend and I was driving home from a physiotherapy appointment near my home on the outskirts of Canada's bustling capital, Ottawa. Three weeks prior I had won the National Championships in my sport, duathlon, and was three weeks away from competing at the World Championships in Australia. Moving my body is what I had done since the age of 10 to manage my anxiety and fears. Racing had become my identity. I was good. I was fast. I held many titles and records as a 5km and 10km road runner and as a duathlete. I had an uncanny ability to push myself to the brink of collapse. Pushing myself came with a cost however… I suffered injury after injury, some of them quite serious, all of them self-imposed through not hearing when my body called for "mercy." After each injury I came back stronger, faster, more determined. The 'comeback kid' they called me in local newspapers. I was a hero to many; yet inside I felt chronically weak, inadequate, an imposter.

As I pulled out to merge into traffic, out of the corner of my eye I caught a glimpse of something red careening toward me at high speed. I felt at once a confusion and narrowing of my vision, and then a deafening sound as my body was hurled to the other side of the car. All I could utter was a series of quiet, "Shit... shit... shit... shit.... shit." I felt a slight tinge in my hip as the reality that I had been T-boned in my driver door at full speed washed over me. Minutes later I heard the piercing sounds of sirens as police, ambulance, and firefighters surrounded me. As they were cutting me out of the car with the Jaws of Life, I relayed that my hip felt a little "off" and I *just* needed to see a chiropractor. As I traveled in the ambulance, I cajoled lightheartedly with the paramedics; all of us oblivious to the extent of my injuries.

I ended up being taken to three different local hospitals and multiple doctors were consulted on my case. Each soberly relayed that I was very lucky to be alive; that this kind of impact injury usually results in a break at the neck of the femur (the long upper leg bone) leading to the jagged bone piercing the internal organs and causing a fatal bleed. On this day, the neck of my femur did not break. Instead, it had busted through my pelvis and hip and penetrated my abdomen.

I was 30 years old. In the prime of my life. The fastest female runner in my home province of 15 million people. The fastest female duathlete in Canada. Moving was what I did. Yet, in that life-altering moment of being told I would be crippled, I lay very still. I did not cry. I did not scream. I felt nothing. I said nothing. I just smiled politely.

I was transferred via air ambulance to a hospital 400km away, where an ankle specialist offered to try to put me back together — he was the only one willing to try. I suddenly understood the nursery rhyme "Humpty Dumpty" in a different light. After eight hours of surgery, with enough hardware in my hip to set off a sensitive metal detector, I was told, "You will walk, but you won't be active, and certainly you will never run or race again." I opened my mouth to say something, but nothing came out.

I was immobilized in my hospital bed for three months, at first in the hospital and then at home. The bed was set up in my living room and the left side of my body was in traction. A full-time nurse, friends, and family provided round-the-clock care for everything from making meals, to getting dressed, to changing my bedpan. Being so dependent and exposed left me feeling incredibly vulnerable. Being ill-equipped to feel that emotional tenderness, I spent my days doing pull-ups on the triangle support that hung above me in my hospital bed and worked away at my computer, helping my boss as he completed his doctoral dissertation.

Finally I was given the green light to transfer from my supine position to a wheelchair. My neighbors rallied to carry me down my front steps in my wheelchair so that I could take a spin around the neighborhood. It was a clear, crisp winter evening. The smell of the pine trees was intoxicating. The sharp, cool air penetrated my lungs. I felt as close to the feeling of aliveness as I had ever experienced.

I spent four months in that wheelchair, after which time I had to learn to walk again. Putting on shoes was near impossible. Sitting for more than 20 minutes, excruciating. At times on a road trip I would have to stop at a gas station and lay on the grungy floor to stretch out my hip and back. I moved through my day with constricted breath, with little access to a full inhalation. The pain in my hip and back were so intense, there were days when all I could do was limp to bed, pull the covers up to my neck, and trust that tomorrow would be a better day.

About a year after I learned to walk again, as I was out for my daily walk, I broke into some running strides. I managed to only run five steps, but they were the sweetest, most exquisite steps I had ever taken. I had accomplished something I was told would be impossible for me to do. I bounded into my house and excitedly announced to my partner that I was going to run a marathon — something I had never done as I had been so focused on 5km and 10km road races and duathlons. The very next day, I began the long and excruciating road of training. Even though my body was being tortured, I pushed through, somehow ignoring the everpresent pain.

About six months later, I drove from Ottawa to New Brunswick to race my first ever marathon. I won the race and in so doing, set a record for the fastest female time on that course — by 16 minutes! As soon as the race was over, I was back in my car as I embarked on my drive home — I didn't even pause to celebrate this achievement. Rather, I just soldiered on, as I had done my whole life, focusing on the next accomplishment — extreme adventure racing, bike racing, completing my PhD in Psychology, and becoming a prolific published researcher. With each achievement I anticipated I would feel elated, worthy, loved, valued, important, or at least satisfied. I never did.

The year I turned 35, almost five years after my accident, I woke up in the middle of the night facing the reality that I would have excruciating pain every day for the rest of my life. That I would never, due to my injuries, be able to birth a child naturally. That running, the one thing that kept me from the brink of a breakdown my entire life, that "protected" me from feeling my fears, my shame, and my self-loathing, was breaking me.

In that moment, my armor cracked and out poured a tsunami of tears that had been frozen within me for decades. Memories washed over me that had been kept locked deep inside my unconscious vault. Memories of passing out as a child when my father came into the room; of laying on a cold cement floor of a large warehouse at the age of 3 feeling terrified, alone, limp as a rag doll; of spending most of my days hiding in my room as a child doing push-ups and sit-ups, or being outside moving my body in some way to avoid the wrath of the strap on my bare bottom; of being made to kneel in the corner of our kitchen where the dogs ate as my 'time-out' if I did not finish my meal; of witnessing my beloved gentle family dog being beaten mercilessly; of being shamed and degraded with words; of being violated by relatives and strangers alike, used as a pawn for someone else's twisted sexual pleasure over, and over, and over. I was such a perfect victim — the one who never spoke up, cried, fussed, screamed, or fought back. The one who dissociated from my voice, my emotions, and my body.

Sitting there in the darkness, I crumbled as I felt the brokenness of not just my body but the brokenness of my entire being. I shattered into a million pieces with shards of me flying in every direction. I cried, shook, convulsed, and screamed for hours until the sun came up.

As the sun rose I quietly whispered, "Help, I need help. I don't know what to do." I didn't know who I was whispering to, I just knew that I wasn't okay. In my mind, I heard the words: "Move to Toronto." Incredulous, I replied "no." I loved my job, loved my community, and loved the city that I lived in. That inner voice would not relent.

Months later, without knowing why, confused and only mildly fearful, I quit my job, packed up my belongings, and moved with my dog and cat to a tiny 400-square-foot apartment on a 15-acre farm. Little did I know this would be the beginning of my journey to heal my physical body, my heart, and my soul.

Within days of moving I embarked on a committed path to working with a gifted healer. I worked with Jacky weekly for eight years. The first year I felt nothing (other than the familiar agonizing sensations from my injury). Yet, something inside of me kept saying, "Stay with it." After a year, my body began to buzz with some aliveness and I started to be able to discern sensations beyond my injuries. What I felt most palpably was a chronic state of contraction that began in my toes and rose all the way to the top of my head. I delighted in the discomfort; it was so much better than feeling nothing at all.

Not long after that, my body began to scream. I can remember being at a Christmas dinner with friends. I felt searing, stabbing discomfort in most of my organs. As I was nearly doubled over in pain, I felt an amused confidence knowing that this was my body releasing a lifetime of trauma. And I felt giddy... for the first time in my life I could feel my whole body! I could feel!

The delight did not last long as I kept being pulled into my suffering. By this time I had been studying Buddhism for 15 years and understood that wanting something to be "other than it is" IS the root cause of suffering. But knowing that did not pull me out of my frustration, anger, and resentment for the physical agony that I felt and how it impacted my life. Until one warm summer day, after almost 10 years of suffering with my pain, I had a lightning bolt moment. As I sat outside with my beloved dog Frisco on what I knew would be his last day in his physical body, I observed him roll in the grass, so carefree and impervious to his physical frailty, then pause to catch his breath amid what sounded like horrible asthma attacks caused by a tumor on his lungs, and then resume rolling in the grass. He did this over and over, for hours. My four-legged teacher, companion, and friend had given me the greatest teaching on his last day: be *with* your pain not *of* your pain. When the vet administered the lethal injection, and he was gone, he took with him a teardrop that fell from my eye into his.

From that day on, even though pain persisted, I no longer suffered. I learned to stop trying to distract from it, to STAY with my experiences with compassion and understanding. Most significantly, as I became more skilled in being with my pain and no longer fought against it, the uncomfortable sensations dissipated. As Carl Jung said, "What you resist not only persists, but will grow in size." My pain was dissolving, not completely but enough to help me to access some luscious full breaths!

As my physical body healed and became more resilient, layers of emotional wounding presented themselves. I released a lifetime of rage, fear, hurt, and disappointment. I did deep inner child work to get to know all parts of myself. Some parts were hidden deep inside, trembling in fear. Fear of not being good enough. Not being safe enough. Not being worthy enough. Not being loveable enough.

Through my deep introspection, I met my little warrior, who showed up as an outrageous image of a 2-year-old with a Viking hat and spear — 'he' is my 'protector.' I met a sweet tender 4-year-old, with pigtails and freckles, who still resides in my chest and who quietly pokes her head out and whispers, "Please don't hurt me." One day, as I lay on my living room floor, I imagined my father coming toward me, his eyes and body intent on hurting me again. My body started to freeze, but in that instant, instead, I looked beyond my defences and saw God reflected in his eyes. In that moment of grace, I felt my heart forgive him.

I learned to embrace all of who I am. The courageous me and the fearful me. The happy me and the sad me. The easygoing me and the controlling me. The me who is generous and the me who can be stingy. The grounded me and the anxious me. The me who wants to be seen and the me who hides. At that time I also became committed to helping others through their healing journey and became a Transpersonal Somatic Psychotherapist, with a specialty in working with trauma, stress, and anxiety.

Around this time I had an experience, during a meditation, of a light presenting itself to me. I had the image of it coming from atop a mountain. It was intensely bright, blinding, and felt like it would completely overwhelm me. This triggered my primal fear of being overpowered. I tried to block it. I was terrified. I called Jacky and said, "What the f*#k! I did not sign up for this." The light continued to flow through me over the next few years, offering the most sublime, tender, and steadfast love and support. Sometimes I welcomed it, sometimes I fought, yelled, and cussed at it. And each time the response was benevolent, kind, and full of unconditional love: "Donna, I am not fighting with you, I love you." I had no more resistance; I surrendered to God's love.

I am full of gratitude for my early traumas and my car accident... they have become my deepest blessings. Without them I would not have learned grit, perseverance, self-love, compassion, acceptance, humility, and surrender. Without them, I would not have embarked on my healing path which has allowed me to serve thousands of clients on their own journey to healing trauma. And without my healing path, I would not be able to provide a safe and grounded adopted home for a little boy with special needs who calls me Mom.

What I have learned about life and navigating difficult challenges is that when all else fails, hope is our greatest asset. It's ok to be angry at God; "He" can handle it. Wisdom is the quiet knowing at the end of an impossibly difficult day that tomorrow the sun will rise — even if we cannot see it. God loves all of us and patiently awaits us to receive the love.

The healing that I was humbled and blessed to experience is available to us all. God promises to keep our soul safe; the job of keeping our bodies safe is up to us. We all have an inner guide, and following that guidance will rarely steer us astray. We can never know why something happened, but we can always bring meaning to what happened.

Healing flows deepest when we surrender to the loving presence of God.

IGNITE ACTION STEPS:

My own healing path, and my work as a healer, flows along certain principles that I call the FREE™ model.

First we must **Feel**. Then we must **Release** the tension, stress, and emotion that are trapped in the body.

Next we want to **Embrace** the tenderness (the wounded children within) and meet with kindness and competence the unmet needs that have been seeking fulfillment most of our lives.

Finally, moving to **Enlighten** the situation by bringing meaning and purpose to it can allow us to feel the deep gratitude for all of our experiences.

Trauma is NOT a life sentence. Rather, healing trauma can be a gateway to empathy, compassion, and living with higher consciousness. And this matters because with higher consciousness we elevate ourselves and our planet to a higher frequency and proliferate the possibility that we can live, together, in greater acceptance, love, and peace.

Dr. Donna Lockett, PhD (Psychology) – Canada
Certified Somatic Experiencing Practitioner
Certified Transpersonal Therapist

Noa Takarroumt

"When you remove the superfluous from your life, you create
a space to welcome the world and savor the journey."

My wish is that this story gives you a glimpse at the liberating power of decreasing our attachment to things and gaining more clarity on what we truly need. It is to touch on the wondrous possibilities that lie behind removing what clutters our lives — whatever that might be. This story is about how I embarked on a meandering yet fulfilling path toward a more purposeful life; may it inspire you to take a step, in your journey, to crafting your own.

Seven Kilograms Around the World

Most of us have, at some point in our lives, felt the need to take a step back. We may go on holiday, indulge in a passion, change jobs, resume our studies… or even do something as small as taking a walk by the sea. I chose to travel the world.

As a child growing up in Morocco, I could spend hours listening to my grandfather's travel stories, from Spain to Jordan, from the Soviet Union to France. I was fascinated by his unfailing wit as well as his ability to bond with almost any individual that crossed his path, partly because he could speak several languages. To me, *Bassidi* — 'grandfather' in Moroccan — was the richest man in the world.

Many years later, several academic and professional opportunities led me to part with *Bassidi* and Morocco to live in France, Bahrain, and Spain, where I nurtured a real passion for languages. An exciting job offer at Microsoft® had me settling in Paris, where I carved a life around a work that I was fond of, quality time with my loved ones, lots of laughter, and an unquenchable thirst for travel.

During my time at Microsoft, I truly enjoyed the projects we were building with our customers. I worked hard, earning a very decent income, getting promoted regularly, and even winning an award honoring top performing employees worldwide. But in the Parisian apartment I called home, I didn't realize I had acquired all sorts of unnecessary things, possessions, and items, as the years flew by.

By the time I was 27, my closets were collapsing under the weight of my clothes, jewelry, books, bags, shoes, and perfumes… In short, everything modern marketing had convinced me was necessary. What I *needed* had become an abstract concept, a blurred image. All these possessions started to feel like a stifling burden, a cloud of heavy dust befogging my sight. While appreciating my life, I felt that I was wandering astray from what really mattered.

That feeling was soon joined by lingering thoughts about a resource that we all have, the most precious of all, in my view: *time*. My days were busy and often planned several weeks in advance. I was not complaining as they matched the lifestyle I had chosen, but investing time being a zero-sum game, I postponed several projects to an increasingly distant future. I frequently heard myself say: "When I have time, I…" and thought almost simultaneously: "Does my lifestyle serve as an excuse for me to stay in a comfort zone, at the very moment the world is offering me millions of possibilities?"

I was taken by an irresistible urge to improvise my days, not to experience the carefree existence an immaculate 'to-do' list and an empty mailbox would offer, but to discover what I would do with my time if I started from a blank page every day — fewer possessions, no obligations of any kind. Being able to listen to myself at every instant, seizing opportunities as they arose, and having the honesty to own what I was not doing, as I could no longer hide behind "the time I did not have."

The summer of that same year, I spent my holidays in Sardinia. There, I met an Italian boat escort. His job was to ship small boats around the globe, which involved inhabiting a few square meters for months at a time with nothing but the ocean dawning on the horizon for company. One day, he invited me and a couple of friends onboard. I remember being fascinated by how useful, compact, and beautiful each space was, from emergency kits to versatile furniture.

These narrow spaces were designed to survive long journeys on blue deserts devoid of shopping centers while remaining as light and compact as possible, yet they were among the most comfortable and beautiful I had seen.

Standing in the middle of that cabin, I was struck by the elegance of the design, so well thought-out, and containing everything that was needed. It was a floating island of luxury, not in material goods, but in clarity and sophisticated simplicity of purpose. Everything superfluous was gone. It was intriguing, so opposite from my clutter-filled closets, that I turned in a circle, soaking it all in. An urge to turn on the engine and head out to sea made my fingers twitch. I felt free. In that instant, it became clear to me that designing my own nomadic lifestyle was the doorway to the answers I was looking for.

So I set out to save money — for the first time in my life. Month after month, transfers flowed to a dedicated account, all labeled "RTW" for Round the World. It turned out to be strangely easy and my savings grew faster than expected. My priorities were clear. My list of "needs" was melting like snow under the sun; the adventure had already started.

During the monthly meeting at the office, I revealed my plans. My boss was surprised as I was off to a bright career. Others voiced admiration, as if I was vicariously fulfilling a dream they never allowed to transition into a goal. Some expressed concern, and I felt like a mirror of their own fears.

A month later, my boss shared that this news had led her to reconsider the priorities she had set for herself. I had not anticipated my announcement would have such an impact, how it would invite others to think about their own lives. It made me both excited and grateful; the adventure was well underway.

A week before departure day, I turned my apartment into a free self-service shop for my friends, then gave the rest of my belongings to charitable organizations with the hope that they would be more useful to them than they had ever been to me. By the time I returned the keys of my place and glanced at the tiny bag that was left, every parcel of my being was flushed by a sense of peace and freedom I had never experienced before... I had nothing left. No more commitments to any institution. No more things to protect, maintain, secure, clean, or store. No more choices to make in an ocean of possible combinations. I had nothing, and soon I would be a mere anonymous soul walking alongside others.

I had nothing except for a seven kilo backpack and a one-way ticket to Ljubljana, Slovenia. A tiny backpack and a one-way ticket, the materialization of the invitation to sobriety and open-mindedness that this adventure was for me; an initiation rite to the life of a mere vagabond curious about this world, free of her time, and intoxicated by the music of Isabelle Eberhardt's words:

"Life on the open road is liberty... to be alone, to have few needs, to be unknown, everywhere a foreigner and at home, and to walk grandly and solitarily in conquest of the world."

Over the couple of years that followed, I explored 19 countries and four continents. Above all, I lived a wide range of experiences I would never have dared to imagine — a documentary broadcasted at the Sarajevo film festival led me to enroll in a university in Istanbul to learn Turkish, which in turn unveiled the beauty of Persian poetry and led me to explore Iran. The struggles of my body adjusting to the road urged me to experience the life of a yogi in an Indian Ashram, study a 5,000-year-old medicine named Ayurveda, and work in a farm in a small village in the south of Japan. In Nepal, a random encounter with an American in Katmandu's airport resulted in weeks of trekking across the Himalayas. Soon afterward, a conversation with an Argentinian inspired a silent 10-day retreat in Kirtipur known as Vipassana. In Tokyo, a talented painter excited by my travel stories suggested a collaboration on an art exhibition project. A few days later, a series of profound discussions with a Singaporean girl led me to spend the month of Ramadan in Indonesia and rediscover my own religion. Further southeast, in Melbourne, a meal at an Iranian restaurant offered me the opportunity to teach Spanish to Australian students for several months, which in turn opened the possibility to contribute to a thesis on multilingualism.

Along the way, I studied various subjects I never thought I would be interested in, met all sorts of characters, and learned to get by in several languages. I also studied photography to better capture the mesmerizing beauties and ironies my senses were perceiving with each step. Like every journey, it had its share of ups, downs, and spirals, moments where I felt lost, anxious, tired, and homesick...but as I look back, this adventure most certainly taught me to carve a path toward a more purposeful life; a life filled with possibilities.

Living purposefully is to be aware, every single day, that our needs are very little, that we all share, deep within ourselves, the same fears, the same dreams, the same desires in the multiplicity of their manifestations. It is the best way I know to cultivate our focus and build deep connections. When you remove the superfluous from your life, you create a space to welcome the world and savor the journey.

Living purposefully is also to realize that each person we meet, every success we celebrate, setback we suffer, wound or doubt we go through… every movie we watch, book we read, song we listen to, every single whisper we hear, nurtures our heart and shapes our mind — both the moments we consider as turning points and those we forgot about. It is to be more mindful of the trivialization of violence, misery, vulgarity, and mediocrity, be it through the power of habit, or worse, that of resignation.

Above all, this journey made me recognize adventure around every corner. I began to see traveling as a mindset, not an itinerary, much less a destination. I learned to take advantage of a red light to look around; of waiting time to meet the neighbor. I learned to walk until the day becomes interesting; to be willing to cross social and cultural barriers; to change plans at the last minute; to talk to a stranger for hours on end without trying to find out his name, origin, or job; to enjoy a tea while observing the people around, imagining their stories, their fears, their dreams, their hopes, and know that they, too, are fellow travelers.

As I was fastening my seatbelt on the plane from Buenos Aires back to Casablanca, I thought again about my grandfather and our shared passion for languages, particularly for their ability to articulate a world view, a peculiar perspective on life. I remembered the day he taught me that one of the possible origins of the word "Insan" in Arabic — which would be translated as "human being" — is the verb "nasa" meaning "to forget." To put it another way, the Arabs presumably placed forgetfulness at the very essence of human nature, which has always made so much sense to me. This might be the reason why I was suddenly seized by the strangest fear, the fear of forgetting what I had learned throughout this journey around the world and within myself.

I started writing and writing, and writing even more. Words were bursting out of every pore of my being and flooding the papers I had left in my bag; I wanted to capture every fleeting moment, every encounter, every single lesson.

"Remember that you could live very decently with seven kilos on your back and little money. Remember your aspirations to keep living simply, as a traveler who rests in the shade of a tree before resuming the road, the traveler you will always be."

"Remember that you have been safe, welcome, and loved, mostly because you were confident, simple, smiling, and genuinely interested in people. Great opportunities are everywhere for those with open eyes, ears, and hearts."

Once in Casablanca, one of the first things I did was fold these pages and head to the post office to send them to myself. It was my way of engraving this milestone, or rather my attempt at not forgetting.

Traveling taught me that I am just passing by. It forced me to remain light and confident, and led me to appreciate what we often take for granted. It also offered me countless encounters and lessons, and gave me a clearer understanding of what was truly important. These are now my most precious possessions.

So, dear reader, please consider taking small steps toward a lighter life and allowing your senses to recognize and welcome the countless possibilities surrounding you. Look around when the light turns red. Get to know your neighbor while waiting for the bus. Walk with no other intention than to explore a parcel of this magnificent planet. Do not be afraid of changing your itinerary everywhere you go. Live in the moment, if only for a moment, just observing and connecting with the human beings around you. Who knows what possibilities it could unveil in your life...

While I never dreaded putting down my bag, integrating the numerous learnings of this journey into my daily life remains to this day the most tortuous adventure, most definitely the wildest ride. I succeed easily some days; forfeit miserably on others. Then I hear back the comforting words of an old lady I met in Ljubljana: "One day at a time, my dear; one day at a time."

IGNITE ACTION STEPS

Uncovering what is essential in your life is truly valuable. It enables you to be more aligned with who you are and what matters most, whether it is in your relationships, your material possessions, or your actions. Here are a few suggestions for your journey to help you uncover what deserves your focus.

- **Keep an updated list of people who really matter** including family, friends, and mentors. Be particularly careful to nurture these relationships on a regular basis.

- **Have a large empty box in your home** that you can fill gradually with any useless things you come across. Whenever someone pays you a visit, think about what could be useful for them in that box, then give or sell the rest of the items to people that will actually use them.

- **Talk to a complete stranger** without asking his name, origin, or job, then part without exchanging any contact details. You would be surprised by the depth of discussions that arise from feeling that you are not put in a box, along with the belief that you will never see that person again.

- **Send a postcard to yourself** — This could also be a voice/video recording to capture experiences you want to remember, the ones where you felt at your best. Go through them on a regular basis and let them inspire your steps, especially when you feel lost.

- **Take a moment every week to pause and reflect** whether your routines are faithful to the life you want. Consider it an opportunity to renew your intentions.

Noa Takarroumt – Morocco
Traveler, Photographer, Writer
noa.takarroumt@outlook.com

MELODY D. BYRD

*"Forgive yourself and others to allow peace to light
your way on the path to happiness."*

I wish for you to have strength to accept the humanity of yourself and others: forgiving mistakes and accepting the past. In this, I hope you will come to love yourself immensely as you embrace forgiveness and the beauty of being human. Know that our mistakes are by design, but they do not define us. We are powerful and can instantly change disempowering memories through forgiveness. Use this knowledge to lessen your emotional burdens and travel lightly through this life as you Ignite your pursuit of authentic self-expression.

MY REGULAR DADDY

Electricity bounced through the room as people jumped to their feet to cheer, the sound growing louder by the second.

"Come on number six!"

In a flash, the horses crossed the finish line and my Daddy knew instantly that he had lost his rent money again.

The booming voice of reality could be heard announcing number seven as the winner. My Daddy's anticipation turned to frustration. He lowered his head just long enough to put on his sporty cap. As we dragged ourselves from the track, my eyes were on him, but he was miles away, mumbling about returning tomorrow to win his money back.

That was the pattern I lived as the little girl of a habitual gambler. My Daddy grew up during a time when education for young, black men was not encouraged. He felt that he had to create his own money stream. He chose gambling. My Daddy loved the adrenaline rush of leaving his life to chance, putting it all on the line just for the possibility of knowing the sweet taste of victory.

In the slow moments between his bouts with gambling, he would see his friends move on to happier lives with beautiful families. In these lulls, he found himself lonely and yearning for a *regular* life. As I grew and saw these same warm scenes in the lives of my friends, I found myself yearning for a *regular* Daddy.

To fulfill his dream of a *regular* life, my Daddy married and had four kids. His first wife adored my Daddy's flashy lifestyle but disliked the way he supported it. They argued incessantly, trapped in increasing unhappiness, until one day my Daddy decided that it was best to live on his own. So, on a cold winter's day, he packed up his car and drove 2,700 miles from the East Coast of the U.S. to the West Coast; convinced he could not be happy nor provide a good life for his family.

My Daddy decided to try and walk a straighter path, landing a job at a pawnshop. He was right at home, chatting up customers with his signature charm and wit. One customer, my Aunt Hyacinth, would introduce him to his future wife. She was a petite, intelligent school teacher living in Jamaica who dreamed of marrying a handsome and rich man in America. I still remember how my mother described it all: a letter-writing love affair complete with pawnshop trinkets to make her eyes sparkle. One day, the trinket was an engagement ring, and the woman who would be my Momi said, "Yes."

In the stories of her engagement, she would talk about how in her excitement, she immediately bought a wedding dress and hired a baker to make a proper Jamaican wedding cake. I marveled at the hope and determination in her heart. I still smile at the fairy tale she was dreaming up as she packed both the dress and the cake and traveled 2,300 miles for her date with destiny.

Two days from touching down, they were married, and two weeks after that, my mother was pregnant with me. I would later learn that my Daddy worried about not being able to support a growing family based on his menial salary from the pawnshop. The impending stress caused him to resort to what he knew best — gambling. My mother, new to this country, was left to fend for herself some days as Daddy disappeared to play his games of chance. She became increasingly depressed, homesick, and regretful of her decision as her fairy-tale dreams did not come true.

By the time I was born, he was like a skipping record, as arguments took over his marriage again. It wasn't long before Daddy fell back into the belief that his family would be better if he was not around. Within a year of my birth, he left me and my mother. This time he moved 2,000 miles away to the middle of the country. Again, he took a *regular* job. This time at an insurance company. I was just a baby and knew nothing of my Daddy's flaws or failures, so it was through my mother's stories of regret that I discovered how he apologized to win back her affections.

My mother took him back and nine months later, my little sister came into my life. We were a happy family again. When my Daddy hit it big, he bought us a new house and a big green car. But the following month, he could not make the monthly payment. Within a few years, my Momi, fed up with my Daddy's recklessness, eventually got a job, moved us out, and filed for divorce.

As a young girl, I couldn't understand it all. I just knew that I didn't see my Daddy for weeks at a time. I missed him coming by to take us and our friends to get hamburgers from McDonald's™. When we invited him to school performances or award ceremonies, he could never make it. We were blatantly reminded of my Daddy's absence as we watched our friends spend time and play with their dads. I was jealous, aching to be reminded of how it felt to be tossed into the air or held tight in his hugs.

My jealousy turned to anger as every week I got a new badge of disappointment to wear. Tired of my badge collection, I began to put more space in our relationship and rarely spoke to my Daddy. When curiosity got the best of me, I would pepper my mother with questions as warm tears streamed down my face. In the beginning, she always had a good excuse for my Daddy's broken promises, but eventually the same stories no longer filled the void in my heart.

The older I got, the more unbelievable the stories became. When my mother finally revealed the truth, I was shocked and upset by the loneliness and fear that plagued her spirit and defeated her essence. In her strength, she refused to let any tears fall. In my heart, I built a wall. I avoided his calls and no longer wanted to visit with him.

When I left for college, I feigned love and respect because I wanted his financial support. When I went home to visit from college, I did not visit my Daddy. Embarrassed by his lifestyle, I avoided discussions about him or kept it brief, only sharing that he worked at an insurance company. I never invited him to family weekend at school, and at my graduation, I avoided introducing him to my classmates.

After college, I began the awkward dance of dating. In my naiveté, I kept men at a distance or moved too fast, with no middle ground and no sense of my true worth. I blamed my Daddy for failing to teach me how a man was supposed to treat me. Some of my friends learned these lessons when their dads would take them to father-daughter dances. Their fathers would open the car door and buy them flowers. My Daddy never did that for me. As I look back on those days, the truth is that fear of more rejection and letdown replaced the invitation to be intimate.

When I was 24 years old, with emotional baggage that I had never unpacked, I met a man who would woo me and support me in the ups and downs of every-day life. He was a tall, handsome man who lived with his two aging parents. He had a *regular* job at an insurance company which reminded me of my Daddy. Yet, he was more stable and I believed he would take care of me the way my Daddy never did. When we began dating, during intimate moments, we would share stories of the heartache we had both experienced. We consoled each other in the fallacy that love would fix everything in life we had yet to encounter.

After a four-year courtship between our inauthentic selves, we wed, hoping that the two of us could conquer anything together. But the more we discov-ered about each other's lifestyles, the more our bliss turned to distress. Again, I put space in a relationship as I realized that we could not build a life of trust, happiness, and responsibility on a foundation of hurt, anxiety, and pain. After just four short years on our non-stop marital roller-coaster ride, we divorced. Again, I built more walls.

With my marriage over, I was back to dealing with the one man who was the inconsistent constant in my life. As time passed and he grew less independ-ent, my Daddy reached out more to me and my sister for help with shopping, running errands, and paying past-due bills. At times, we would help him. Other times, we would ignore him in an attempt to pay him back for the mistreatment of our mother. When I did take him to run errands, I rushed him and spent very little time with him. He probably felt like an inconvenience as I huffed at every request, snarled at every question, and sometimes met his attempts at conversation with silence. My unresolved bitterness and ever-growing walls left no room for compassion.

Then in April 2005, at the age of 40, I got a call that my Daddy had a stroke. I visited him in the hospital out of obligation. Over the next two months, I watched him decline until he passed away. Ironically, he died without having insurance, even though he had worked in the insurance field. Perhaps out of guilt, I decided to keep his ashes at my house as it was always his wish to live with one of his daughters.

For years, I would reminisce on bittersweet memories of my Daddy and have pretend conversations with him. I desperately wanted to ease the pain and move forward in my life, but I did not know how to do it; I was trapped behind my walls. With anger and bitterness as my best companions, I almost passed up the opportunity that would end up transforming my life.

When a guy I was casually dating talked to me about living a happy and healthy life, I was sure it was impossible. In an effort to quiet his pleas, I agreed to listen to a presentation that focused on transformation. Taking a gamble that this might work, I signed up for a three-day class that I never intended to finish.

On the first day of class, I attended as if I was a robot; stiff, quiet, and indifferent. I sat and pretended to listen to other people's problems. I half-heartedly watched the skillful classroom leader as he coached people who shared private stories of heartbreak. Then, unconsciously, I started to pay attention as I saw myself in these other humans. I began to listen intently and focus on the poignant words of the people in the room with me. I moved to the edge of my seat and began paying attention to the leader.

With direction to do so, I took the advice from the leader. When he said to separate the story from the facts, I did. When he said choose your mother and father just the way that they are and are not, I did. When he said love yourself, love your life, and give people the space to be human and make mistakes, I did. I hung on every word and became engrossed in wanting to know more.

During breaks, I began smiling at others. I introduced myself and exchanged telephone numbers. I started to let down the walls and slowly let people in. I even went so far as to speak on the microphone and allow the leader to coach me. I felt the drama disappear and the warmth of compassion creeped in.

My story wasn't so different from the others that I heard. In fact it was a *regular* story of hurt I carried for so many years. Just sharing allowed me to see that I could accept my life. It doesn't have to hurt. I don't have to remember only the defeating experiences. Changing the way I viewed the story helped me change my life.

On the final night of the class, I do not remember driving home; only that I made it safely. I walked in the door without taking off my coat, and ran to my computer. I immediately began typing…"Dear Daddy, I forgive you…" The letter had been brewing in my mind the entire drive, or perhaps in truth, much longer.

At the age of 44, typing those five words ignited peace, clarity, and a sense of acceptance. Tears of joy mixed with tears of regret, as I felt love pushing away the burdens on my heart. I took deep breaths and stared up to the ceiling as if I was a little girl looking up at my Daddy. I mouthed the three magical words: 'I love you.' I never remembered saying that before but I knew it was never too late. I looked toward his ashes and smiled, hoping that he could read the lips of his little girl and forgive me too.

The letter allowed me to regain my personal power and choose forgiveness as a possibility in my life. Realizing this, my next clear step was to forgive myself. I called old friends to make confessions and ask for forgiveness. I no longer wasted time on pity and wielded my newfound talent to quickly forgive or apologize in a moment's notice. I chose to use my precious time wisely to create loving memories.

Along with forgiveness, I chose acceptance. I tore down my walls and released myself from the trap of negativity. I gladly told of the rides in my Daddy's luxury cars, eating at fancy restaurants, and shopping till my heart's content. I bragged about my Daddy's flexible work schedule and the wads of cash that sometimes filled his pockets. I inherited my sense of style from my Daddy and my ability to be congenial. Like my Daddy, I take risks and sometimes I win and sometimes I learn. I have accepted that as a way of life, especially with making mistakes. As I embrace my humanity, I know that the experience of true happiness is in letting go of the painful memories and emotional burdens. I choose forgiveness to light my life's journey.

Choose to accept your past and you will come to know the peace I found when I finally forgave my *regular* Daddy. When you find inner acceptance, you can create love and fulfillment. Life blossoms in your favor and victories become possible. True joy is derived when you forgive others and *yourself*. Life is full of winning moments, claim your own. It's the *regular* thing to do.

Ignite Action Steps

Forgiveness is instantly available, at any time and anywhere for anyone.

- **Be selfish about forgiveness.** Do it for yourself. Unload the burden of painful memories and create the space for you to cherish those memories which make you smile.

- **Forgive and change your narrative by sharing positive memories.** This is the best place to focus your energy to produce happiness and healing. Be the love light that others are attracted to and want to emulate.

- **Ask others to forgive you.** Make this an annual goal to aggressively pursue forgiveness with yourself and with other humans as a way of life.

Cash in on your winning ticket. Once you make peace with your past and fully forgive and accept yourself, (along with those around you), you light your way on the path to your greatest happiness. That is when the richest of all possibilities becomes available to you.

Melody Byrd – United States of America
Speaker, Author, Life Coach
www.melbyrdrocks.com

KATHERINE VRASTAK

*"Life is a GIFT — Set your voice free and allow your
light to shine through the darkest times."*

**It is my hope that you see you can rise above anything. Breathe through
it. There *is* light on the other side and you will make it there. The silence
within is where all the answers live. Your life is a gift… embrace it with
love; it is the best gift you can give to yourself. Forgiveness has the power
to heal and enlighten you. Please know the power of forgiveness is so vast
and available, if you only give yourself permission to surrender and allow
it. Forgiveness frees you to realize the power was within you all along. Life
happens for you, not to you!**

EYE OF THE STORM

Have you ever lived through a perfect storm? I have. The year that changed
so much for me could have easily been a write-off, but instead, I used it as a
propelling force — a catalyst for change.

That year had me on the fast track to rock-bottom: triggering memories of
my brother's horrific murder, much needed hip surgery, devastating divorce,
coping with a very sad teenaged child suffering from suicidal ideation, and our
home caught on fire just to cap things off. I felt like my life was a crude joke
or God was trying to awaken my sense of awareness by literally bringing me
to my knees. Most would say that my life was determined to be in shambles.
Yet, in truth, by then I was already well-practiced in the art of going within and

rising above the pain that came at me. Growing up I felt unheard and unseen, having other siblings with particular needs. Therefore, I was raised by a mother who left me to suffer in silence. I chose that circumstance as a gift and a source of empowerment. I rejected the tendency toward self-pity, and instead worked toward fortifying my inner strength.

It was quite devastating when my mother, brother, and two other people were all tragically killed in a very unfortunate motor vehicle accident: a truck driver fell asleep behind the wheel. You can't imagine how I felt, since I had the blessing and the curse of being bestowed with a sixth sense as a young child and actually predicted this awful chapter in my life. I was left abandoned as an orphan at age 13 and even estranged from my extended family. By the grace of God this actually taught me self-reliance in a way that would make everything possible as I grew.

Several years later, a new devastation came with the loss of my fun-loving brother, who at 37 was someone that captured the breath of life within him. He lived his life truly in the moment. The shock was intense when he was killed by someone who intentionally drove into him when he was riding his bike. I was the person who ultimately had to decide to pull the plug to end his life. This travesty led to my personal seven-year journey of countless court appearances to enact justice for his five children. The trauma of this hateful crime fueled my despair and desire to prove his killer deserved to remain behind bars.

During that ordeal, I had slogged through it all, losing touch with my children and their father who remained distant. When you're trapped in that pain, seeing a way out can seem next to impossible.

There I was, in the year that wouldn't quit, reliving the trauma of my brother's death while coping with everything else that just kept piling on. I had left my marriage and my old matrimonial home behind, trying to step into a new life where the strong, resilient woman within me was standing in the sunlight.

Then, barely a month after I moved into my new home, a major windstorm hit the neighborhood one night! I was awakened by a loud thud, and looked out into the darkness to see if it had been a nightmare. I saw nothing, and went back to bed. The next morning, as I backed out of my driveway, I glanced to the left and couldn't believe my eyes. An enormous tree was leaning on the corner of my home. My first thought was, "Oh my God, can anything else go wrong?" Struggling on crutches from my hip surgery, and eager to get to my medical appointment, I checked to see that no one was hurt. I put the critical weather out of my mind. I had too much to think about and was sure I could deal with it when I returned. As soon as I arrived back home, I walked to the tree to see how bad the damage was and immediately called a contractor for help. While waiting, I pruned the tree a little to see if it had damaged anything, when suddenly it shifted — the storm-struck tree freakishly fell right on top of my head! I fell to my knees and let out an agonizing scream, "Oh my God, help me please!"

My phone had fallen to the ground and cracked, but thankfully still worked. I called everyone I could think of but no one was able to come and help. After desperately calling three more contractors, I found one that was willing to assist me. Before he arrived I had been able to crawl out from under the branch. I stayed outside, although my head was pounding and my world had started spinning. I wrestled with the tree to prevent damage to my neighbor's car that was inexplicably parked right next to it. They chose not to help whatsoever, but stood on their rooftop taking pictures. I continued to prune the tree, which now thinking about it, I can't believe I kept doing. Before I could care for my injury, I had to wait for the contractor to arrive. I sat on my front porch in total despair, feeling completely alone. My injured head struggled to focus while it throbbed uncontrollably. Since I was always about serving and helping others, my own well-being was not my priority even in that moment of pain, anguish, and fear.

After I finally was able to handle the external damages to the home, I was then able to focus on myself. A friend came to drive me to the hospital. She dropped me off. I sat in the waiting room with a neck brace on, all alone with no friend, no family, and no one to call. It was quite agonizing — noises and vibrations were all extremely irritating and painful. I was scared and lost... again on my own.

I was given the diagnosis of a concussion and no medication after a CT scan ruled out a skull fracture. I was told it would heal with rest and time. I got up out of the hospital bed, walked away with every noise making me freeze in excruciating pain in my head and neck as I walked, sat, or lay down. While the doctor had been so dismissive, my head injury was much worse than I could have ever imagined. I had two life-threatening scares after the initial trauma and was taken in by ambulance due to the pain in my head. I could not even handle the humming of my fridge on the other side of my bedroom wall when I tried to sleep. I was so sensitive to abrupt sounds and other vibrations that when there was a house fire across the street that made my house vibrate, this caused me to be rushed into the hospital and be placed on IV meds for migraines.

Through my pain and desperation, all I wanted was to be able to look at sunlight and daylight and focus on my two children again. I was unable to function, to eat, or sleep. My life was spiralling downward like I was in a tornado. Divine intervention gifted me with a female doctor who supported me on my journey by supporting my healing protocol. Ultimately, I did find an effective naturopathic doctor to have a holistic healing approach. I sought out network spinal analysis, physio, acupuncture and homeopathy, and nutritional supplementation, all of which helped me find a fraction of comfort. I changed my diet, consuming holistic, plant-based foods to heal from the inside out. It was proven that sitting in dark silence meditating daily with only my salt lamps on was quite calming for my parasympathetic nervous system which propelled my healing process forward.

In my thirst for knowledge on how to heal compound concussions, I discovered an online concussion rehabilitation course. Additionally, I became involved in an exercise regimen with my local gym. The daily workout regimen involved a one-week training in Wim Hof breathwork then a golden opportunity to take an Evolved Neuro-Linguistic Programming (eNLP) course that would propel my healing journey forward exponentially. That course was the most intense three months of my entire life. I purposely dove into doing one session after another, earnestly to reach full healing, so I could have my life back. I took weekly sessions with my classmates and much integration to allow head to toe full release to my nervous system. The huge challenge was memory and being on the computer while trying to heal at the same time. No easy feat. I still was earnestly determined to rise up and be able to walk and even run again in sunlight.

It wasn't as though I hadn't been putting in the work before. My seven-year journey to reach this profound forgiveness involved voluntarily sitting in two healing circles that the courts had arranged. I read my three victim-impact letters to the murderer and those who were supporting him. During the cathartic process I emptied out all the emotions I felt to the depth of my core. Yet, I was left feeling no hope for justice to prevail, as the murderer was given full parole. I walked away worried about my children and my brother's children, frozen in fear and broken in pieces. I knew that I had to make peace and let go, so I went on an earnest quest to set my own prisoner free in my mind, body, and soul. I desired to live for my children who were my lifeline, yet I had grown apart from them because of the deep-seated anger and fear that had pulled me away from reality. I had to go to the depth of my core to heal all limiting beliefs, shadow archetypes, and physical dis-ease in my body. This was truly a welcomed journey, as I knew my life was worth it, and my children deserved to have a mother who could help them to raise their children. I passionately desired to leave a positive legacy.

On the day of my NLP recertification, I received a profound powerful forgiveness healing from head to toe. Thank God, my whole body released on a cellular level. All of my five senses had literally come alive in that moment. My sensory acuity had changed dramatically. I broke out into a full body sweat, head to toe, and I required an ice pack on the back of my neck as I fell asleep for the night. I had gone so deep within my being, earnestly desiring to save my own life, to find the piece of my heart that was missing.

I surrendered to my subconscious and tapped into my higher self. I woke up the next morning able to pull back the curtains to look at sunlight not to mention also walk, speak, and hold my head up for the first time in 11 months! My whole entire body awakened to a huge sense of expansiveness. I felt so alive; joy, peace, and self-love like I had never experienced in my entire life!

The freedom I felt was deep and profound. I was able to finally forgive those that took my family... including my brother's murderer. Up until that moment, I had been held hostage to my repressed grief for so long that I lost the true value and connection to the world around me. Sadly, I was detached from all emotional connections and was living purely on autopilot. In reaching this epiphany I could celebrate, as I finally released the prisoner that actually was me all along. All the emotions of anger, fear, sadness, guilt, and shame were released at a cellular level, right down to the molecules and spaces in between. I went into the gap, the void of peace to find the resilience that was there all along inside my core essence.

After my transformation, I took full responsibility over my health and gave myself permission to reclaim my life so I could find joy again. I finally released the pain and forgave the man that murdered my last brother. That forgiveness was huge! I released all the anguish from my cells, so my heart could heal and love again. While the murderer's freedom was not going to be freeing for me, my heart knew I was NOT going to continue to let the unforgiveness affect my body and relationships. I set the prisoner inside of myself free by forgiving. I could now live in my light instead of the darkness of grief. I had to go to the darkness of the inner child to rise up and embrace freedom and be Ignited in my power. Now, I clearly embrace the fact that my birthright was to be a light and a GIFT to the world.

Thinking back, it's quite fascinating that my gift had been incubating for all my life. The consistent theme that has been interwoven throughout my entire life has been the need for self-care which has been represented by the deer totem. The symbols of both the tree and the deer were indeed a reminder of my need for self-care. During my actual journey over the past year, both a deer and tree had physically fallen before me. As they had fallen, so had I. As the deer's spirit journeyed beyond, I had to do the same... rising up from my circumstance into something greater. I was brought to the clear self-realization that no matter what type of storm I had encountered in life, I must honor myself to achieve my unlimited highest potential.

Upon reading my story, my hope is that some of you will relate to having a soul truly seeking to belong and to live fully, despite any trauma or adversity — to survive and thrive on all counts. To do so, we truly must forgive. I forgave myself for allowing the painful experiences I have just revealed to violate my sense of joy and abundance in this lifetime. I value my innate gifts and talents for helping others who might struggle with grief and trauma or who have not grown up with a loving homelife.

I feel that for those of us on the road less traveled to transformation, our soul has a sacred contract. This journey can be challenging, stressful, alienating, or lonely, but it is by going into the eye of the storm that we can Ignite a sincere spiritual rebirth. It's in this space where anything is possible. Had I not encountered these difficult challenges, I would not have arrived at my current and absolute knowing — I am here only to love and be loved in return.

Gratitude is paramount. I look at the tree… that which might have destroyed me; yet now, all I have is gratitude. When I look at my home and all I have, and all that I am, especially coming home to my innocence, I am grateful, at peace, and full of joy. My sincere prayer is that I leave a legacy to touch and embrace the power of forgiveness. As a result of this trying, yet illuminating life chapter, I am now able to share with you my transformational experience. I do so in the hope that you can derive a deep sense of connection, transparency, and alignment with your infinite possibilities.

When we are open to explore, question, and seek possibilities for what our soul has conjured up in this lifetime (one of many lifetimes and generations), hearts can be opened with an honest desire with sincerity to confront the pain. Looking into the past is truly where we can move forward through all the challenges and eventually come to terms with the true possibilities. I am loved and I can love... life can be beautiful if we allow unlimited possibilities.

IGNITE ACTION STEPS

Earthing in Mother Earth: put your bare feet in the soil and hug a tree.

- Practice daily gratitude in a journal. Write and recite positive affirmations and create a vision board, of your future higher self, using all six of your senses to bring to life your infinite possibilities through visualization.
- Write your five goals and five values daily to become a master of your destiny!
- Make a sacred contract to show yourself deep self-compassion, self-love, and self-forgiveness. Fill your cup up first, for you are only as good to others as you are to yourself.
- Recite the Ho'oponopono Forgiveness Prayer daily: **"I'm so sorry, please forgive me, I love you, thank you."**
- Explore Evolved Neuro Linguistic Programming (eNLP). Transforming your life with eNLP will create infinite possibilities by clearing denial, reframing, forgiveness, and so much more.

Katherine Vrastak – Canada
CEO & Founder, Sacred Roots Coaching
www.sacredrootscoaching.com
@sacred_roots_coaching

RYAN WILLIAM MANNION

"Create a spark that Ignites the one life you have right now."

I want you to understand that your reality is actually so common with your peers; in sharing with others, it is therapeutic for not only yourself but for them as well. It can connect you with the perspectives of each unique individual going through similar events in their lives. This connection will bring you a sense of oneness with others, and comfort in knowing that what you are dealing with is not unique; it is only unique to you.

SEEING THE WORLD AS ONE

My name is Ryan William Mannion. My father committed suicide when I was 7 years old. I vividly remember the heartbreak on my mom's face when she shared his passing. I even remember getting home from school that day and how different it was.

After that my mother and I had conversations that a 10-year-old shouldn't have to have.

For a while we had no household income other than what was given to us from my dad's passing. I heard my mother hiding in her car crying many times. I talked with her about our house being in pre-foreclosure from the bank. I was involved in the problems we had financially, and was my mom's shoulder to cry on.

In high school I was scared of girls, and shy around guys. I didn't have sex, drink, or do drugs until I was 18. The first time I had sex…. Okay you get the point… I was shy, intimated, and here I am, only 10 years later, writing vulnerably about the power of communication in the story I share with you today.

Growing up, I have fond memories of the kitchen table. It was where my mother, brother, and I formed a deep bond.. It was a simple table, made of light wood and fit for four, an arm's-length from the stove, just enough for my brother, Connor, my mother, Karen, and myself to sit and have dinner.

The table overlooked a beautiful six-by-four-foot window over our mostly private backyard in Danbury, Connecticut. The kitchen ceilings and other touches were Victorian, and immaculate. Both my grandfathers were handymen and our kitchen reflected the love they gave my mom after my dad's passing. I paint the picture of the kitchen to share with you what a place of beauty, bond, and connection it became for our little three-person family, and thanks to the amazing grandparents we had.

It was in this beautiful kitchen, and at that table, where I first learned how to communicate. The forced communication started. I still tease my mom about being in the hot seat at every meal.

"What did you learn today?" She'd inquire. "Did you talk with the teacher about gym class?" "Did you share we will be late for homeroom tomorrow?"

When my answer was, "Well, yes kind of," I would hear something along the lines of, "Ryan, it's important that you know this for certain… Will you go back and confirm that you won't be in trouble if you are late tomorrow?"

I was then held accountable the next day for my actions, while we ate our frozen fish sticks and mac'n'cheese. It was a blessing. I was exposed to so much. My mom spoke with her heart and soul and gave us the attention that you can only dream of growing up as a kid. To this day I speak about her often and speak so highly of her influence; she will always be my greatest mentor in life. I love her so much and appreciate all she has done for us, and the person she always has been.

When my dad passed, I can remember talking a lot about a lot. My mom and I talked at the dinner table every night. Sometimes about little kid stuff and sometimes about grown-up stuff and sometimes about little kid grown-up stuff.

When I spoke with my mom, I probably could have found ways to squeak out of the conversations. I could have lied. I guess I could have made my mom upset by moving away from the conversation, but reality is, I was always forced to share.

During our discussions, odd occurrences became relatively normal. Nothing was too horrible to tell Mom, and there was an unconditional love and bond that developed between the three of us, associated with the power of communication.

As I prepare to write this story, I think of all the stories I could tell. The amazing friendships and flings that I have had. The three years I 'started' for what became a Top 25 college football team. The three months I have spent in Colombia living my best life as I write this. I could talk about earning almost $400,000 USD at the age of 27, working directly under the CEO of a $400m company. I could express what it took to leave that job and my best mentor. I could also share the humbling situations and massive platform I have created as a co-founder for BookThinkers™. But I'll park that for now.

I could write about the responsibility I face today by knowing that I am a vessel of "God's work." It weighs on me at times. We could talk about the very real conversation I had with my life coach just four months ago about closing off my personal life to everyone. I remain scared of being an influencer, and the judgments I receive from people that do or don't know me. Or the scarcity beliefs I still have as I remain that shy kid that chooses to move through my fears. But I'll pause on that also.

As I write to you today, I cautiously love this girl in Colombia (as a friend and potential partner), and because of these feelings, I have my life coach forcing me to communicate with women as beautiful as she is. We do this so that I remove my scarcity beliefs and see all the options of women that I can partner with one day. This is not to remove myself from this girl, but to benefit myself and my current and/or future partner in the healthiest way possible. Approaching some of the world's most beautiful women from a place of pure openness scares me every time.

I share this so you can see how human I am. Experience the highs I have, and the apprehensions that linger. I want you to see the growth one sees on my life resume, and the struggles and fears I feel on the inside.

What is most important to share with you is a love story, not a traditional romance but a dance with vulnerability. As I reflect on life, communication has given me everything. What started with sharing with one person (my mother) took a turn and has brought me to today.

Before we go into it, it's important you know how I roll. I share from my unique experiences, and I see everyone as unique. I do not intend to come from a place where I tell you what you should do, nor do I assume that I know anything about you, or what is best for you. I simply want to share a powerful story of communication, and ultimately find love in communication.

It was in my teenage years that I remained shy and sheltered. People only glimpsed my personality because my childhood friend Christian would hang out with the popular kids, and so when I found myself with him, and with them, I had to speak. When I did, they recognized my humor, but this only came in small rooms outside of school.

Until I consciously had my Ignite Moment. (Just to let you know, I share this Ignite moment with tears welling up in my eyes for the power it has had.)

My Ignite moment, my decision, came to me as a freshman in college.

I arrived early for football camp where I met 100 new teammates. Every single player was stronger than me, and almost all were more outgoing. There were a lot of egos flashing around.

I slowly worked my way in, and in the night when practices were over, I strolled through the beautiful cliffs overlooking the ocean where my school sat, propped up against the Victorian mansions in Newport, Rhode Island, USA. It was a beautiful place to be and a whole new world for me to explore.

I had remained my quieter self that I knew all too well. It was early, but at this point my football coaches called me more by my number than my name, and when I was called on, I was quietly moving through the back of the line, finishing up the drills.

It was the fall semester of college a few months in when my personal epiphany occured. As I strolled past the mansions that line Salve's campus, I remember a sense of gratitude and warmth. It was a new home for me and a new opportunity to be different, to leave my labels and experiences behind.

Then came Stephanie. (Steph whose last name will not be revealed). Steph has dark hair, dark eyes, long legs, tan skin, a bubbly personality, and a smile and look in her eye that carried several expressions... dangerous for any man...

It was just outside of the cafeteria as I strolled along the sidewalk one late morning when this pretty colleague of mine walked by me. I had just looked up, and Steph and I locked eyes. Her look was so friendly and kind, and yet so intimidating. I froze at that moment. I wish I could have recorded how I looked; I know the feeling was ugly. My eyes widened and my mouth went dry as my throat tightened.

In that moment, I was blessed with a thought that would change my life forever. I knew that I had a decision to make, and there were three paths.

Path #1 was to remain quiet, and have what will be a reserved college experience. I will drift through it, and attempt to stifle the regret of never having really lived true to myself.

Path #2 was to say "hi" when I felt comfortable. I instantly ruled this one out. Is there anything more awkward than only saying "hello" briefly? This feels like lockjaw, and a whole bunch of weirdness and indecision in my mind and in my expressions.

Path #3 was to say hello to everyone and do it always. On this path there is only one decision, and that decision would be made in one moment. No "thinking," or allowing our creative, fear-based minds to prevent me from making an effort to communicate.

I chose this path #3 and started saying hello to everyone.

The original driver, frankly, was my desire to never let the woman of my dreams float away into someone else's arms because I never introduced myself; only to regret losing out on her love. I know this because this was happening to me time and time again until I made this courageous decision... I was the man she would want to meet!

As I found this to be an option, I also realized that if I built out my communication skills, then no matter what degree or career path I pursue (yes, I was uncertain), I would always have a foundation of communication that I can lean on. This foundation of communication will create success for me regardless of how my life will come to be, and what my passions and career evolve into over time; businessman, doctor, husband, father, teacher, etc.

At that moment I had no choice but to pursue my path and take control of life. I know we only have one life, and I wanted to experience it fueled by the person I truly am.

As I said hello to everyone, I was surprised to receive warm greetings. I got rejected by some people, but mostly I offered and actually received really good energy, and I saw a world of goodness open up.

The events within my journey have birthed an incredible inner love story. The power of communication helped me see the world differently. I pursued deeper communication, but the realization is one of a love story, for myself, and for my peers, based on commonalities that are found through this communication.

To this day the best compliment I have ever received came from a colleague after seven years of working together. She said, "I feel comfortable being able to share anything with you." Hearing this made me feel like crying. Along with my eyes, my heart was full. For someone to want to, and feel comfortable, talking about the challenges they have, and to feel safe and willing to share is incredibly rewarding for everyone involved. You can be the one who shares or the person that they lean on. Or you can do a touch of both. I say this because I have found so much gratitude with both.

The heartfelt words my colleague spoke to me and the environment that I create touches and humbles me at my core. Yes I have taken the leadership role by sharing vulnerably and consistently, but what I have heard from others is what has put my life in perspective.

In the years since college, I've spent time connecting with people. I have some amazing takeaways and bonds from these experiences. I have found these bonds by being an ear for someone else, or by lending my thoughts to them. I knew from experience the more I shared or heard, the more that the weight lifted from my shoulders. The more comfortable I became, the more I experienced fulfillment and realized our deep connectedness and oneness.

Every person I approached had a story...

- The 'weirdest' kid on the football team was actually awesome.
- The friend whose mother died in high school seemed fine.
- The 30-year-old whose father is alive but not present looks secure.
- The cool kid that looked secure was completely uncomfortable in his own skin.

Whatever it is, the list goes on and on, and on and on, and on. We all are going through something and it is what we are going through that makes us who we are.

To be heard or to hear, together with just one person, is to see the commonalities that we all share. There is power in seeing you are respected and loved despite the chaos of your mind. It is so awesome to love your unique story and see the positive imprint that you can make on your peers because of your past experiences.

I realize now this sense of oneness is always what I experienced with my mother. She has always allowed me to be myself, and I knew that was okay. She showed me how to have the courage of being open, and vulnerable, while listening, showing love, and sharing my authentic self. She always told us that others have it worse than we do.

As far as the girl in Columbia, and the prospects of being with her, I am grateful for my mother's lessons. I continue to share my feelings openly and believe that with courage, vulnerability, and positive manifestation anything is possible...

As I summarize my thoughts, I am moved by the prospects of humanity, and the strength in the people around me. I believe that it is through communication that together with our neighbors, we can unite under common causes, under a deeper love, and create a spark that Ignites the one life you have right now.

I personally, will forever view our world as one.

With Love,
Ryan

IGNITE ACTION STEPS

Spend One Hour Being There for Someone Else. This will bring a sense of comfort and realization that what you are hearing and sharing, regardless of the depth of feeling or thought, is okay. Don't abandon the conversation before the time is up. Keep talking, get deeper, and be comfortable with it being awkward and you or the other person not responding in a perfect way. You can share or you can listen, just spend an hour being vulnerable in your communication.

It's Your Decision. You only have one life. What do you want your life to be?

Ryan William Mannion – United States of America
Co-Founder of BookThinkers
@RyanWMannion
Www.bookthinkers.com/RiseWithRyan

HEGE ELARA SALVESEN

"Believe, and all is possible; for we are all god/goddess and immortal."

I want to inspire you to awaken to your god/goddess self — that innate powerful being that you are. Often we give this power of light and love away to others. When you take back your power, you can manifest what you want to design on all levels as a master creator. Do not let other people shut you down, shut you up, or write you out of creation. My hope for you is that you feel and be your god/goddess self — fully embodied and WHOLE.

WE ARE ALL GOD/GODDESS

Lying in a hard Norwegian hospital bed surrounded by silence, I knew I was secure at last but still felt so fragile and haunted. The sterile stark white walls were a vast contrast to the colorful, yet deadly streets of Tijuana, Mexico that I had endured only a week before. I had been caught in a web of abusers; patriarchal oppressors and depleters of my soul and energy. My body had been broken nearly beyond recognition. Yes, I had finally found refuge in this hospital; but unsure whether I would recover, I was still in turmoil.

Then, the energy in the room shifted as my love touched my heart, giving me a breath of welcome relief. He appeared energetically through the hospital window, and I felt him whisper, "Don't worry, my love."

Slowly our energy fields start to align. His face appeared from the other side of a giant matrix, an energy field connected to the Earth. "I will help you. I will come into union with you and spin you out of their grip," his deep, charismatic voice comforted me.

"Thank you, my beautiful twin flame," I whispered, relieved. "The patriarchs are threatened by us. They are trying to control and destroy me and the feminine principle of creation. Don't let them shut me down or kill me, or put me in exodus."

My thoughts drifted back to Mexico just a few days before when I was looking out at the sun through the opening of the mausoleum in a Tijuana cemetery. I wondered what time it was. I lay there, having fled in desperate search for refuge. I knew the violators were hunting me and this was the only place I could sleep without being assaulted continuously again. I had eaten nothing and had nothing to drink for days apart from a few drops of the polluted water in the cemetery. Alive but barely breathing, I could feel death calling me, coming closer. I called out for my love, 'the Lion,' and the French templars from my past life. They were the only ones who could help me survive this.

Days blurred into one. It had been weeks, perhaps close to a month since I arrived in Tijuana. It was a city of death, with one of the highest crime and death rates in the world. I sighed. I wish I had known these statistics when a friend convinced me to go there from Los Angeles to 'help me renew my US visa' after my passport and visa were stolen. I had to exit the country to reinstate my documents and he assured me Mexico was an easy place to do that. I was so trusting; too trusting. Tijuana was like a war zone. I felt violated and abused by the hostile energy in the air. Many of the men in the street treated me horribly, as if I was a possession; calling me a whore and chasing me until finally one of them cornered me and raped me. More than one violated me after that and forced me into submission. Then they drugged me.

Only a month before, I was living a clean life in LA as a yogi, an environmentalist, a healer, and a tantric goddess. I was a health freak, but now I just looked like a freak. My skull was open from being beaten almost to death, blood still showing in the gash on my fractured head. A giant wound covered half the left side of my face, leaving it swollen three times its size. My head was clouded with the drug they made me smoke. I was limping, open sores on my foot from when they hit me. My own shoes had been stolen and the ones I now wore, given to me by a stranger, were falling apart. I had been left with nothing. No passport, no food, no money, no clothes.

On the brink of death, my past life memories flooded through me in the streets of Tijuana, tormenting me. I became aware that I had been here before in another life. The intense and horrific experiences in my present life mirrored those from that prior life in which the abusers had killed me. In this life, they couldn't. I wouldn't die.

In a haze, while fighting for my life, my dad's words from childhood roamed through my head and my body. I shook as I heard his echoes: "You can't do anything and you know nothing. You are a loser."

He was the biggest patriarch of all; an abuser on every level: emotionally, mentally, energetically and worst, sexually. He had stolen my life through rape — used and abused me. I wondered if that was why these new abusers continued to treat me like I had no boundaries or sovereignty. I once again felt both enslaved and enwhored.

As I layed there left for dead, every ounce of my life force spoke to me: "Seize your power and your body temple."

I didn't have to die at the hands of a man, nor for humanity, religion, or sacrifice. I vowed that one could no longer use me, nor could anyone abuse me. "I claim myself back," I uttered, then I stepped outside of their grip, subjugation, and abuse, and said, "NO! No to any control over me, and to all the patriarchal abusive energies that have hurt me. I seize my power back from all the abusive men I have been with and all the violators on the planet. I take back myself, my power, my energy, my essence, and most of all my god/goddess bodies. I am free and I am me! Thank you," I said, the last rays of the setting sun touching my face. Tears flooded down my cheeks, this time from gratitude. I was going to be safe. I could feel it. Safe… I didn't have to die.

I stared out over Tijuana and wished the same for every other woman who was stuck in an abusive situation there, or anywhere. A giant shift took place inside the left side of my body, the feminine side, as I released the wounds and reprogrammed my mind. I saw a deep place inside my brain where an old program my dad had implanted was running, repeating: *You are nothing and cannot do anything.* He had taken my power and my life force when I was a child, so, I reprogrammed it, shouting out loud, *"I can do everything and I can be anything!"* I hoped the sky would carry my words as I declared, "You no longer own me, nor does anyone."

I was immersed in knowing that we don't own one another, we share and co-create. That is the new paradigm; co-creating — the feminine and masculine principles of creation; god and goddess together. If *all* were co-creating in union and communion, there would be no wars, no poverty, no diseases, no abuse, no control, and no subjugation — just joy, ecstasy, peace, truth, trust, equality, and equanimity.

"That felt good," I murmured, my lips dry from lack of water. I sighed. Now I just needed to get out of the cemetery and reclaim my life. *"Mon amour, viens tout de suite, je ne veux pas mourir,"* — my love, please come now, I do not want to die.

A light filled the end of the tunnel in my life and I felt an immense possibility of who I could be. A vast liquid love and divine light matrix flooded through me. I turned golden and expanded. The patriarchs were not going to beat me down in this life — nobody could. I would live and be my goddess self. Like the Phoenix, energetically I rose through the ashes of the dirty streets of Tijuana, off the cold floor of the mausoleum.

As I reclaimed my god/goddess self, I opened my heart to those who heard my cries for help and rallied to my rescue. My brother and my sister had contacted the embassy and police, and friends had tried countless methods to make sure I was found and pulled from the grips of those abusers in Mexico. As I was recovering for the next six weeks, I came to know with such gratitude the love that had flowed from the people who helped me. I came to know my love for them.

I felt free. And even in my physically battered state, my strengthening spirit knew the world could be free also. In the days that followed my rescue, as my body healed in a Norwegian hospital, I became increasingly in tune with my ability to expand my personal story to become that of the Earth. I was reminded that my wider purpose was to connect others to their own divine innocence. As a healer and a planetary worker, I had to shift things for the Earth and humanity, and now I had turned the spiral of creation the right way, out of abuse. I resolved the world would no longer be enslaved and oppressed.

I sighed with relief, gratitude, and quiet determination as I sat up and sipped on a cup of tea in my hospital bed; the sun's rays through the window reflecting the rays brightening within me. The spirit of my love, the lion, appeared again. Slowly we merged together through several layers of energy, into a labyrinth, and began to spin together once more. My face changes into that of Mona Lisa. My head turns with hers until I become her, slowly unveiling myself... my authentic self. I rise up through the Louvre in Paris with him, my love, my true love. We raise the grail together through the pyramid of the Louvre up into union and communion as the true star of David; the masculine creator principle together with the feminine creator principle. I explode with a love so great; I had never experienced it before. It was like melting chocolate with rose petals and champagne, and my entire body and energy field fused with liquid love. I radiated a golden essence that had been stolen before by the patriarchs. My feminine elixir, liquid love, was restored, and our love essences were so great that they fused together an entire universe and melted the hearts of humanity into love.

We continue to float above Paris in a giant golden vortex of love that slowly descends into the city and rises up from the Earth. The Earth and us explode in love as the grail raises in Paris through the heart of creation. My body continued to vibrate gold and my energy field was illuminated with pink, golden elixirs.

At first, I struggled to hold this frequency because so many patriarchs told me not to, still wanting to control me and the Earth. But now, with my love's spirit melded into mine, I could hold it. I didn't have to die. My love had saved me. Wishing he had his arms around me, I texted my love, my twin flame, from the hospital: *I love you so much. We are coming together into union and communion.*

The Universe whispered that the starry heavens would grace us with our union codes and love. "The twin-flame portal of creation will now grace the planet with your energies and create a fertile new Earth in harmony, communion, truth, trust, equality, love, and peace." Our spirits descend in Paris and ascend from the Earth; Da Vinci and his muse, his love, arrive in union.

I also feel my niece is smiling and laughing. "I am helping you," she says. Energetically her pure innocence and eternal wisdom have been a conduit to bring me and my twin flame into union with one another. She playfully gave me his teddy bear, the one he had as a child, so that I could help heal all his childhood trauma through this connection. She gleefully gave him my little toy dog, all chewed up on the ears from when I was little, so he could heal me. This beautiful exchange helped us heal one another. That is what twin flames do; they heal each other and with it, they heal the Earth and humanity.

I turned my life around from dying to being with my twin flame and stepping into a state of being god/goddess and embodying liquid light and liquid love, some of the highest frequencies we have on the planet. I defied death. I always say I am immortal. That is how I feel.

After healing in the hospital, I began to welcome love fully back into my life, I started to paint and write. I hadn't painted since I was 12 after my teachers discouraged me from using this talent to its fullest, but now I knew I might as well do all the things I had put off for so long. I didn't die, and I had to fulfill my life's mission. The books I had put on hold, deemed too controversial to write, I was going to write: I was alive, so I had to! My fears had dissipated as I had defied death. I was no longer afraid of anything.

As my creativity was reborn, my thoughts turned to my love. He had been with me energetically through all my pain, and now I trusted that he would come to me physically as well. I channeled this feeling into a painting. I stared at the canvas with joy as I painted a naked couple floating in a rainbow starry sky. It was us, seeing our wedding in Bora Bora: I am walking slowly down a pier, with my niece in front of me carrying a pillow with two rings. I am dressed in the most magical wedding dress with flowers in my hair. The sun is soft pink and gilded, close to setting, and guests are watching from the shore and on the pier. Some shed tears. I walk with such pride and love. I am radiating golden love and finally I feel safe to get married. This time, it is real. My bouquet smells of fresh frangipani from Bora Bora: white, pink, and yellow.

They adorn my hair with a beautiful crown made out of flowers with a veil at the back sloping down over my dress. The white chiffon and silk dress is low-cut, sexy but virtuous. It is fitted to my curves. The cleavage is low in the front and back; it sits perfectly on my hips and then drapes slightly on the Earth behind me. I walk slowly smiling, radiating, I have never been as happy as I was in that ethereal moment. Our twin-flame love consists of truth, trust, equality, equanimity, love, compassion, and harmony, anchored in a union and communion star of creation.

I painted several paintings bringing in a new reality; celebrating my womanhood — abstract, golden, and ornate with flowers as if to restore my divine innocence after what had happened to me. I created art to represent my reproductive organs; I painted myself pregnant, feeling my children still coming. Piece by artistic piece, I reclaimed my body, insisting it would not belong to a church, mosque, or synagogue; nor to a priest, Iman, or Cohen; nor to a cemetery. It belongs to me. As I painted and wrote, I continued to restore myself, piecing together the fragments of the puzzle.

My next choice was to step back into my role as a healer for the world; to spread my love outward again to others. I had reclaimed my body and I wanted to help others do the same. Many people on Earth today have been disconnected from their god/goddess body because of some religious practices or have been written out of creation as I was. When I give healing sessions, I often connect the client to their own consciousness and higher bodies, freeing them from anything that has taken over or blocked them.

I AM WHOLE. Fully embodied. I am my God/Goddess me! I am often in a state of ecstasy, a state of constant bliss. I call it the divine orgasm — nirvana. The state of enlightenment can be compared to a constant state of orgasmic bliss. Every pore and cell of your body feels alive and conscious and breathes with love and light. Your chakras are connected to the portal of ecstasy; the highest masculine and feminine aspect of self in balance, with the divine child within. The challenge for humans is to trust that this is the path forward in the physical body and that the enlightened state comes from within and from fusing the masculine and feminine aspects of self together, and bridging heaven and Earth in divine union and communion.

As you embody yourself with light and love, anchor your own god/goddess aspects and all your other soul and spiritual bodies with the intention of doing this for the highest good, you can create in line with your higher self and your blueprint. You can design what you want to make happen. This level of being comes with great responsibility. Your awareness should not come from greed, anger, hatred, or any negative thought forms or emotional states. It is essential that you create from a place of love, joy, compassion, equanimity, equality, truth, and trust. When you are constructing your own reality at this level of consciousness, aware of your conscious and subconscious thoughts and emotions, you can create at a level of true awareness that is good for you, the Earth, and all humanity. Go out, my god/goddess, and seize life!

IGNITE ACTION STEPS

- Seize your power.
- Say NO to abuse.
- Say yes to life and live it fully.
- Move away from 'block people' who put you down.
- Move toward those who support you.
- Stop self-sacrifice; instead, stand up for yourself.
- If you know somebody in need, help them.
- Become you and be your god/goddess self.

Hege Elara Salvesen – Norway
Healer, Writer, Actress, Environmentalist
www.hegeelara.com
🏵 *hege elara solar rays*

Marshanelle Horne
APRN, FNP-BC

*"Imagine the grandest version of yourself, create
the life you want to live, then Thrive."*

My gift to you in reading my story is to have unwavering belief in yourself. Your current circumstances never dictate your future. I have come to understand that life is a river of impermanence, forever changing. The river doesn't run backward, and neither do you. Run toward your fears. Erase the thought of fear from your mind and go after what you want like failure doesn't exist. No isn't an answer, and Plan B isn't an option. Nothing is impossible. The only luggage to carry in life is joy in your back pocket like a passport to happiness. You have everything you need within you to create and achieve whatever you want in life. Know what you want, ask for it, believe you will get it, and manifest your life!

Living the Thrive Life

All my life, I've been a nurse, taking care of others, but I was never one to take care of myself. My own joy took a back seat to everyone else's needs.

Being a young black girl growing up on the west side of Chicago with an open creative heart, big imagination, family secrets, and a mind full of fear was not easy. As the oldest of eight children, I always felt the need to be a caregiver, be responsible, and be reserved because my younger siblings were always watching. Fear always showed up. I was a worry worm all the time, worried about being good in school, about being a good role model for my brothers and sisters, worried about the need to help my family. Fear became the catalyst — the fuel to living the life I thought I wanted to live.

Whatever I imagined or visualized, I would try to create it. At the start I would go after what I wanted full steam ahead, good or bad, but my subconscious fear made the journey difficult. I would push myself to reach my goals. The fear of not doing well drove me. I was doing what was necessary but it didn't feel rewarding. I was not *thriving*. If I would have learned to let go of fear earlier in life, maybe I would have learned how to thrive sooner.

In my early years, I never felt like I fit in, creativity and imagination became my best friends, which later led to me being an introvert. I often stumbled over my words and developed a slight stutter in elementary school — here comes the speech and extended-reading comprehension classes. Embarrassed, I decided one day not to talk anymore. I remember answering questions asked of me in my mind with no verbal response. I would have full conversations in my head and watch my teachers ask, "Why don't you answer?"

I would laugh thinking, "There's nothing wrong with me, what's wrong with you!"

The armor that protected me from subconscious fear and awkwardness was silence, studying, and reading. And I read a lot! In silence I would learn more about myself and other people. While I was in observation mode, I would pick up on others' feelings. I could tell just by the way people interacted, by the way they moved, that they were off-balance with something. When I felt that in a person, I wanted to fix it. But back then, with me being silent and fearful of being rejected, I would keep that willingness to help to myself. Unfortunately, that didn't stop me from absorbing that heavy energy internally.

My creative ideas, imagination, and curiosity made me want more than my current situation. A few months after I stopped talking, after speech therapy helped me slow down my speaking and gave me the confidence to express myself, I decided to talk again, but the fear still lingered.

In high school I played it safe. I only had a handful of friends and I pretty much stayed to myself. I didn't take any challenging classes, I did not hang out after school. In fact, I got a full-time job miles away from school and home to keep me more than busy. I would take the train and bus to work straight after school and work until the last bus was scheduled to head back to my neighborhood. I liked this because friends knew I was working and would not bother me to hang out and be social. That pattern was my safe spot. I was comfortable there. Soon, I was made manager at my job at a gourmet bakery and sandwich shop in a high-end shopping mall.

I would watch the fancy ladies stepping in to order their gourmet coffee and sandwiches dressed to kill with their designer bags, high heels, flawless makeup, bloodred acrylic nails, and lambskin leather coats or furs. I would look at the families that came in with their children in designer strollers looking like parenting was so easy, while their kids would throw $15 sandwiches on the floor. I couldn't even afford the sandwich with my employee discount. I would laugh and think to myself, "This can't be real." It was a lifestyle that I was not accustomed to. Things weren't the same where I was from.

I shared a room with my little brother. He was my alarm clock. He would whack me with his plastic "He - man" sword every Saturday morning. There were no fancy sandwiches for lunch, lunch meat never lasted more than two days after mom went to the grocery store, and you better be home when dinner was made or you were out of luck. My mom cooked oatmeal for breakfast on Saturday mornings and made coffee for my stepdad, in an old pot on top of the stove. No fancy clothes for us either, Mom made breakfast in an old slip that she converted to a nightgown with one nipple poking out which traumatized us all from eating oatmeal forever.

I had been working at the bakery since the summer before going to high school, but three years later it all fell apart. The company moved and I was let go. My boyfriend at the time cheated on me, I guess because he was way more popular than me and played high school football, and I was the absent girlfriend. Two big hits to my sense of security in such a short period of time led to a sense of abandonment and trust issues, and added another layer of fear. In a sense, I thank my fear because it kept me out of trouble and somehow shielded me, all while helping me to be exposed to a broader reality and a different way of living.

After losing my job, I felt weird going straight home after school with nothing to do, so I put on my armor of protection again — silence. My thoughts were a hurricane of thinking about the life others lived, how they lived, and the joy they seemed to have. I wanted that for me and my family. I started shopping at that mall with the money I had saved and thought in my mind, some day I too will have a husband to sip gourmet coffee with and have children snacking on sandwiches while sitting in a big fancy stroller. I had no goal of going to college or doing anything else after high school but working and saving money until 'my king' found me. That was my goal. I asked for it, visualized it in my head, and imagined the life I wanted each time I was able to go to that mall.

Two days before my 16th birthday, I walked around the corner to my cousin's house, rang her doorbell, and got no answer. That was not like her so I decided to just wait on the stoop at her front door until she showed up. I had nothing else to do. While I was sitting there, a blue Celebrity car pulled up in front of me, the guy driving had the cutest cheeks and the brightest smile.

He asked, "Are you Lisa's cousin?" My introvertedness kicked in and I said yes while trying not to look at him.

He asked, "Can you cook chicken?" I thought to myself, "Hell yeah, I got four baby brothers and sisters!" But I just smiled and said yes.

He smiled at me again and said, "You hungry? Let's go get some BBQ chicken."

When I finally looked at him, I felt his energy, and it just felt safe. I felt light, almost floating like a feather. Free of fear. I couldn't resist his smile, his cheeks, or the chicken, and fearlessly, I hopped right in. We ended up getting BBQ ribs instead, and he took me back home and ended the night.

The next day, I went back to my cousin's house. Lisa told me that she hadn't heard the doorbell the day before because she was getting ready for a date, and that she had hooked up our other cousin Kim with a blind date — her date's best friend. Kim was getting over a breakup and was feeling bad. But the blind date never showed up. I described the guy I had met in front of her house and she screamed, "He took out the wrong cousin! You stole her date!!"

Every day for the next two weeks, that blind date showed up at my bedroom window calling my name, "Ney Yo! Ney Yo!" I didn't answer because he was saying it wrong. He must have asked my cousin my name again because she has a little southern accent and that's how she says my name. That feeling I had when we went for chicken was still there, but it couldn't be right. How could I trust it? I figured this can't be my king if he can't even get my name right. For two weeks, he showed up at my window, and every day, I ignored him, running away from the happiness and from what felt good.

One morning my mom asked, "Are you gonna say something to that boy today?" I was undecided. I knew that he usually showed up midafternoon, and as soon as she said that, we heard a knock on the door. It was him! I was nervous and feeling a little scared.

"I've been looking for you. Why haven't you answered?" he said as I slowly opened the door. He was standing there looking handsome, sort of glowing from the bright-colored jacket and matching hat he was wearing.

I was nervous and his presence threw me off. I stuttered slightly as I fell into his gaze. Then I got my confidence and replied, "Because you're saying my name wrong!" Then I told him how to say it correctly. He smiled at me again with those cheeks and that was the beginning of a lifetime. No one could tear us apart after that, everything went warp speed. At the time, I was in my senior year of high school and he would drive me to school and pick me up. He felt like my safety net, my safe space, my happy place to be. I told all my friends at school that I was getting married next year right after school (he hadn't even proposed, but I imagined it).

One day we were at the mall and walked past a jewelry store. I said, "I would love to have a ring out of there." On Valentine's Day he picked me up from school and asked me to get something out of the glove box. Inside the glove box, there was a little burgundy box from the same jewelry store we had walked past a few months before. Inside, sitting on white satin, I found a ring. It felt surreal that I was being proposed to. I wanted it, and said YES! But my fears made me wonder if it was actually possible. Even though it was exactly what I had imagined, my fears made me question if I was good enough to have this life.

We immediately started planning our wedding. I visualized how I wanted my wedding and it happened just how I imagined it the next year. But there was a surprise growing inside of me and I was afraid of what my family would think. Because we were so young, I had the fear that everyone would assume he was marrying me only because of the baby. That was in my head — the fear all the time of what people were going to say. We kept our secret until after the wedding. I was about to barf the wedding cake all over everyone but I didn't because that would have been a dead giveaway!

The years started flying by and baby number two came three years later. I was semi-living the life I had so clearly desired. We had the designer strollers, a nice apartment, and I was sipping gourmet coffee with my man and children at the mall I used to work at. However, it didn't feel like I imagined. It was hard. He was working nights and I was working days and going to school. Fear was in front of me every step of the way. Fear of failing, fear that I would prove everyone right by getting married too young. Fear of not being a good mom or wife. Fear of having to move back home. Fear of not being smart enough to pass my classes. Fear of learning new things. Fear of dying from depression and exhaustion. Fear of being left with two kids alone and becoming a single parent before 25 years old. The people who were in college with me didn't have any of that. They just went to school and hung out with friends, while here I was, leaving school to go take care of a whole family. I did not look or feel the same way I did prior to marriage, and eating BBQ chicken was no fun anymore. I had lost confidence in myself.

I hit a wall. As I finished up the pre-nursing classes in the junior college I was attending, I became afraid of applying to the university afterward. One day, I told my microbiology professor that I just wasn't university material. He told me to snap out of it and believe in myself. He believed I could do it and encouraged me to apply despite my fears. I resisted, but he persuaded me to apply, and told me on no uncertain terms that if the university accepted me, I had no choice but to go.

"If they believe that you can do it, why don't you believe it yourself?" he asked me.

When he said that, it made me feel empowered. I felt a heat rush through me. Those words lit me up like fire. I applied to Concordia University and West Suburban Hospital nursing program and got accepted. And I had no choice but to go. I fought my fear by pressing forward, putting on my armor of silence, surrounded myself with work, school, and reading to shield myself and family from the world. The years passed.

Close to turning 40, I walked past the wall mirror at my front door. When I looked at my reflection, I didn't recognize what I saw. I didn't know who that woman was. I had consumed myself with creating the life I wanted through the toxicity of fear. I had gained weight and felt emotionally toxic. Staring in the mirror, I knew I needed to change. It was time to take control and live the life I wanted, and I needed to manifest it without fear, but wrapped with love for myself mentally, physically, and emotionally. I knew without a doubt I was ready to use my voice to pursue my purpose.

My transformation began the very next day. I began living healthier, making small steps by focusing on me. I put down the Pepsi™ cans. I started walking a trail near my home daily. I became obsessed with living a healthier life. I watched what I ate, exercised, and began meditating and practicing yoga again. My family supported me and cheered me on, and I poured into everything I wanted for myself. I verbalized it, believed it, and had faith that I was good enough to have it. I lost weight, but what I gained was immeasurable. I gained the self-control and the strength to push through fear when it shows up. I wanted others to feel this way too, so I started my business, *Thrive Life Wellness Center*, and every day I *Thrive* and I help others do the same. Now I'm living an intentionally created life. I share my story so you can know that whatever it is you want, do it fearlessly. Fear will show up, but you have to do it anyway. If I believe that you can do it, why don't you believe it yourself? Imagine the grandest version of yourself, create the life you want to live, then go *Thrive*!

IGNITE ACTION STEPS

Listen to that little whisper that says you're in a safe, light, energetic place. Follow that whisper and see where it leads you. Don't be afraid to jump in the car and go for BBQ chicken! You can take small steps every day to move yourself closer to a life lived with intention and joy. What will it take for you to thrive? Start doing that today, even if only for five minutes. Then, throughout each day practice the *pause*, check your *energy*, *element,* and *environment.* Keep your state of mind focused on positive energy. If you are feeling unbalanced, imagine connecting to your balancing element, be fully present in your environment. Remember to take time to imagine your biggest life possible and take steps each day to make that life happen. The most important thing is, nourish yourself. Incorporate YOU into your life and imagine the grandest version of yourself. Create the life you want to live, then *Thrive.*

Marshanelle Horne APRN, FNP-BC – United States of America
Board Certified Family Medicine Nurse Practitioner,
Business Consultant/Coach
200hr Certified Yoga Instructor
Founder and CEO of Thrive Life Wellness Center
tlwcenter.com

ATTA EMAMI

*"Fall in love with the present moment and let it
show you a myriad of possibilities."*

**My wish for you is that you are inspired to create more possibilities in your
life by seeing how I navigated through challenging circumstances in mine.
I will share with you how I came to see more possibilities when there were
none present in my external environment. No matter what is happening
in *your* external environment, you can create new possibilities by falling
in love with the present moment and connecting with your heart.**

SHINE YOUR LIGHT INWARD AND
UNLOCK YOUR POTENTIAL

It was almost the end of day on a Monday afternoon. I was standing on the
conference level of the hotel I was staying at, just about to go into the training
room, when I felt like I got hit by an 18-wheeler truck! Moments before, I had
received a call; an unfamiliar female voice saying something like, "This is an
agent... from the FBI." Thinking it was a prank call, I hung up. The phone rang
again and this time when I answered, using a firmer voice, she commanded, "Grab
a pen and paper, call the FBI San Francisco offices, and dial this extension." She
had me repeat the extension and hung up. Following her instructions, I dialed the
number to find out she was indeed an FBI agent! My knees involuntarily dropped
into the floor and I was between worlds. Nauseous, dazed, and confused, my face
on fire, my heart racing, and my body fired up with a jolt of adrenaline getting

primed to fight. It was an inconceivable nightmare I hoped to wake up from.

The FBI agent informed me that I was a victim of an investment fraud. She told me my victim ID number and that ALL my investments, including my entire retirement savings, were gone. My world as I knew it shattered into pieces in an instant.

I never expected anything like this would happen to me. For most of my career, I was thriving. I excelled at finance, management, and leadership to deliver more complex large-scale initiatives. I was good at leading information technology projects, and competent at utilizing processes and systems to resolve challenges and rally the project team members to complete their tasks. Being a victim was an unfamiliar role and it did not sit well with me. It was a hard pill to swallow at that stage of my career.

At the beginning of my career, I was entirely focused on the deliverables, processes, and managing the projects, but deep down, I had an inclination that there was something more. Then, I stumbled onto something that completely shifted my perspective on life, work, and leadership. It was a brief conversation with one of my MBA professors. He shared a story of working with an Olympic-level athlete who calmed her nerves before performing in front of a packed arena. The work wasn't focused on her physical or technical performance but on her mental and emotional performance. I thought, if that works for an Olympic athlete at the world stage, it would surely work for me and the people I work with at the corporate level.

I started looking into ways to learn more about human development, leadership, and high-performing coaching. I started educating myself on adult development, neuroscience, executive coaching, and how to facilitate transformational change. As I began applying them, I realized that beyond the processes, project deliverables, financial models and operations, there are human beings "gluing" all the pieces together. The more complex the project or goal was, the more important the interactions between the humans navigating different aspects of that collaborative effort became.

At some point, I had over 20 astute and disciplined people on my team responsible for managing the entire portfolio of projects that were initiated within our organization, and we were quite successful at delivering results. Life was good! I was still climbing the corporate ladder and reaping its rewards; however, I started focusing more on the 'people side' of the assignments. I was witnessing the positive impacts of the pivot every day. Whenever I saw people NOT paying attention to the human aspects of business, their projects suffered. And mine were thriving. Even so, I was shying away from revealing it to the leadership team and project sponsors. Part of me wanted to remain in the old and comfortable 'MBA guy' identity I worked so hard to portray.

In parallel, as I was entering the world of executive coaching, I also included embodiment practices such as yoga into my training. It was beautiful to see the growth my clients were experiencing through my coaching. I was especially intrigued at the positive impact that embodiment practices had on my business clients and the topics they raised during our sessions. Adding a few asanas (yoga postures) to a client's practices supported them in seeing improvements in getting to their desired state faster. Their positive changes inspired me so much that I opened my own boutique yoga studio within a few weeks of graduating from coaching school.

I was experiencing the power of shifting peoples' mindset and how that massively impacts whether a change effort will succeed or not; be it in a one-to-one coaching contract with a senior leader or a large-scale transformational change impacting the entire organization. I wanted to facilitate this type of work and be more of service. It felt like a calling.

I left my cushy corporate job and my not-quite-a-corner office, and stepped more fully into the Executive Coaching, Facilitation and Organizational Change arenas. I set an intention for myself to facilitate the initiatives I was leading with a more explicit focus on the intricacies of human dynamics. I wanted to facilitate how human interactions inform and impact the dynamics between teams, departments, and the organization as a whole.

I loved delivering both the one-on-one coaching with executives, and the team coaching for change initiatives, achieving breakthroughs for the entire organization. It was clear to me that this is my life's work.

I will admit though, it was challenging work. But, when I witnessed people coming to the realization that we are all in this game of life together, it was so rewarding. We need to break down our silos, connect, open our minds, hearts, and wills to see possibilities. We should aspire to listen more and help each other to navigate through the uncharted territories that arise in any transformational change. As the 12th century Persian poet Sa'adi eloquently says:

"Human beings are members of a whole,
since in their creation they are of one essence.
When the conditions of the time brings a member (limb) to pain,
the other members (limbs) will suffer from discomfort.
You, who are indifferent to the misery of others,
it is not fitting that they should call you a human being."

I thought I had found my footing after a wobbly transition to the consulting world. Things were going great. When I won a contract at a multinational corporation to facilitate change initiatives impacting over 25,000 personnel across two continents, I was overjoyed. I was doing exciting, impactful work and things were going according to plan.

Until I got the call from that FBI agent!

As someone who holds multiple academic degrees, including an MBA from a prestigious business school, I considered myself smart and easily justified moving my investments from where they were to a new investment firm in San Francisco. After all, I always did better in my stock market investments than my sophisticated investment team. After that phone call, realizing that I was lied to and had fallen for a ponzi scheme, my ego was completely crushed!

Over the year that followed, catastrophe after catastrophe ensued: I lost my entire retirement savings and more, my personal banker rejected my mortgage for a townhouse I was legally committed to, and I had to return my favorite sports car with penalties back to the dealership. It upended my personal life, putting a major dent in my relationship with my partner on a very low 'trust battery.' Then it attacked my body. I got a severe case of shingles and could not get out of bed literally for weeks. It caused me to lose a contract, hitting me in my already depleted wallet. The five stages of grief were unfolding right in front of me with one exception. I was cycling through *denial*, *anger*, *depression*, and *bargaining*, with no *acceptance* in line of sight.

I could not see any possibilities; there was no clear way back to my normal routines. My confidence wavered going into the polished boardrooms talking to the executives. I couldn't face my colleagues as I felt like a failure. I remember being in line in a grocery store one day hoping my credit card wouldn't bounce. I had hit my version of rock bottom! As I was drowning, I desperately sought a way to breathe again.

Then, *something* shifted. More than one *something* in fact. In reality, the most important shift happened when I realized that the more I let myself live fully in the immediacy of the present moment — connecting to my Heart — the more I would notice all the opportunities in my daily life. When I was not fully present, when I was busy running by my (old) habitual patterns, I would miss these opportunities. I was too busy being in the past. I was too busy living a repetitive, predictable future. Or worse, I was ruminating on the challenges life brought me with that ponzi scheme, hoping for a major breakthrough while missing all the mini breakthrough moments that were happening right in front of me.

I started meditating more after my body collapsed with shingles, and I was on bedrest (not by choice) for a few weeks. Meditation had for many years been a routine practice, so I used it now to deconstruct my thoughts and beliefs around what had happened and what I should do next. I began using a technique in Zazen (seated meditation), asking who or what is having these thoughts? I started going to Zen meditation retreats, but as powerful as that was, even that wasn't helping at first. I needed to make a stronger shift.

I committed to deepening my Zen meditation practice no matter how hard it got to sit with my thoughts. Seated on the meditation cushion one day, I recalled the exact moment with that "investor," and how my Heart had raised a flag. At the time I had dismissed it. I then recalled all the other times when I ignored my Heart's wisdom, and there were many. I started practicing being more Heart-centered. Every time the negative thoughts started ruminating I would bring my focus back to my breath, connecting to my Heart — and eventually the space surrounding my Heart and body. With perseverance and continued practice, I felt a shift in my posture. A shift in my thinking. In my *being*. The dark thick cloud that consumed me was still in my subconscious mind, but I realized, when I'm coherent, connecting to vast infinite space, I am the entire sky! The dark cloud became a small dot in my periphery. I started seeing opportunity, instead of just zooming in on negativity.

Sometimes, I still fall. The echoes of my old self still equate falling with failure and I beat myself up in those moments where I fail to follow through with my positive routines. To bring myself back, I rely on my vow that no matter what, I WILL get up and go at it again! I used to say when you fall seven times, you need to get up eight times. But my 8-year-old son corrected me, saying, "When you fall seven times, you can only get up seven times, Daddy!" His childish wisdom reminds me to be gentle and pragmatic with myself.

Living through the aftermath of that phone call was like surviving a tsunami. I felt an enormous guilt for bringing this on my family and the consequences it had on my passion project that would impact the hundreds of yogis that practiced in my yoga studio. It almost destroyed my life, my family, and my reason for living.

But, with hindsight, I know that my heart got cracked wide-open as it wanted me to listen — really listen — more fully to its messages. It was an incongruous and unexpected invitation to bring all my training, and the practices I was sharing with my clients, "online." I have now learned to fall in love with the immediacy of the present moment and let it show me a myriad of possibilities unfolding during the day. The events of that year also taught me the importance of having a support system. I am fortunate to have a group of friends and incredible mentors and teachers who helped me when I needed it the most. To this day, I feel extremely privileged to witness a community of yogis coming together, growing together, and working on their holistic health and transformation at my studio.

We often forget to ask for help when we are under enormous amounts of stress, or we just think we don't have a support system. I have been around long enough to know that it is just our ego playing tricks on us. I would remind myself of the enormity of what Victor E. Frankle and Nelson Mandela endured in their isolation and it gave me a boost of inspiration to continue with my practices.

To see the possibilities in life, all you need to do is to come back to the present moment by connecting to your Heart. Another powerful tool we all have at our disposal, yet we often forget, is our breath. With daily practice, Breath will quickly bring you to the present moment, requiring no external stimulus, and completely independent of your external circumstances.

You should not wait for a serendipitous moment, because life is filled with those moments every day. You can wait for a miracle, or realize it is already here — right in this moment — in the life you lead. With disciplined rigorous practice, you can reprogram your personality and see opportunities regardless of the situation you are in. Fall in love with the immediacy of the present moment. Let it show you the possibilities unfolding every moment of every day. Learn to see beyond your current circumstances, current environment, and things and people that together create your current way of showing up in life. May you connect, and fall in love, with your Heart, stay more in the present moment, and realize and live your *true* nature.

Ignite Action Steps

By connecting to your breath, you activate your Heart and find your center again no matter how many times you are thrown off-balance by life's circumstances. Connect to your Heart, and no matter how impossible the situation is, with practice you will see possibilities showing up. We are most creative when we are fully present. What are you willing to give up in service of living life from your highest state of Being?

Heart-centered Breathing:

Step 1: For 10 minutes every morning, bring your attention to the center of your chest at the same line with your physical heart. As you take smooth, slow, and soft breaths, imagine your breath is flowing in and flowing out of the center of your chest. Do this breathing in a rhythm that's comfortable for you.

Step 2: Set a few reminders for yourself throughout the day to practice this Heart-centered breathing, e.g. everytime you turn on your computer, go to a meeting, sit at the dinner table, etc. No one will notice you doing it, and with practice, you will bring more coherence into your life.

A quick guide to enlightenment:

This is a simple — not easy — yet powerful practice that will improve your odds in life.

Avoid the **three C's:** refrain from complaining, comparing, and competing with others.

Atta Emami – Canada
MBA, Integral Master Coach, MSc.
www.ChangeFacilitator.com
https://www.instagram.com/atta_emami/
https://www.linkedin.com/in/attaemami/

Dr. Yasmine Saad

"A lotus bud in muddy water doesn't doubt that it will transform into a beautiful flower."

Trust that the miseries of life are there to propel you to your next greatness! Keep trusting in life and hold space for hope. Misfortunes can be hidden blessings. Seize the opportunities and possibilities that are coming your way and see what happens!

Misfortune to Fortune: A Transformational Journey from Pain to Empowerment

Have you ever felt devastated by an event in your life just to realize a few years later that it was the best blessing in your life?

I always thought I am protected; life has my back and I have always been able to turn a negative into a positive. And then I had a miscarriage. I had gone to the OB/GYN for a regular prenatal checkup. I laid back on the examining table as the physician's assistant moved the wand over my belly, moving it around in many directions trying to find the baby's heartbeat. The seconds felt like minutes as I waited in angst, holding the hope for the baby's life, but the only thing I could hear was my heartbeat and the rest was silence. They told me the baby was no longer thriving. They couldn't find a heartbeat.

I was so devastated. Why would life prevent me from having a child? Was my body defective? Was I not good enough to be a mother? These questions had me thinking back to my own birth and comparing myself to my mother and the example she had set. My mother had been pregnant during the civil war in Lebanon, bombs falling all around her. Yet, she made it to the hospital all alone and gave life to me, protecting my life when I was born. Why couldn't I protect the life of this child to give birth to him or her when my mother was able to give birth to me through the war? I was crushed. I never imagined I would have difficulty having a child. I am very motherly and take care of a lot of people. I knew that I was meant to be a mother, so what did this mean for my life going forward? Was I not going to be a mother after all? Was I mistaken about my motherly instincts? I had been knocked sideways and the truth I knew about me — and life — was broken.

I always wanted to have a child. When I met my husband, I suddenly desired so much more than having a child, so I postponed pregnancy and took an exciting detour. I was having so much fun with him that I wanted to live MY life: travel, go out, enjoy each other's company… and we did that for eight years. By that point, it was time to decide… child or no child? I couldn't imagine going through life and not experiencing what being a mother would be like. I always dreamed of a family of my own with two children and a home filled with hugs, togetherness, and joy. It was time… time to give birth to a baby!

How was I going to make it all happen? I was working an insane number of hours: I had my full-time job at the hospital and was seeing patients in my private practice after I was done with my teaching and hospital work. I literally started at 10 AM and ended at 10 PM. Thinking back to my dreams growing up, I remembered the life that 16-year-old me wanted: having my own private practice and the flexibility to go see my patients and come back home to be with my child. As much as I loved my work at the hospital and my teaching engagements, I had to let these go to create a balanced life where I could be there for my child. I decided that I would give up my hospital work and teaching, and move full time to my private practice. I also felt a need to go somewhere powerful to rebalance my body from the hard-working hours. I worked on having my husband take two weeks off so we could have another honeymoon, this time an exotic trip to Bora Bora, and get pregnant. What a magical place to start the baby's journey!

Everyone thought I was crazy, telling me, "You cannot decide when you get pregnant," but I kept thinking, "Why not?" Life had my back and I found an amazing deal for a package with flights and hotel in Bora Bora. I followed my plan, indulging in a blissful two weeks in Bora Bora, and I did get pregnant!!! I was over the moon! I knew right away that I was pregnant as my body was not acting as usual. I had some digestive changes, it just didn't feel the way it usually does when it processes things. I am very sensitive and attune to my body, so I knew! I went to my OB/GYN who confirmed it: I was pregnant! I always imagined that pregnancy would be a great time: how fun would it be to feel the baby move inside of me, talk to him or her, and have 24/7 company.

I was so happy on my way to one of my prenatal visits, and then I lay down on the paper sheet covering the table, only to feel the angst of the physician's assistant who could not find the heartbeat; only to be left with my own terrible grief. After the miscarriage, I was shocked, hurt, and puzzled. I never imagined I could have a miscarriage. Did I damage my body by working so hard that it could not carry a child? Did I wait too long to become a mother? I didn't know what to think. I was hurt. Why would life give me this? Why would life let me go through the joy and the hope just to be let down, and be left with tons of uncertainty? As painful as this was, that was just the beginning of a difficult journey.

After the miscarriage, I developed sensitivities to all foods. The only thing that I could eat was quinoa. I couldn't eat anything else without having a rash or arthritic-like sensation in different parts of my body. My sensitivity was not limited to food; I became sensitive to everything — food, people, and even places. Sitting with my patients, I would develop all kinds of symptoms such as intense fatigue and headaches, to name a few. Entering a supermarket would trigger an immediate headache that would be relieved as soon as I left. I had no clue what was going on. I was told that it was the hormones in my body, but this lasted for months on end and didn't go away. I went to see all kinds of specialists with no conclusive results. Being tossed from one specialist to the next, I felt lost, and worried for my life and health. My world had become very restrictive in what I could eat and what I could do. How was I going to function? How was I going to continue to see patients, eat, and enjoy life? My body reactions became my laboratory: I was constantly analyzing my symptoms and trying to draw correlations between what I did or ate that triggered a reaction.

Although the analysis of what was happening in my body consumed my days, my main goal was to figure out a way to have a child. Beside the emotional and physical pain, the miscarriage had highlighted my desire for a child and being healthy was the road to get there. Even more than health, I needed a reconfiguration of my whole life to hold space for myself, for a little one, and for my patients. I was determined to have a baby and wanted more than ever to be home to take care of my child. I saw no pleasure in spending my days working and being away from him or her. I wondered how I would make it all happen. I had to work to support our family. I also knew that I would need to be able to afford help, as my mother lives in another country and my husband is a very busy professor. How could I have my dream come true: a child and my practice, with the flexibility to take care of both?

I looked at what I had in my life that could make this happen: I taught and supervised the next generation of psychologists and psychiatry residents. I had a steady flow of patients and referrals. I suddenly remembered the words of the internship training director at the hospital I worked at, when I left: "You are going to go create a group practice." At the time, I thought, "Who does he think I am? I am not Robert Leahy," (a famous psychologist who created a very successful group practice at the time and has written several books). The director got me thinking, "What if I build a group practice? He thought I could do it so maybe I can do it. What do I lose? Money, okay so worst case scenario I lose money. I could live with that. If I lost my savings, I would just not have savings. That is not the end of the world." I just had to mix all these ingredients together to make a new recipe.

That is when I realized I could make it happen! I decided to see myself through the eyes of the director; someone who saw more in me than I saw in myself. I took all the ingredients that were already in my life and embarked on the journey of creating a group practice.

With a group practice, I could help so many patients get better help, and I could inspire the next generation of psychologists to elevate their therapy skills and learn the ins and outs of private practice (something not often taught at the time), supporting them in achieving their career goals.

I am a giver, teacher, and healer. I can create a cycle of people giving to each other: giving wisdom to the psychologists who will then help their patients, which will give me the balance and freedom I needed. I would hire the best of the best and give the best of the best. I would be freer and, through this cycle of help, I would have flexibility so that I could take care of a child of my own.

It was a bold move. At the time, there were very few group practices. I didn't know my value then and was wondering if I could pull it off. In my moments of doubt, I would close my eyes and remember the words of the internship training director and all my other colleagues who believed in me.

Now, how was I going to make it happen? First thing first, I needed to find an office space for this group practice. I already had a beautiful office that I loved on a floor where no one ever moved out, and I didn't want to give it up, but I needed a new space where I could be next door to my trainees. Little did I know that life had my back: a few weeks later, the office right next to mine became free as the psychologist who occupied it had to relocate to another state.

This was my opportunity! I seized it and rented the office. I was now in the business of creating a group practice! It was time to find a name for the practice, set it up as a business, and start hiring the first psychologist to come on board.

I was still going through all my health issues and not knowing if I would be able to have a child, but I was sure the group practice would be the source of all the freedom I craved. In my mind, if I didn't have a child, at least I would have my health as I wouldn't need to work so many hours. Little did I know I would start working so much harder to make sure everyone was taken care of and that the group practice ran smoothly. I wanted to make sure that the patients got the best treatment they could get, and that the psychologists I hired were blossoming. I often wondered at the beginning if I would ever work less. Was this group practice really such a good idea?

In the meantime, I was still struggling to feel good emotionally and phys-ically. Once again, life had my back. One day, about nine months after the miscarriage, I had gone to my acupuncturist's office. The acupuncturist was part of a training school for Qigong. There were pamphlets laid out in front of me on my way in for each acupuncture session, but I never paid any attention to them. I was single-mindedly pursuing my treatments.

That particular day, a Qigong practitioner who was there that day handed me a DVD of *Dragon's Way Qigong* by Master Nan Lu. I asked, "What is this?" The answer was: "It might help you."

I had no idea what Qigong was. I was a math major who had the guts to follow my passion and became a psychologist instead of an investment banker. I was not into meditation or yoga and I liked being stimulated intellectually. I was not into energy or anything esoteric, but I needed something that worked when nothing did, so I decided to watch the DVD. I put the DVD on and fol-lowed the master as he was doing the slow, gentle movements that looked like nothing. A slow kick forward, a toe twist, a shift of the hip… and it was like magic! I had no more aches, no more pain, no more rashes. How could this be working? It looked like *nothing*! I was like: "What is this?"

The next time I had a rash or arthritic like sensation, I tried it again. I did the Qigong movements and once again it worked!!! I was like: "What is this? I need to study it, learn it, and understand it."

I want to say that that was when my life began. In reality, life had been supporting me all along and my miscarriage was the vessel for my next personal and professional growth.

I healed myself through Wu Ming Qigong and started integrating the heal-ing principles of traditional Chinese medicine into my psychology practice. I had no symptoms and felt great! My patients reaped the benefits of my newly acquired knowledge, and since a lot of them were doctors, a lot of them found their own holistic approach and in turn helped thousands more patients.

I started a movement of practitioners of medicine and psychology who are now integrating holistic approaches to treat their patients. My group practice grew, and we have now more than 15 psychologists on board, with many more who have left to open their own group practices and teach to other psychologists the benefits of integrated Eastern and Western healing traditions. Many practitioners have blossomed in their ability to help others more effectively, and thousands of patients have been helped in a profound and long-lasting way.

The biggest blessing for me personally came from going further in my Qigong journey. Qigong gave further clarity to who I am: I am a giver, a healer, and a teacher. When my father was not doing well physically, I decided to get further training so that I could use Qigong for healing both of us. The training was going to significantly elevate my energy. The thought popped into my head that if I were to get pregnant after this training, this would be the best way to welcome a child into the world. Life had other plans… better plans!!! I became pregnant two days before starting the training and went through it while pregnant. It was the best pregnancy ever! I was feeling great and was able to balance symptoms that came with being pregnant. The desire to heal both myself and my father was enough to set the path to a healthy new life growing inside of me. Healing my past healed my future.

I can now say that the miscarriage was the best thing that happened in my life. It put me in touch with my priorities, opened doors that I would never open myself, and it literally put me on my path. I now have a beautiful daughter, a booming group practice, and I am a more powerful healer and teacher… of others and of myself.

Can you imagine what my journey would have been like if I knew all along the blessings that my miscarriage was going to bring me? All that time spent on pain and doubt would be gone. I would have just lived in the expectation of the wonderous possibilities this miscarriage was going to bring me. I would grab every opportunity with excitement and trust with no doubt in my mind. I would feel so empowered and so supported by life, all along the way, instead of just at the end of the journey. We never know what each event we go through is going to bring us so why not believe from the beginning that it will be great and beyond our dreams! Let go of your desire to understand with your mind and let yourself be open to what comes your way. Seize it all and see what happens! Connect to the love of the Universe that is supporting you.

Stop listening to your mind who wants you to be prepared and wants you to solve problems. There is no problem worth solving, only opportunities to take and enjoy! What is bad might be great and what is great might be bad. It is your trust in life that shapes how you shape your life. Be open to possibilities and embrace what comes your way even if your mind does not understand it.

Trust life!

IGNITE ACTION STEPS

Stop listening to your mind. It wants you to be prepared and wants you to solve problems. There is no problem to solve, only opportunities to take and enjoy!

Look for the good in the bad. Ask yourself what good you can make out of the bad. Make a positive out of a negative by opening your mind and discovering new territories.

Seize it all and see what happens! What is great might be bad, and what is bad might be great. It is your trust in life that shapes how you shape your life. Be open to possibilities and embrace what comes your way, even if your mind does not always understand it.

Follow your heart. Your desire will show you the way and you already have all the ingredients to make it happen. Trust Life.

Dr. Yasmine Saad – United States of America
Licensed Clinical Psychologist, Founder and Owner
of Madison Park Psychological Services
https://madisonparkpsych.com

Reverend Sheila Black

"Your soul is eternal and the essence of who you truly are."

My intention for you is to know that the sadness you feel at losing a loved one can be replaced with the empowered knowing that your loved ones and your Spirit Guides are always with you. I believe that with focused intention and practice, you can be divinely guided along your path. Embrace life to the fullest and know that you are loved unconditionally and that you are truly never alone.

Signs From Spirit

I walked solemnly along the river's edge, my footsteps slow and deliberate and my heart filled with great sadness. The sound of the booming waterfall couldn't drown out the clutter of my sorrowful mind. Gazing up at the sky, I longed for a sign from my father. A cloud formation, a shape in the river, an animal like the blue jay that my father adored; but nothing. Dad was gone for over a year and I haven't seen him since his wake.

His wake was held at my parents' party room in their posh condo. The afternoon was filled with glorious tales of Dad's antics over a dram of Glenfiddich™ scotch, straight from the freezer. Feeling distant, I slipped away silently up to his room. I pained for him, as I gently caressed his favorite soft woolen sweater and basked in the scent of Old Spice™, his favorite aftershave. All of a sudden I looked up and saw him, in spirit, standing there with a big smile on his face. I was elated to see him but then he disappeared quickly. Sadly, I didn't sense his presence again for years.

The last time I saw my dad alive — a stoic Scotsman with kind, gentle, and mischievous brown eyes — was at the hospital before his surgery for a routine hernia operation. I was with Mom. I picked her up as she was a nervous driver at the best of times; actually, I think the rest of us were more nervous when we knew she was driving!

Mom was rather haggard and worried about Dad. Dad suffered with emphysema and painful shingles that he described to feel like razor blades across his shoulders and down his spine. He suffered for years with issues breathing, but overall was pretty healthy. During the operation, he was supposed to remain awake with a local anesthetic but in error the hospital gave him a general anesthetic and knocked him out. When he awoke after surgery, Dad was coughing so violently that he had a fatal heart attack. Imagine the shock of it — Dad died! I was in a total daze. I couldn't believe he was gone. I spent the night devouring photos of him, not able to join the family at the funeral home the next day. Everything seemed to feel numb.

I was daddy's little girl, the youngest of five children. One of my fondest memories of my dearest dad was when I was 13 years old recovering from a major scoliosis back operation. Strapped in a specialized medical bed for a month, eight hours looking straight up at the ceiling, endlessly counting the dots in the tiles. When I was laying facedown, my face would be squished in a little opening and I was only able to look directly down at the sterile floor below. My father would lay below me on the hard floor, as my tears poured over his kind and gentle face. No one else would do that but him. It created a special bond for us.

Twelve months of missing Dad had led me to take my riverside walk, searching for a sign from him. I reminisced on all of our beautiful memories; crying heavy sobs and searching for a way to soothe my aching soul. I slowly walked out of the park to the quaint main street and into the general store. It was filled with all types of knickknacks and the floor creaked as I walked.

Suddenly, I heard my dad's favorite song "Amazing Grace" playing. I looked up, held my breath, and cocked my head to listen; trying to find where it was coming from. I quickly ran by the candy displays to the back of the store looking for the source of the music. I started to feel light-headed, I rested my hands on the wooden plywood walls, feeling my knees go weak.

I followed the song to a jukebox and just as I got there, the song stopped! I eagerly searched the playlist but didn't see it there. I was not surprised that it wasn't one of the songs the jukebox could play, I just knew. There it was… my sign from Dad.

I felt so happy and content that I got the message I needed to know that Dad was with me. I was grateful that I was able to use our connection to receive that validation from the spirit world.

Soon after Dad's passing, Mom moved to a retirement home. Quickly she became very depressed and tried to kill herself several times. I was so stressed; trying to cope with the loss of my father, working at a very demanding job with young children at home, and dealing with my mother trying to repeatedly end her life by suffocation, with pills, or with knives.

I remember one of the visits to hospital after a failed suicide attempt. I told Mom that if she killed herself, she wouldn't be able to go to heaven to see Dad. I felt horrible saying this and I truly did not believe it, but the trick worked and her attempts at killing herself finally stopped. Thank goodness!

A few years later, Mom was rushed to the emergency room with what was thought to be a stroke. I remember going to see her, feeling the love and sadness overwhelm me. I slid in beside her on the tiny and hard cot, snuggling close, holding her cold hand, and feeling the fear that was deep within her.

Mom and I were always very close. Being the youngest, I was fortunate to spend time with just her. As a young girl, I always came home for lunch from school to enjoy Mom's delicious 'cheese dreams.' We also loved to watch scary shows together and, petrified, I would reach out one of my feet to touch and cuddle with one of hers for comfort and reassurance. As I matured, we traveled together and had more of a sister relationship. In the last few years, It was difficult to see her decline and watch her suffer with such sadness.

In the hospital, the staff discovered that she had not had a stroke but that she had a week's supply of medications stuck in her throat. The hospital staff, in all the confusion, didn't purge her esophagus of the pills; in error, they forced all of them down and that triggered an overdose.

The overdose of medication had her hallucinating and screaming, "Help me! Help me!" Her green-blue hazel eyes were huge and full of fear. Mom was never the same after that. It was heartbreaking and I started having insomnia as a result of it. I would come home and see her scared eyes on my bedroom ceiling each night and hear her screams for help.

She ended up being sent to a nursing home where, for her safety, they tied her to her wheelchair or to her bed. On one particular visit, to cheer Mom up,

I brought her a delicious chocolate and caramel ice cream cone. She enjoyed every morsel, the chocolate dripping down her face, and it made me happy to see her so joyful. As soon as I got home, the phone rang. It was the nursing home informing me that my mother had just passed.

I rushed right back to the nursing home. The sight of Mom laying utterly motionless on her bed brought out the little girl in me. I cried, "Mommy…" I haven't called her that since I was a wee little girl. I bent over the bed to kiss her and hug her, then they took her away in a body bag. That image is seared into my brain forever… her lifeless body stuck in a bag seemed so surreal to me. I had just seen her smiling and it was impossible to comprehend that she was gone.

I remember speaking at her funeral. I wrote a tribute for her entitled "My Mom, My friend." I chose the songs to be played and noticed that the most gut-wrenching one was planned just before I spoke. I thought to myself that I was not going to be able to speak after that song. Instead, the funeral home played the wrong version; it ended up being a funny country version, which made us all laugh. I know my dad helped me with that. He worked his magic from the other side of life. Thanks Dad!

Months before her passing, I had booked a workshop to make an indigenous native hand drum. It ended up being the day after Mom's funeral. I didn't want to go as I was way too emotional, but my friend insisted. Making your own hand drum is a very spiritual and sacred journey. While I was constructing my drum, I pulled the pliable yet hard deerskin to make the ties and it snapped. I was devastated. Drums are often referred to as *Grandmother* out of sacredness and respect. That drum, to me, represented Mom. The elder told me that the damaged drum symbolizes my broken heart and that she and my friend would help mend it, which they did. I was relieved and it gave me hope.

Three weeks later, I was in my backyard, sitting in the shade of my large Linden tree, carefully sewing a bag to hold my newly made drum. The bag was a soft purple corduroy fabric on the outside and I lined the inside with Mom's favorite black and white leopard print blouse. I was missing her terribly and felt so lonely and alone. I decided to go back in the house and draw a bath. My soaker tub is my sanctuary. There, I can go in and lock the door, talk to my Spirit team, meditate, and pray.

I filled the tub with Mom's favorite scent of lavender, then lit incense and a white candle in her honor. I slid in and let the silkiness of the water caress my tired body. As I got out and dried off, I looked at myself in the mirror. Standing behind me was my mom.

I quickly wiped the steam off the mirror to make sure I wasn't imagining it, and I saw her smile at me. She was quite a bit shorter than me but I could see her clearly. A bright smile lit up her face, the gentleness of her love enveloping my entire being. I felt her soft hand on my shoulder, noticing her signature red nail polish. I burst into tears, but this time not of sadness but of great joy to be able to see and feel her tender touch. She stayed with me for several minutes and I was so grateful that she was there.

I could see and feel Mom so clearly and the healing that I received was profound! This pivotal moment changed me forever. It directed me to my soul's purpose. I knew I was meant to devote my life to Spirit and to help others heal their grief.

I have been spiritual my entire life and always felt a connection with all of my guides and angels. Connecting with my parents showed me my abilities and awakened me to what else was possible; however, I felt that if I was to do this professionally and support others, then I needed to master and hone my unique mediumship skills.

This led me to visit my first spiritualist church soon after Mom's passing. The ministers at the Spiritualist Church of Canada were all mediums and healers. Their core belief is that life is eternal. It felt so liberating to be able to talk to like-minded people without having to turn around to see if someone was judging me and looking at me like I had three heads. I felt like I was coming home.

I took many courses with tutors from the United States, United Kingdom, and Canada. At my ordination service, I surprised many of my family by demonstrating mediumship for them for the first time. It was my opportunity to "come out of the closet" and let my light shine in a beautiful and heartfelt way.

In my career and day-to-day profession, as a corporate manager, I was praying daily for an exit strategy that would let me practice mediumship full-time. Then, on the very day my *beonewithspirit.com* web page went live, I was in a terrible car crash. I regained consciousness in my smashed up car, in the ditch, confused, and realizing that I was not breathing. I was having an out-of-body experience, on the verge of crossing the veil. As the rescue crew arrived, my life force was brought back to my body. I made the choice to stay and fulfill my life's mission of working with Spirit.

I suffered a mild traumatic brain injury and had to stay home in bed for six weeks. Due to the injury, I was depressed and crying, compounded by the hypersensitivity to light and sounds. The company I worked for was pressuring me to come back. This forced me to leave the company permanently. I did get my exit strategy after all, though not exactly as I expected.

Within six months of recovery, I started to work in my spiritual practice and have never turned back. I knew it was my calling and that I needed to help people with their grief and to empower others to develop this kind of spiritual connection for themselves.

Throughout my journey practicing and teaching mediumship, I have had some beautiful affirmations of my calling. Recently, the sweetest 11-year-old girl with Down syndrome came through for me to give messages to her mom. She was the brightest soul I have met, and her innocent and loving personality shone through. Her Mom gained immense healing from the experience. It gave her peace to know that her daughter was okay on the other side.

As I started teaching, one of my students lost her 8-year-old son. Shy and grief-stricken when I first met her, after taking classes with me, she became more confident in herself, trusting her own divine connection, and learned to communicate with her deceased son herself.

While it was Mom that inspired me to focus on my spiritual training, it is my father that is one of my strongest guides and helpers. I am grateful to my parents for all they did for me while here on Earth, and am still grateful for the love and support they provide me from the Other side.

I love all aspects of my Spiritual Practice. It gives me such joy to see others empowered. My story shows that anything is truly possible. I feel that anyone can be a medium; it is not unlike playing the piano. You may have more of a natural talent for it or you may have to try harder, but results come with effort. There is always something for you to learn and develop. You too can be of service for humanity. Never come from a place of Ego but one of Love. Trust yourself, believe in your gifts, and embrace them.

Ignite Action Steps

Meditate — Quiet your mind. Prayer is asking for help while meditation is receiving answers. Experiment with different types of meditations. I recommend you listen to quiet music or be silent and expand your soul to blend with the spirit world. I love to have walking meditation and connect to my Spirit team as I hug trees and connect to Mother Earth's energies.

Join like-minded groups — There are many groups available whether in person or online. It is wonderful to gather with people who 'get you' so you can share your experiences and come together for the higher good of all.

Build your Spiritual Toolbox — Take courses and let the studies integrate with your Soul before moving on to the next course. There are so many different teachers out there and so many types of Spiritual growth. Focus on what you are most passionate about and do that!

Don't care what others think of you — This, too, could be your soul's purpose. Embrace your Spiritual Self with your entire being!

Reverend Sheila Black – Canada
Ordained Minister, Accredited Spiritual Healer, Certified Medium
www.beonewithspirit.com
❑ Be One With Spirit
❑ Rev Sheila Black

MARINA SIGALOVA

"Your highest expression is needed for the new story of humanity, and at the highest expression is LOVE. When you put your full essence behind vision, strategy, and your actions, everything is possible."

I know this is going to sound like a full-blown fantasy to you, but hear me out. Not only is it possible, but achievable as I have already walked the path ahead of you. There is an alternative to the endless stress, exhaustion, and hidden suffering of high-achieving leaders. All you need is to connect to who you are at your core, your highest truth, and fully express your innate authority with purpose, passion, and love.

UNLOVING BEGINNINGS, MAGNIFICENT MATURING

I wake up on a tired gray sofa, in a dingy little flat in a dodgy neighborhood, the rain beating a rhythm on the window, and my whole body itching. What the hell is happening? Confused and exhausted, covered in bites, I slowly slid off the sofa onto the floor. Panic sweeps through my body as I sit frozen and mute, my breathing shallow, my chest hardly moving. I am a corporate executive working for a top accounting firm, living a life of misery in this infested flat. My rent contract in a beautiful Abbey house is over, and this flat, a 15-minute walk from my office near London Tower, is my temporary home. It was offered to me by a colleague, who is shamelessly profiting from my misery. I feel used. And itchy. The sofa is severely infested with bugs which have spread to all my belongings. I want to crawl under a rock and never come out again!

I wonder how long I have to live in this never-ending struggle, where no matter how much I strive for a fulfilling life, I never seem to be able to get there.

I desperately scroll through my phone book to call people I can stay with, but no one will have me. Swamped in my drama, I feel bitten not only on this couch, but by life; unloved, abandoned, and desperate. I think about calling my therapeutic healer, hoping she can get me out of this and knowing that a session with her will give me a moment of peace and bliss. But, thoroughly pissed off, not only by how much money I have spent on healers but also my dependence on them, I don't call.

As rage took over me, I squared my shoulders, lifted my chin, and my eyes blazed. It was so infuriating to realize that I had worked myself to the ground in a job that was draining, unfulfilling, and meaningless to me. I remembered my failed relationships one after another, making me feel alone, totally disconnected, and unhappy. My whole life was shit.

The feeling of loneliness started when I was a child and has stayed with me. Several times a week I would drag myself to music lessons after school. My father forced me to take music, which I wholeheartedly hated, and the unbearable anxiety of it made my heart tremble. I would stand in the choir, knowing I was the worst singer in the group. Excluded from competitions, I felt invisible. I was never able to get the right tone and every time it was my turn to sing alone, the pity in my teacher's face reflected and amplified my humiliation. I felt fundamentally flawed.

My father, the enforcer of my attendance at choir, was the most influential figure in my upbringing. He sought to raise an independent and successful woman, but the way he did it destroyed me. Home resembled a communist army more than a safe and supportive space: restrictions imposed upon me, shouting, physical and psychological abuse.

To make sure I progressed in my piano-playing skills, my father rehearsed my homework with me. As I bumbled through the notes, he beat the rhythm loudly with his palms; and if I got lost, he shouted. My mind was focused but my body was in survival mode. My heart beat like a bird trying to escape from my chest, and my touch on the piano keys was slippery from the sweat of fear on my palms. I was terrified to disappoint him and taste the weapon of his control: a long brown leather belt with a metal belt buckle. Trapped and defeated, I concluded: "I have no choice, I don't matter, I must be perfect and comply to be accepted and loved..." And that's just what I did for over two decades. Scraps of approval became my definition of love, my motivation in life, and I forgot there was any other way.

The resilience and inner strength I developed allowed me to become a highly successful woman. But I felt that there was something intrinsically wrong with me. No matter what I accomplished, I pushed myself to work harder, learn more, and do everything to be worthy. For years I'd force myself out of bed, shower, glance in the mirror at a tired depressed face, and arrive at work. All on autopilot.

One day, I stepped out of my office to get a coffee from the bland and featureless cafeteria downstairs when my boss called me to come back. Radiating stress and dissatisfaction, she prohibited me from leaving my workplace and created a big fuss in front of the higher management about my temporary absence. Without a rock to crawl under, I shrunk into myself instead. I felt small and helpless, squashed under her heartless boot. Later that week when she informed me of her plan for my work for the next year, I felt rage start to boil inside me. My heartbeat quickened, blood rushed to my face, and the silence became dangerous. The image of being stuck there for another miserable year stabbed my eyes. Deep inside of me I said: "No way!" The next morning I handed in my resignation.

It was the first time I gave myself permission to reject the intolerable.

However, I did not step straight from permission to paradise. So far my empowerment had only won me a dingy little apartment full of bugs, a new setting for that feeling of rage boiling inside me. But something was different on that cold, rainy day as I sat on my floor and cried for help. This time, I was ready! With a firm intention, I chose to become the absolute sovereign master of my life. Something buried deep inside of me, yet unbroken, knew I was meant for more. It called me to heal myself and one day help others to do the same. The amplitude of that decision washed through me with an incredible warm energy that opened up new possibilities for me. I felt it empowering me, energizing me, and giving me the impetus to move forward. And, it was telling me that *it was time*. In that moment, at the end of my tether, I intuitively felt a push to sign up for the courses I have been thinking of taking for a very long time.

I have always been spiritual and wanted to contribute in my own way to a better world. Deep inside I felt there was a potent light force that was yearning to be awakened. But I was littered with limiting beliefs about my capabilities that held me firmly disconnected from my potential. The course I had been wanting to take for a long time, that I finally enrolled myself in, set me on the path of my divine timing. There I learned how to transform my inner story through energy healing and how to go from victim to master of my life. I had always had strength and courage, and now I was activating all that courage to make my life into something I could truly love.

A month later, I took a trip to India to visit the Ashram of Amma. Amma is known famously as "the hugging saint." I remember going up on the stage to receive a hug, called *darshan*, with a letter I handed over to the Swamis, who stood by Amma's side. As one of the Swamis was reading my letter to her, my heart missed a beat in awe of the moment, and I knew something very important was happening. I was seeking her blessing and support to fulfill my heart's greatest desire — to be a healer and live an utterly different life from the one I had known. Her kind smiling eyes were emanating the highest form of love that pervaded right to my core. My body moved toward her like a paper clip to a magnet, and I was enveloped in a surreal cosmic motherly embrace. She whispered love into my ear, "My daughter, my daughter, my daughter..."

After my hug, I sat behind her. Suddenly, sadness and grief took control over me and I burst into tears. The force of love turned my tears of hurt into tears of liberation, and then those of joy of being reconnected to love. It brought me back to peace. I felt alive. I clearly heard 'the message,' that I was going to do exactly the same, reconnecting people to love. I flinched from the amplitude of that statement, not feeling worthy of it just yet. The idea scared me, but I got it! Everything I've been through has a purpose. I lived through those trials so that I could know true freedom and lead others toward it.

The next morning, I walked through the doors of a beautiful stone temple to the goddess Kali for an early 5 AM prayer. After my prayers, I went to meditate on the beach. The ocean was calm and soft little waves were gently embracing the ridges of the stones alongside the shore. The beauty of the rising sun was reflected on the water, welcoming me with a magical streak of glittering light and warming my face. As I went within, I felt like I was becoming a pearly white light. The edges of my being no longer sharply defined me but blurred into everything around me. Fascinating visions of me teaching in front of a big crowd showed up… a burst of joy and light lit me up from within. The heavy burden of the imposed projections about myself slid down and disappeared into the ocean. Relief and confidence downloaded into my whole being and rooted in deep. I knew at that moment that things were going to be so much better. I had the tools and knowledge to transform everything. I could live the most magnificent light and love-filled life. I declared deep inside: *This is the life I've been working toward and I feel ready now. This loving energy that wants me to be here is calling forth my message and there are souls who are eager to hear it. This IS the upward spiral of love, for our highest good and joy. All I have to do is return home to myself and allow my essense to be fully expressed.*

I felt it in every nerve of my body. I am connected to my soul, I know who I am and why I am here. There was so much ease in this feeling! It felt light, warm, and peaceful. It Ignited me with hope that I could fulfill my vision with ease. The moment I understood that, I set myself free.

The energy of freedom rippled through my body. My skin started to tingle from the crown of my head to my toes with such force that I felt my etheric wings unfurl. No longer were they crumpled, atrophied lumps under my shoulder blades but beautiful eight-foot high wings of shimmering golden light I could feel moving rhythmically as I breathed — not the anxious shallow breaths of before but full deep, calm, liberating inhales of life. It wasn't even me breathing, I was being inspired by a greater force that was loving me back into wholeness. When I opened my eyes there was a new sparkle in them. I had expanded so much and in so many ways that I could never go back. It was time for me to be who I am at my core.

On my return to the city, I clearly knew I had to quit my job and go after my dream. The unknown was scary but nothing was as terrifying as an endless repetition of what I had already lived. It took five months before I could divest myself of my old job and really begin living.

Every morning without fail, even if it would make me late for work, I meditated. Sitting by the fireplace, in my bedroom, in yogi position, legs crossed with the backs of my hands resting on my knees, I touched the feelings of confidence, hope, faith, assurance, and support. Bathing myself in loving energy, I envisioned my new life.

I committed to myself, but I didn't take the journey alone. Many times I was guided to receive the assistance of other healers and teachers. It was an evolution that is still evolving, as my commitment deepens. I disciplined myself not to get up from those mediations until I got a full body sensation and confidence that I loved my life.

My trust gave birth to courage and five months later I threw caution to the wind, packed all my belongings, and left London for Bali — the place that I believed could truly nurture me into my fullest power as a woman and energy healer.

Living in Bali was such a dream! I chose to stay in the heart of the island, Ubud, the magical jungle town, nestled among lush green rice terraces. It wholeheartedly offered me a unique combination of a spiritual atmosphere — timeless vibes of ancient temples and waterfalls, tantalizing, divine, heavenly living foods, and nurturing, healing massages. In stark contrast to the bug-ridden flat, this was the place for my mind, body, and soul to be nurtured into wholeness.

My heart center was gently opening up in this land that resonated so much with the vibration of heart due to its healing and nurturing qualities while my roots were growing deeper and stronger in the fertile soil of Mother Bali. I was invited to lead sound and theta healing ceremonies with large retreat groups and that made me glow with happiness and satisfaction. I was in love with my life and became my own soul mate!

There's one particular day that stands out in my memory. I explored Besakih Temple, the largest and most revered complex of temples and shrines on the slopes of Mount Agung, the holy volcano. The guardian of the temple, a healer, met me at the entrance with a welcoming smile and guided me to my destination, a temple higher up. At the top of the dragon stairs, fresh mountain air opened up all my senses. I could smell an astonishing array of colorful offerings left by the locals. My mind was pregnant with two questions: How could I further develop my powers to become an outstanding healer? When would I meet my life partner? After the prayer ceremony, I found myself alone with the healer. He looked in my eyes and answered my questions without me having to say a word. He patted me on the shoulder, reassuring me that I am on the right journey.

Straight after our talk, I sat on the very top of the temple, surveying the mystical vista of the lush green valley. In complete serenity and gratitude for this beauty, I closed my eyes and immediately felt an incredible wave of light passing through me. It went directly into my womb space, Igniting my feminine energy in such a potent way that it was pushed up all the way into my heart. My heart was bursting with so much love and joy. Love was coursing through my body, shifting my vibration so much that I felt myself as a Living Goddess on Earth, a manifestation of the divine female energy. That very moment, I knew I was fully initiated into Love. I not only intellectually knew that my true essence was love, but actually felt and lived it. Love is who I am at my core and I was one hundred percent ready to let human love come into my life.

That same evening, at the most popular vegan cafe in the middle of nowhere, a tall gorgeous man was naturally drawn to me by some invisible force that allowed him to notice me immediately. My golden goddess dress was flowing in the source of the light radiating from within, bringing my beauty to the max-imum. That day I received the gift of human love, my long-awaited soul mate.

The vision of the new me and my new story made me fall in love with my life before I even created it. In return, life fell in love with me and Ignited exciting possibilities. I left Bali for Europe, having been rebirthed into the highest version of myself to give birth to my mission into the world.

That mission is to share with you, that just like me, you are worthy and free to create the life your soul is yearning for. Once you are aligned with Truth, you open yourself up to an infinite flow of pure love. It's this flow of love that will Ignite exciting possibilities for you. You can turn your vision into reality via synchronicities and opportunities. Miracles will take place more effortlessly and your manifesting powers will skyrocket. All you need is already inside you.

IGNITE ACTION STEPS

To create higher vibrations of love in your life, enjoy the following activities.

- **You live by what you believe you are**. Examine your life and jot down the old stories that currently run your life. Keep asking, "Is this the highest truth? Is this really who I want to be?" Tune in for the answer, then jot down your new story and who you are at your core.

- **Write down 100 regrets, resentments, and rejections on a piece of paper**. Dig deep to find the things that you have been holding on to. Then imagine each one being released from you and dissolved into a sparkling light of love. To complete the process of removing them from your life, burn the paper and forgive yourself for holding on to them for so long.

- **Fill the new space you have created with a higher vision of yourself.** Be open to the unknown. Along your path into the unknown is where you will find the reality of your heart's desires. Receive assistance with this process from a healer, coach, or mentor who has walked the path ahead of you.

Marina Sigalova – France
Healer, Teacher, Advisor, Strategist
www.marinasigalova.com
marina_sigalova
Marina Sigalova

Meghan Huthsteiner

"Let go of your ego; rise above your thoughts and commit to listening to the unique individuality of your heart."

May you have the will and strength to accept truth even when it is uncomfortable. Search and you will find answers yourself; don't be swayed by others and take on their ways or truths out of fear of possible failure. Dreams are the essence of life, and to gauge that you're on the right path, embrace the unknown to allow beauty to show itself willingly and honestly. Scrutinize, challenge, and investigate purposefully before you adopt something as your truth. Embracing the journey and finding your own answers will lead to a revival of joy, bringing freedom to live life in the manner that you were perfectly designed for. That is faith in the possibility of human transformation.

The Bruised Fruit Makes the Sweetest Jam

The long, brown black-out curtains hanging from the windows of the fifth floor penthouse in the Hollywood Hills were moving gently from the breeze. The air around me was so smooth that if you were naked it would be the perfect temperature. I was curled up on the tufted round couch that was usually so comfortable, and I could see the city lights as though they were the stars. But that particular night, my heart laid heavy. My eyes burned and my nose dripped as I couldn't hold back the tears. It was 2 AM and all I wanted to do was sleep and escape the thoughts of loneliness and never finding someone I could truly trust to start a family with while surrounded by the takers and shakers of LA. Like in previous years, the days came and went and the feeling of emptiness hovered. That night, the echoes of the intoxicated pedestrians from the street below mimicked the city's selfishness; if they didn't sleep, neither did I.

The wooden 'kingdom' double doors flew open and my business partner and owner of the house walked in. I frantically tried to get back to that perfect appearance I put on display each day before the black-out curtains would close for the evening and I could comfortably hide my broken spirit.

"Hey, Meg! The boys are going to Vegas!" he shouted, and headed down the hall to start packing. A relief came over me knowing I had a few minutes to pull myself together.

"Can you help me pack?" Patrick shouted from down the hall. "I'm leaving right now so we can get there by dawn. If we get going right away, we'll get a good three-day stay."

"Perfect," I beamed, excited to have three full days for my self-pity party in this perfectly manicured penthouse that I worked so hard to match my outward persona to. Maybe I would be more open to receive some kind of guidance if I was all by myself.

Upon return from Las Vegas, a charmingly quiet new friend of Patrick's had accompanied him through the kingdom's doors and caught my attention carrying four bottles of champagne and a package of strawberries. He was a perfect distraction to my agonizing thoughts of not ever being able to start a family at this age. That distraction turned into a year of an off-and-on long-distance relationship.

It was no surprise when the issues I had prior to that relationship showed up again. This time though, it was physically manifesting itself as health illnesses and sickness in me. It was also going to force me to readdress my internal 'issues.' Needing to heal my body, which was rapidly giving up on me, I said to him, "Since we have not committed after a year, now we need to move on so I can focus on healing myself." He asked me to move to San Francisco to be with him. "If I was going to die," I thought, "what's the harm in spending my last days with a guy that at least enjoys my company?"

Making the move to San Francisco didn't cure anything. Day by day and hour by hour, I was getting worse and worse. It felt like life was being sucked out of me. Running up and down mountains was a thing of the past, but the memories oddly comforted me and I had no regrets. After a few months of denying the 'cancer' I was certain was consuming me, I worked up the courage to go to the doctor to receive my diagnosis and treatment plan. Routine tests had been done prior to the doctor entering the room. The four white walls that confined me in that sterile tiny room were making me exceedingly anxious. How am I going to break whatever the devastating news is to my family? I cringed at the thought.

And then the medical assistant walked into the room and blurted out, "You're pregnant!"

I was so mad at her for her incompetence, I snapped back, "NO! I have stomach cancer. Go redo the test." She returned 10 minutes later, tilted her head to the side, and said with a bit more confidence, "You're pregnant."

I couldn't believe a doctor's office could be so irresponsible when diagnosing such a tragic cancer. "This was not a joke, I'm seriously dying and all I would like is to know how severe it is and if I am too late in catching it. Please, please," I begged, "go do it again, maybe the cancer has altered something." She stepped out of the room a third time. I'm certain she only stood on the other side of the door to give me a minute to absorb the news.

How could this possibly happen? I felt as though I was the biggest failure. I did everything that looked right up until then, but now everything was backwards. I didn't even know if the man loved me! How could I be pregnant before I got married and not have a house to raise a family in? I'm Christian and this is not what a Christian does! The shame was so overwhelming I wished an accident would just take me on my way home. Cancer, to me at that moment, would've seemed like an easier diagnosis to digest. I saw all my dreams and hopes take wing and fly off, regretting they had ever wasted their time with me.

Failing to address my issues head-on and maintain my dreams only allowed my mind — or rather, my ego — to continue to make horrendous life-altering decisions. It didn't take long to wash away all the years of discipline and sacrifices I had made, all for the protection of my pride. Unbeknownst to me, I had opened the gateway for the wandering darkness of my thinking.

The monsters lurking under my bed that were once small had grown to a size I was no longer a match for. I started yet another Youtube™ binge-watch for all hours of the night to shorten the terrors of my dreams. Most nights, walking from the hallway to my bedroom, I could feel the monsters watching. Asleep, I would see a dark unidentifiable figure coming from beneath my bed with arms reaching over, dragging me to the underworld where I belonged. My voice is seized, my last attempts for pleas of help go unheard before I am about to be taken under to my final destination. Forced moans of terror turn into loud unrecognizable cries, I'm certain my neighbors could hear.

This happened so often over the next few years that it seemed to no longer faze my daughter's father, rather it annoyed him. All I really desired was to create a God-loving home. It would be considered a success to sit in front of our beautiful bay window, while rocking our baby and singing her a lullaby as the thunder clouds rolled by, but my cold reality was an infant, a male roommate, bare white walls, and a poorly furnished apartment. My picket fence dream was going to stay just that; a dream. I had been stripped of my power and freedom as a single driven woman to create my own caged reality. Defeat had married my fear of not having a loving home and taken up permanent residency in my mind. That belief built castles, ruled kingdoms, and reigned over me. Bowing my will to its whispers until I surrendered; a slave too terrified to disobey or disagree. All I had were the chains of memories and screams from the prison of my mind. Beautifully crafted rational excuses became my knitted safety blanket.

My whole life all of a sudden felt like it was a prank. The daydreamer I once loved and believed in that had all the promises in the world at her fingertips had been punked. Each day, it became more and more apparent that a happy God-loving family who created memories in a home we built together was and will be just a fantasy. It was too crushing to bear. My ability to control my emotions was an afterthought. I despised who I was becoming. It didn't reflect an ounce of who I knew I was. I was crippled by the choices I had to make in order to heal. More than anything I've ever set out to achieve in life, that reality took me down to the deepest, darkest crevice in the ocean. It was my punishment for not being patient.

Alas, I had a dream where I am standing at the pearly gates surrounded by the brightest whiteness. It was glorious. I wasn't standing on anything, nor was I floating. I was just there, waiting to enter. And then a voice spoke the soul-crushing words with divinity: "Depart from me; I do not know you."

Instantly, I knew my fate. There was no need to ask how; I knew full well. I was neither hot or cold. I've lived my life right in the middle where it's nice and comfortable; where all accountability could easily be passed on to another. I couldn't argue with God's divine words when I knew them to be true. How do you know someone when you never know their true stance? I myself would say to people, "Pick a side!" At least then I knew where they stood, regardless if it was with me or against me. And yet, here I was, refusing to step to either the left or the right. My divine sentence was a result of my lack of choice.

I woke, terrified. God's sentencing of me didn't coincide with my heart's true desire. How did I get life so wrong? How can I possibly fix this when I felt so stuck? Being seperated from my creator, no matter who you envision your creator to be... why would anyone in their right mind be okay with that?

I had to make sure that that wasn't going to be the case. I felt the urgency to restore my relationship with God. There is no feeling more tragic than wishing I had tried harder, and knowing I was failing to meet my creator's design for me. I knew I had to live not better, but more intentionally. I had to be bolder and not waver.

In those years of dysfunctional communication I knew to the depths of my soul that if I didn't get the courage to make a change, it would be the literal death of me. My body was manifesting the degree of poison I was mentally ingesting. I made every excuse why I couldn't leave, but the truth was I was afraid of accepting who I became and what would become of me because of my pride. That dream of being rejected by God was the greatest gift and catalyst to open my eyes and see that I had actually made my own choices to put me in that prison. The moment I woke, I surrendered my relationship, child, friendships, career, health, and happiness to start living for Jesus, and choose to go where He wanted me to go regardless of comfort. Yes, very painful because I knew how much I had mucked things up, yet, I was amazed to find that the years of chains just fell away once I continuously decided to pick a side… the doors flew open!

I was comforted that He was there for me and where there used to feel like there was no way, God made the way. I rested on the promise that God could restore the years that I had lost if I relinquished my control of my life and let Him take the wheel and carry me through. Standing on each and every one of His promises became my true possibility. It was then I asked, "If my life isn't being lived fully in your design for me, then take anything and everything away until I humble myself, secure my place in heaven, and make the most impact here on Earth."

My failure to listen to good counsel left me unguarded to bad opinions. Because I am responsible for my actions, I stopped the cycle with having to believe I had to be validated to be heard. It didn't matter who was right or wrong in this relationship. There was no need to be angry at lessons badly learned or poorly embraced. Being angry was just another bad habit. I've embraced my experiences like notes in a symphony, being played by multiple instruments with different intensities. I've pleasantly become attuned to the importance of dissonance and harmony in each sound throughout my life's composition.

For years I swallowed my voice with what I'd have to say to not upset someone out of fear of disrupting their world while sacrificing my own. Coming back to life, I have no other choice than to get to know this girl once again. I needed to acknowledge the pain and learn how I have allowed myself to take wrong turns, all the while giving grace and mercy like my father in heaven has. I'd rather have a love affair with the one who has created everything than with one who stands to lose everything. I want to put my head down at night knowing that I have done my best to fulfill my life's purpose.

I feared that the world would look at me and say I'm a wretched person for wanting to live that way. Now I see that this is my ego's fear and not my heart's reality. I refuse to dim my light in order not to offend the ones who are still living like judges at the guillotine. I don't need to be a perfect strawberry, lush, beautifully shaped, and free of flaws. I can be a bruised fruit. In fact, bruised fruits are those who have learned from life's experiences rather than shying away from them. They are my favorite sorts of people.

I hear a lot of people talking about how the Universe will give you everything you desire when you're authentic, open, and willing. When we inspire others through our mistakes, we essentially show them that our circumstances don't define who we are. They're just circumstances. It's all circumstantial and that's just life. When you start consciously making it about YOU, then it's just YOU. It's not the ego. Your thoughts become purified. When you get your priorities right, it's incredibly freeing. You find yourself able to open up in a vulnerable and real way with everyone you meet. Life becomes a shared human experience instead of a superficial Instagram™ reel.

Rid yourself of ego. When it's about your personna, you're alone. Sharing stories with profound messages that are enlightening and helping others to find their message and share theirs also is truly living. That knowledge is so freeing and wonderful. I made so many bad choices because I didn't want to be seen as a failure. I let my ego tell me I should be ashamed of who I was, but instead, I needed to rise above it. And when I did, one thing after another started to fall into place like clockwork. When I started being grateful and living fully each day... each day felt like it had *days* worth of experiences crammed into it. My life expanded exponentially, and I felt wonderful!

No longer is there a question of my purpose. I freely allow myself to walk in the unknown. My prayer to God isn't revealing a purpose for my ego to glory in, but making me walk in my purpose every day without having to know each step God has for me.

When I think about what history really means, I break it up into two words: it's *His Story*, a beautiful tapestry for us to witness and learn from Him. It comes to me as a miracle that the Bible, *His Story*, is the most read story in the world. It is an egoless story gifted to bring the world together. My greatest takeaway is that He desires an intimate relationship with each and everyone of us, as do we all with each other. Just as He is the divine example to each of us, we are to one another. I'm committing to that intimate relationship; that open and unguarded opportunity to be a reflection of Him. With this new knowing, all possibilities for you and me are endless.

IGNITE ACTION STEPS

Don't run from your thoughts; listen to them. Identify your enemies. If you don't know your enemy, how do you prepare for war? Aim to stop lying to yourself and others that you have it together. Each day face your pride and stubbornness and address it till it runs clear like purified water.

Every bit of learning is a new death. With each death is a new birth. Don't ever sacrifice what you could be for what you already are. Never stop learning.

Allow the best in you to serve the best in others. The biggest pleasure in life can be mentoring. It beats any other form of reward. Be a lighthouse in the midst of the storm.

Good counsel will always trump opinions. Counsel comes from those who have gone before you and have had their experience. Opinions are from people who just have a thought of how something should be. Be wise in choosing your counsel.

Meghan Huthsteiner – United States of America
Holistic Health Practitioner, doTERRA Essential Oil Advocate, Clinical
Aesthetic Medical Assistant, International Best Selling Author, Director of
International Business Development at Ignite Publishing
circadianhealth365@gmail.com
@circadianhealth
Meghan Huthsteiner

BEEJAL COULSON

"Discover your creative essence, nourish your soul, and set yourself free."

My deepest desire is for you to creatively connect to your inner temple and allow it to be a stepping stone to discovering your authentic self. Life is a process of becoming; honor that. Surrender to the synchronicity of infinite possibilities that await you. Commit to the journey knowing its purpose is to find your way back to you.

EMPOWER THE CREATOR IN YOU

My feet absorb the coolness of the water as I step tentatively into the sea, mesmerized by the reflections of the patterns created underneath the water. Knee-deep, I look up and am welcomed with the breathtaking sight of the landscape right before me — the beach and the sea against the backdrop of the mountain range. The visual picture of Port de Soller, Majorca embedded in my mind gets sharper each time. My body acclimatizes as I move deeper into the clear turquoise water until it reaches my waist. My heart starts beating faster. I immerse my whole body in and after the initial shock of the cool water, my heart expands and some warmth permeates my skin cells. I feel invigorated. The magic sprinkles shine beneath the afternoon sun, laying a shimmering golden path I swim right into. I turn to float on my back, captivated by the piercing cerulean sky. The soft wind gently bellows in the nearby port and the sail posts of the boats move and clank to form a melodic sound. I stand up, neck-deep in the water, and wade back to the shore. The glow from the sun absorbs the droplets of water running down my skin. I take yet another photo of 'that' view and smile with appreciation. Nature has indeed become my muse. I decide I am going to capture this moment and recreate the essence as a painting in my next art class. I lay down, as it's time for an energy healing session. Earphones in, the track that I co-created, "Love, Peace, and Light," playing on my phone, eyes closed. Tuning in to the frequency of my client in Canada, I see shapes — lines, waves, spirals, circles… I journey into another realm.

As a very young child, I had grown accustomed to living by the sea amid the beautiful nature in the tropics of Mombasa, Kenya. I moved to the suburbs of London when I was 4 years old; a stark contrast in terms of climate and landscape. My journey into grayness was more than geographical and while the yearning to be by the sea never left me, I can still feel the inner and outer conflict that marked those years.

As a young girl, I enjoyed anything creative: daydreaming, drawing, painting, and making things with my hands. It's no surprise that art and music were my favorite subjects in school and I displayed great talent in them. My creative side was celebrated at school and used initially as a means to appease me at home, but by the time I turned 7, the creative experiences lessened. I begged my parents to let me attend extracurricular activities that my friends had the opportunity to experience — singing and dancing classes, learning to play the piano and flute — but it was a flat no and nonnegotiable. There was a strong cultural belief in the Indian community that anything related to the arts was not going to give me a career so there was little point to engage in them. Sadly my parents were part of this conditioning, concerned about what others would think, and acceptance in the community was far more important than individual desires. The denial of myself as a creative being was like having my oxygen supply slowly cut off.

At a young age, I remember being chastised for being defiant yet again. This time it was about me being left-handed; the left was my dominant hand. My mother had demanded I change to using my right hand as it was deemed inappropriate (I was shaming the family), but 5-year-old Beejal retorted back that unless my mother could prove both hands were not equal, I would not change. This angered my mother. I saw the rage rise up in her face and her eyes widened. It was an Indian cultural belief that being left-handed was unlucky and unsavory. Even though I refused to change from being left-handed, this was an early message to me that I was not accepted for who I was (and on a subconscious level it had turned into a limiting belief). I discovered years later that my father had been caned at school for being left-handed; he had no choice but to conform. My parents know better now. They accept, support, and celebrate me for who I am and my creativity. So much has beautifully been learned.

Years later, when I researched deeper into creative skills as an academic, I learned of the connection between creative abilities and being left-handed. Left-handed people make up about 10 percent of the population, and studies have found that they score higher when it comes to imagination, daydreaming, intuition, rhythm, visualization, and linguistics.

More than a decade went by before the opportunity arose to explore this creative element of my soul. I enrolled in an art course during my summer break after my second year studying for a university degree in science. I discovered that being in the art studio was similar to the delight I experienced when in a fairground as a child. It was so much fun experimenting with mixed media and a variety of art techniques. On the final day of the course, I was immersed in a lush green landscape — a beautiful lake surrounded by English countryside. I was about to paint on a canvas with oils. A color caught my attention — an earthy terra-cotta tone called Burnt Sienna. My future daughter's name was chosen; 'Sienna' — a reminder now to me everyday of creative expression.

That art course became the catalyst for the journey of my creative awakening. I devoured books on impressionist artists, modern art forms, and all there was to appreciate about them for the next few years. I could not continue to pretend that I was going to have a career in the field of science, yet I didn't have the prerequisites for a creative qualification, so I opted to change from a science to a business degree.

Seeing the work of artists in galleries became my favorite pastime especially while on travels. French impressionist painter Monet's artwork in the *Musee De L'Orangerie* in the Tuileries Gardens in Paris was impressive; I was surrounded by beauty in the two oval-shaped rooms that created the infinity symbol. When I observed the sheer magnificence of his life-size masterpieces, I could resonate with the quote: "I dream my painting and I paint my dream." The blue reflections of the sky, green vegetation in the water, and weeping willow around the water's edge fascinated me.

Soon after my studies, I landed a job in the creative industry in advertising, but it was as a media planner/buyer and I found it restrictive and very numerical, so I dabbled in art by enrolling in a watercolor painting course one evening a week. I then became a lecturer in marketing, which was very interesting as I had autonomy and was able to teach in creative ways. I felt a deeper resonance to the arts in my work when I progressed to teach fashion marketing. Even though I was not creating art, I was surrounded by creatives and my creative style of teaching was very welcomed.

In my late 20s I decided to do something radical. I left my life in the UK for a year to travel the world solo. Just before I left, I took a week-long art course. That week revealed to me that art is something that shows up inside out. I had the intention and desire for what I wanted in life, but the materialization did not appear. My artwork uncovered that there were blockages; I felt powerless and restricted. My travels took me to New Zealand where I experienced a sense of freedom that I had never felt before through the power of nature. I experienced the kingdom of heaven in this place and the beauty of life uncovered the hidden secrets within myself.

On my return from travel, I embarked on a personal independent growth process. I was intrigued by all things to do with the mind. When I started training as a coach, I learned about growth mindset. It was fascinating how I had been operating from a limited, fixed mindset all these years. I focused on knowledge to empower myself to achieve my desires and engage in practices that took me closer to my goals. I went back into academia, specializing in arts marketing with a greater awareness that creativity was important in my life. I enrolled in a year-long part-time art therapy certification. This course created a huge shift for me. It was a cathartic healing process, revealing the true light which emanates from within me and the secrets of my heart and soul, highlighting the significance of creativity. I realized I had to honor my creativity and make it an integral part of my life; it would no longer be something peripheral.

I faced challenges in giving myself permission to create despite being pro-active. I enrolled into art and African drumming classes and attended craft workshops, but situations kept arising in my outer world to reinforce that I didn't have permission to create. I even created an art studio at home, but it started to accumulate unfinished projects. Just facing the blank canvas in the first place was a mission in itself. There was hesitation to make the first mark. My body tensed up as the critical mind started — "What if this is not going to turn out great? You are not a trained artist. You don't even know what you're doing." This carried on until my inner voice whispered, "It's fine, there are no expectations," and my body let down its guard. My hand eventually learned to choreograph the paintbrush into a dance onto the canvas. Soon, waves of peace gently spiralled up in me, chakra by chakra, and inspiration beamed down through the crown of my head and landed in my heart. When I create, time stands still. It feels like I am in a hypnotic state. I am in 'flow.' The canvas takes on a life of its own where the inner world meets the outer and consciousness channels itself through me. I smile. The results are impressive. My critical mind is speechless and my inner voice silently praises me.

A big opportunity came when I suffered a burnout and was in an abyss of the unknown where my life and career path would unfold. It led to *healing* and a career shift into this area. The creative world contributed as my healer and my coach. I learned that everything in the world has been taught from the beliefs and imprints that have been passed on. The move to a growth mindset was key for my transformation and evolution.

Meditation became a game changer. It awakened my creativity to another level in my artwork and in my career. My higher self was collaborating with me now and my possibilities were expanding. My new roles as a rapid transformational hypnotherapist, coach, and energy healer were infused with creativity. I created a modality called Quantum Life Technique™ that enables clients to discover their highest potentials with their higher minds and aligns them to their future lives. My own life changed vastly as a result! Lifelong dreams materialized. I became a successful hypnotherapist, coach, and healer serving clients globally; a multiple best-selling author; the owner of a second home in Spain; collaborated with a music producer; and officially called myself an artist!

When my family and I arrived on the Spanish island at this horseshoe-shaped bay called Port De Soller for a long weekend to celebrate our birthdays, it was love at first sight. We had a sea suite in a boutique hotel with the most amazing views of the bay. I woke up to the sound of the gentle waves lapping on the shore. We decided to go for a morning walk before breakfast. Tall palm trees lined the promenade, the beach golden, the sea turquoise blue, the majestic mountains in the distance, and cobalt blue sky. My mouth gaped wide-open in surprise as I caught sight of a distinctive red rose etched in one of the rocks on the side of the bay. I had seen the rose dimensionalized in my mind during a meditation a few months ago. My heart and soul connected to a deep sense of knowing that this rose was indeed a sign. Butterflies fluttered in my solar plexus. I just knew that this was the place where I would live in the future.

My lifelong dream of a second home by the sea came true; this magical Baleric island is my creative haven. We found our perfect home and these days I wake up to the view of the mountains in the background and the sea nearby. The rooster in the distance is singing his morning song and the familiar sound of bells on the goats close by is ringing. The sun is rising, giving off a beautiful glow to the houses and apartments up on the hills, the mountains in the backdrop. I walk with a spring in my step to the local weekly market selling fresh fruit and vegetables. I pick out a selection of fruit including a box of mouth-watering strawberries, fresh juicy mangoes, and a bag of local Sóller oranges. I chat to neighbors in Spanish. I attend art and pottery classes in a nearby village. I go to the beach in the afternoons and swim in the sea. I do therapy or energy healing with clients virtually all around the world. I sit out on my terrace as the sun is setting. I repeat the following affirmations to myself: "I accept myself. I am unique. I am a creative being. I give myself permission to be happy, creative, and free." There is a beautiful pink glow on the mountainside and I take in the breathtaking views before me. This is me now living the dream.

The impact of self-acceptance and permission to create has flowed into my work and my gifts. I've had the profound realization that when I Ignite possibilities within myself, this Ignites possibilities in others in unimaginable ways.

During my first transitional energy healing, I was in an inferno with bright flames burning; I could sense organs starting to burn. Waves of energy cascaded through me as I felt the fight for life, the letting go and surrender, then freedom and bliss. I felt a tear release from my right eye, representing the liberation of a soul. My client transitioned in peace and I walked to the port area listening to Seal's music track, "Future Love Paradise." The smoldering red sky was hauntingly beautiful. Nature had painted an exquisite picture.

My journey back to art has been an interesting one with many twists and turns. I was denied my creativity as a child, and later in life, I denied myself my creativity. Still to this day, I go through the motions with my inner critic whether I am drawing, painting, making pottery, or writing. It's easier now because I have learned to trust and surrender to the experience.

My time in Majorca is teaching me something fundamental: the essence of who I am as a creative being. It is through the practice of art that I nourish my soul and flourish in my life, especially in unlocking the ability to help others profoundly. To not be creative is to deny who I am. Art has been my healer and coach. It has brought me full circle.

Creativity is a stepping stone to self-acceptance and authenticity and the synchronistic path to freedom and fulfillment. It propels a self-awakening, a transition, a right of passage toward oneself and raises consciousness through successive stages.

Creativity can be a vehicle to Ignite the potentials of your soul's purpose. When you Ignite your possibilities, you have the power to Ignite them in others. Infinite possibilities exist when we give ourselves permission to create and create for the sake of creating. Empower your creativity to activate your soul evolution — release, surrender, transform, heal, awaken, and raise consciousness.

IGNITE ACTION STEPS

1. Go out in nature and tune in to the array of colors, tones, and shapes you see; the various sounds you hear; and the scents around you that you can smell.

2. Artist Date — sign up to a creative endeavor on a weekly basis. Do something you haven't done for a while or something new that you've been interested in experiencing.

3. Meditate focusing on your sacral chakra to begin with. Imagine your creativity activating and rising up to your throat chakra as the expression of your authentic truth. Then do something creative! Drawing, painting, writing, dancing...

Beejal Coulson – United Kingdom & Majorca
Creator / Founder Quantum Life Technique
www.beejalcoulson.com

Amy Lin

"Be strengthened by the future you define,
not weakened by the burdens of your past."

My intent is to create an awareness in you that encourages you to uncover who you truly are. The essence of who you are is perfect, and you have infinite potential within you. You are meant to live an opulent life; a life full of prosperity, happiness, and wealth. It is my goal to show you that you are not defined by your past, and you can make a committed decision *today* to become the best version of you from this point on. BE the creator of your life. In every moment, you have a choice. You have the power to choose how you want to feel, what you want to create, and how you want to live your life.

Becoming *Extra* Worthy

"How are you feeling?" I heard this booming male voice behind me. I turned my head and looked at him. Speechless and in denial, I wished I was anywhere else, instead of sitting in a steeply-climbing airplane with a stranger strapped to my back. I couldn't hear anything except my pounding heart or feel anything except my sweating palms. "There is no turning back," said the frantic voice in my head.

With adrenaline rushing through my body, I looked across the plane and saw four other groups of people strapped together just like me. Coming to my senses, I noticed a guy around 30 years old, sitting directly in front of me.

Surprisingly, I saw there was no one strapped to his back. He should have been as scared as I was, but he was smiling and calm. He leaned over and opened the airplane door. A cold breeze rushed in and the wind blew on my face, then off he went, disappearing into the vast blue sky.

Stunned by what I had seen, I wasn't even aware it was my turn to jump. The stranger strapped to my back yelled again, "Are you ready?" and my entire body tensed up.

Before I could respond or think, he stood up and dragged my body with him toward the open door. Out we flew. My eyes were shut tight and the first thing I felt was the cold air rushing against my face. My goggles pushed up against my cheeks and my facial muscles flopped out of control. My hands were gripping hard to my vest like my life depended on it.

I was falling… falling from 13,000 feet up.

"AHHHHH!!" I screamed, terrified. I dug deep to find courage as I realized there was nothing I could do at that moment. I finally opened my eyes, choosing to enjoy and be present. I appreciated the mountains, seeing them from a bird's point of view. I noticed the vast blue sky and I felt the crisp fresh cold air on my face. I had stepped into the unknown, and the sense of surrender that overcame me felt so freeing and liberating.

Before I knew it, we had landed on the ground safely. I saw my friend who had been in the same plane and landed nearby. We ran toward each other.

"Oh my God!!! We did it!" he shouted.

I yelled, "What's NEXT?" I felt invincible now that I'd faced my biggest fear: a fear of heights. I'd never felt so empowered in my life.

I've taken that power into so many experiences since. I've walked on fire over hot burning coals in the middle of the night with 20,000 people. I've put fire in my mouth and swallowed it. I've trapezed from a pole as tall as a five-story building and jumped off a 143-meter Tarzan swing in Costa Rica. These were all powerful ways for me to push the limits of my capabilities, move beyond my fears, and bust through limiting beliefs that were holding me back.

I didn't always feel this empowered.

From my youngest moments, I had a nickname that silenced my little voice: *DuōDuō*. This name, 'The Extra,' was a reminder from my father that I was unwanted. In my traditional Asian family, as in many others, there is a belief that's been passed down from generation to generation that boys are worth more than girls. I am the youngest of four kids: there's my oldest brother, my sister, my second brother, and then me. Before I was born, my mom miscarried — a boy that was meant to be her third son. Back then, there were no ultrasounds, so when my mom got pregnant again, all they could do was hope it was a boy. As time went on, my dad went from hoping for a son to expecting one. To his surprise and disappointment, I was a girl.

Similar to other kids, all I wanted was love from my parents, but I didn't get the love I deserved as a child. In fact, I felt like I didn't belong. From my earliest memory, I always thought I was adopted because of the lack of love and affection I had received from my parents. My helplessness and loneliness were only made worse by the fact that I was bullied by my siblings. Unfortunately, my parents weren't around to witness any of this because they were working two jobs to raise us four kids.

Some part of me believed my parents would have put a stop to it if only they had known, but I couldn't tell them how I was feeling. I wanted to speak up, I wanted to tell someone, but I was scared. My oldest brother would beat us up when my parents weren't around and I didn't dare to tell on him because I was sure if I did, a beating from him would follow. I was living in fear most of the time during my childhood. I was so scared that I decided to be disconnected from the family both emotionally and physically. I often refused to go home after school, finding whatever safe space I could to hide away from my brother's hostility. I'd do anything to not go home just to avoid the possibility of doing something wrong and setting him off.

I found that safe space in the home of my nanny who was our neighbor. I had a very close relationship with her and her father. He was my godfather and like a real father to me. He had dark skin, with a receding hairline, and a smile that made me feel safe and cared for. He seemed so big, like a shelter where I felt protected and secure. He would take me places after school, let me sit on his motorcycle, and treat me like I was his own daughter. I really enjoyed my time with him as he made me feel loved and cherished.

One day when I was around 6 years old, my godfather passed away. My whole world came crumbling down. I no longer had someone I could depend on. I was too young to understand what death really meant. I felt the sorrow of losing someone I loved; the pain of being alone again. I was back to feeling unwanted, unloved, and scared. Whatever self-worth I might have felt with my godfather was slowly chipped away as I continued my life as the *duōduō* of the family.

I carried this feeling of unworthiness into my adult life. It set the stage for how I would attract love. Because I felt unworthy, I unconsciously attracted someone who treated me disrespectfully. I often overlooked his actions and allowed him to undermine me. I thought I was going to spend the rest of my life with him, so I let him get away with lying to me over and over again. I didn't care about everyone else's warnings; I simply looked past his behavior, in denial because it was my first time ever being in love.

I ignored all the signs that I was in an unhealthy relationship and, because of my low self-worth, I denied my own intuition. It was one of the longest romantic relationships I had ever been in. I lost myself in that relationship. I had forgotten about me for the sake of a beautiful illusion. The trust between us was broken repeatedly until I finally chose to put an end to the toxic relationship that I had accommodated for six years. After the relationship was over, I felt a part of me was gone along with it. I didn't know who I was or what I wanted to do. That's when I started looking into personal development events, to find out who I was, what was important to me, and what I wanted to create from that moment on.

Over the next three years, I immersed myself in various personal development events and seminars. I discovered so many things about myself that I wasn't aware of. One of the biggest lessons I learned was that I am the only person who is responsible for my life. Facing that hard truth and getting honest with myself sparked my self-reflection even more. I recognized how my low self-worth was not just sitting inside me, but vibrating out of me. The outside world reflected this back to me, reinforcing the feeling of unworthiness through the circumstances and people I attracted. Through my journey of personal growth, it dawned on me that it all stemmed from my days as a little girl, living as *DuōDuō*.

This reflection took an even deeper turn during an advanced personal development course I was taking. I sat surrounded by 200 other people in a grand, open auditorium. The instructor onstage asked us to recall a memory where we felt a loss in belonging. Immediately my memory took me back to my godfather, and I thought surely his passing was the most significant event from my childhood. The instructor had us go find a partner and share with them what happened. I got out of my chair, walked toward the first kind face I saw, and asked if she would be my partner. She agreed and we pulled up two chairs and sat across from each other. We were instructed to look into each other's eyes and pick one person to go first by tapping on their knee. Out of habit, so used to letting others go first, I tapped on her knee.

Although the lights were dimmed for this exercise, I could still see her face as she spoke. She began by describing her memories as a 7-year-old child at a family gathering with her parents and siblings. Then her story took a shocking turn as she said, "I was sexually abused by a relative."

Her voice was so calm, almost as if she were telling someone else's story. She went on to describe how she volunteered to watch her younger relatives at gatherings so what happened to her would not happen to them; and how her family just assumed she loved being around the kids. I was looking into her eyes as she was telling me the story. She showed no emotion as she explained all the ways that event impacted her life, but I could feel her pain. I thought, "I cannot imagine what she went through. If I was in her position, how would I handle it?"

That's when it dawned on me — like a huge lightning bolt striking over my head. Buried deep in my unconscious memories was the revelation that I DID know what it was to be in that position. My memory flashed back to when I was little, though I don't recall how old I was. I was in my oldest brother's room having a sleepover and he sexually assaulted me. I was too young to understand what was happening, but even then, I had known something did not feel right.

The next second, I was back in the conference room. As my partner continued with her story, I became aware of my sobbing. Tears were rolling down my face. I felt shaken by the sudden unlocking of a trauma I had hidden so deeply away. After so much time not wanting to feel it or think about it, it was brought to the surface and I couldn't deny it. A deep sadness came over me. I felt my inner child screaming and in pain. I was crying so hard that I began feeling light-headed.

My partner still continued with her story as I transitioned from tears to anger. One minute I was sobbing and the next minute I was furious. I went from feeling sorry for myself and feeling sad for my inner child to declaring internally: "No way am I going to give my power away because of what happened!" Remembering that shocking event put me in touch with all the past experiences that made me feel unworthy. During that moment, I decided to gain my power back. I was not going to allow what happened to me to hold me down any longer. I learned that the only way to overcome trauma and painful experiences is by not avoiding them; rather, it's important to feel it through: feel the anger, resentment, guilt, shame, self-pity, and bitterness. Feel it all. Like turning on the light switch in a dark room, once I was able to see, I could finally do something to change it.

Once I knew that hiding away from my scared feelings and past pain was holding me back, I made the choice to start facing my fears. I began embracing opportunities to conquer everything outside my comfort zone that I had been avoiding. This new determination to discover what was possible for me is what led me to jump from that plane, and do everything that followed. I chose to define my future for myself, rather than let my past determine my path.

The experiences of my youth made me who I am today. However, now I make sure to not *allow* them to define me. They do not have power over me any longer. It was easy to blame the circumstances; it was easy to blame other people. The moment I took responsibility for myself, I felt empowered. Now I have a choice. I can choose who I want to become. I can choose what I want to create in my life moving forward. This conscious decision of owning my power is a beautiful feeling of liberation.

Now that I have come to this realization, I know that I AM the one who determines my worth; not anyone else or anything else external. I have also discovered that my purpose in life is to do what I love and what I am passionate about, which is to help people to become the best versions of themselves and step into their greatness. As an Opulent Coach, I help people uncover what is holding them back so they can choose to move past it and start living the 'opulent life.'

You deserve to live an opulent life; a life full of all that you desire. An 'opulent life' means having an abundance of wealth full of richness. Wealth includes three aspects; spiritual wealth, intellectual wealth, and material wealth. True wealth in life is to identify yourself with the spirit of Opulence, and it all starts in your mind. It is the ability to think freely, lavishly, and liberally. It is available to anyone. All you need to do is to let go of the past experiences that don't serve you; let go of the limiting beliefs that have been holding you back.

I went from a little Asian girl who was an *extra* in her family with low self-worth, to discovering my true self-worth. Today, I am someone who gets to decide her worth and I show other people what's possible in their lives by helping them discover their self-worth. One of my favorite quotes by Dr. Joe Dispenza, says: "You are either defined by the memories of the past or a vision of the future."

I'd like to support you in being gentle with yourself and being grateful for *all* your past experiences. If you truly understand who you are and the essence of who you are meant to be, then you'll know that you do have *perfection* in you. The essence of who you are is unlimited. It is infinite, it is opulent, it is divinely you. You get to decide! YOU measure your worth!

Make the decision that all the things in your life that are *extra* are the things you love. Extra joy. Extra happiness. Extra Faith. Extra self-confidence, self-care, and self-worth. Most importantly and opulently, make the decision to live a life full of *extra* self-love.

Ignite Action Steps

- Write out any trauma or experiences that you've been holding on to that happened in the past. Write out the emotions and experiences in their entirety. Burn that page, purging the emotions within it. Then, write down how you have come to feel after doing so.
- Write a letter to that person who hurt you in the past, or someone you hurt in the past. Forgive those who hurt you, and forgive yourself. Give that letter to that person(s) or burn the letter.
- Do one thing every week for yourself; one thing that you love to do and that brings you joy. Look at yourself in the mirror every day and say, "I LOVE YOU."

Amy Lin – United States of America
CEO & Founder of The Opulent Academy, Speaker, Author
www.theopulentacademy.com

LINDA M PARKER

"Everything you desire starts from within YOU!"

The foundation of everything is what we choose to see in ourselves. My vision is for all individuals to be empowered through self-love and self-acceptance. When you learn to love yourself, anything is possible. The self-defeating dialogue you have in your head is what keeps you closed off from possibilities. By reclaiming control of this conversation and turning your inner critic into a superpower, you can create a life of happiness and abundance.

POSSIBILITY STARTS WITHIN YOU

My husband was driving recklessly on the treacherous, winding mountain roads that were covered deep in snow. My sister, her husband, and I, fearing for our lives, yelled at him to "Cut it out!" He laughed at our panic and ignored our pleas, being ambivalent to our concerns. We almost crashed into the side of the mountain, swerving into the opposing lane, and only then did he stop the car. We all jumped out. My brother-in-law, furious, walked up to me and said, "You need to divorce this piece of crap!" and climbed into the driver's seat to take control of the car. Me and my sister moved to the back seat. I gazed out the window as if this wasn't my life. I was like a zombie having an out-of-body experience; not really there. We got back to the hotel and I made my way to the lobby bathroom with my sister. She slapped me across the face and said, "WAKE UP! You need to divorce him."

It was New Year's Eve weekend of 1996. I was in Lake Tahoe, California with my husband and five other couples for what was supposed to be a fun holiday ski trip. I'd been married about three years, but the thing is, I didn't even want to get married. I just wanted to have my baby, but at that time marriage was still considered something I "should do," especially since he was willing. My love for my 3-year-old baby girl was what kept me there, but I was totally unhappy with no self-worth.

On that trip, no one wanted anything to do with this obnoxious man I'd chained myself to. I was finally awakened to the toxic relationship I was in and the unhappy life I was living. I knew this wasn't me. It was a long few days until we were back home. The very next day I sat at my mother's dining table and leafed through the Yellow Pages™ looking for a divorce lawyer. Within a year we were divorced but the verbal abuse didn't end. After a couple of years of constant fighting and threats, I decided I needed a different approach to deal with him so I could be happy. I had to do a lot of soul searching to become the person I needed to be for my daughter. I looked within myself, trying to figure out what my role was in creating that relationship where I wasn't being loved.

I asked the question that so many people in doubt do: "How did I end up here?"

I always thought I was a strong person. I mean, I had bought my own home at the age of 24. Doesn't sound like a person who wasn't confident or strong does it? Here's the thing, my inner conversation was one of unworthiness. I told myself I was not good enough, fat, stupid, and so on. I never went to college because I was told in third grade that I would never be good at reading or math. I know now how much that derailed my desire to even try to learn.

Here I was, 30 years old, a single mom working two jobs to provide for my daughter. I needed to keep her in a loving and caring environment since she only experienced turmoil whenever she was with her dad. "How am I going to do this?" I wondered, "Is it even possible for me?" I was running on probably five hours of sleep a night, while my daughter had night terrors. I was in constant fear and dread dealing with this relationship that was emotionally draining. I had sleepless nights, not knowing when the next fight or disappointment was going to occur. I had to continually support my daughter and create a positive and loving environment. As she got older it was the dreaded phone call of her crying wanting to come home when she had to stay with him. There were many times I felt I couldn't even breathe from all the anxiety it caused.

I knew I had to do something. It was up to me and this is when my discovery of personal growth began, and it has taken me over 15 years to tap into who I am today.

When I started this journey, I realized that my inner conversation was what was making me feel so unworthy, not good enough, and not smart enough. Once I was able to unpack all the untruths that were embedded in my subconscious, I was able to start living a life where I liked who I was.

As I was learning more about me, I overheard my daughter who was only 8, telling herself she was fat and ugly. I immediately told her she was beautiful, and she replied, "You say this to yourself all the time." It dawned on me that our kids are following in our footsteps without us even knowing. At that point I needed to show her, *not tell her*. I needed to be the person I wanted her to be.

When you love yourself, you start showing up differently. You begin to attract different people, relationships, and opportunities. As my journey toward self-acceptance progressed, the new energy I put out drew in the real man of my dreams. By the mid-2000s I was happily remarried, living in a beautiful home, with my daughter, his son, and our new little girl. We were the modern Brady Bunch. Life was good, the kids got along great. My career was thriving, my husband's business was thriving, and we were financially secure.

Everything looked picture-perfect from the outside but it definitely was not. I was miserable and I really had no idea why. I was embarrassed, even ashamed to let anybody know how I was feeling. I thought, "How dare I?" when I had so many advantages around me that other people didn't have. Who was I to want more or to feel unhappy? I tried to ignore these feelings but they did not go away.

Over the years I had done a ton of personal growth and self-improvement reading: journaling, vision boards, goal setting. All these things did help me get to where I was but I realized I was only doing 'surface-level' work, nothing deep to get connected to who I am and why I feel the way I feel. I was not happy. I was easily frustrated and angry, and took it out on the ones that I loved.

Then the external stress mounted. In late November 2008, the real estate market came crashing down. I was head of the Mortgage Underwriting Department when shit was hitting the fan and it seemed like the world was crumbling around us. We had one of our usual boardroom meetings to address the next steps for handling this housing market crisis. At 9 AM on a Wednesday morning I walked into the cold boardroom. I was wearing my traditional black dress pants with a navy blue top and a black blazer, carrying a water bottle, pen, and paper in hand. In the last few meetings everything was just about finger-pointing and passing blame. Blah blah blah… I wasn't the least bit interested. I tuned out, feeling totally disconnected and didn't even care about what was going on in the room. I swivelled my chair and I stared out the window looking at the brown, leafless trees moving in the wind, thinking to myself, "What's going on with my life? Is this all there is for me? Just banking?"

No! I knew there was more, I just wasn't sure what that was.

That night, laying in bed, I kept saying to myself, "God give me a sign. There's got to be more for me." I was grateful for all the opportunities that my job provided but I just knew that there was something more for me. I could feel it, I just didn't know what it was, so I kept asking for signs. While in meditation all that I could hear was, "It starts from within." This phrase kept coming into my mind for the next few days.

Okay God, I need to start from within me. I wasn't really sure what that meant or would look like. I started doing a little research and came across life coaching. This seemed like a better option than therapy, because if I went to therapy then there would be something 'wrong with me,' and I wasn't going to allow myself to think *THAT*. I ended up hiring a business coach, figuring I'd just start my own business. I had been in network marketing before and online marketing was a huge up-and-coming thing. It was within the first couple coaching sessions that I realized I was not living my life for myself.

When I took a look at my 'core values' versus what I was actually doing, I could see the huge disconnection. I was living by default based on others expectations and just following along with how my life 'should' look. I started working on who I am: what do I want, what do I believe, and what do I stand for. This is a lot of deep work. It wasn't easy because who wants to admit that they're responsible for the life that they're living? I know I didn't. I was so resistant because there was no way on earth I set out to be in an abusive marriage. But ultimately I realized it wasn't the marriage, it was more a matter of me not loving myself. I confronted the fact I was responsible for the conversation I was having with myself and all the decisions I was making. These two things were causing everything that was showing up in my life. It took me a couple of years to own the fact that I was 100 percent responsible for all of it.

When I started to journal about my feelings and what I wanted out of life, I saw that banking wasn't what I was meant to do. I knew there was a higher calling for me and that yearning wasn't going to get me anywhere.

I returned to the self-actualization tools I used before: journaling, meditation, vision boards, and goal setting. As I got deeper into this work, I started to show up differently. Friends took notice, asking me what I was doing, and I shared my tools and practices when they were interested. We started doing classes in my living room, deciding to meet every other month. This grew and grew, taking off until friends were calling me and asking me to come to *their* house and create goals, life visions, and vision boards for their friends. They even started paying me! That turned into hosting actual workshops and I realized I had found my calling.

Helping others see what thoughts are holding them back and determine what their own true beliefs are was where all the inner work I taught began. These limiting beliefs were very common. Most women have this underlying thought that they're not worthy; something that rang true for all of the women I was working with at that point, including myself. What I loved about this work was seeing how these women transformed themselves. When they had someone stand for them and see them in a way they couldn't see for themselves, they were empowered to take action toward embracing new possibilities.

With all the work that I was doing and all the conversations that I was having with other women, it dawned on me: it all started from within ourselves. That's when the light bulb went on! That's what God was trying to tell me. I was meant to share with other women how starting from within themselves is the key to them living the life that they truly want.

There was one unexpected area of my life where these lessons would prove most crucial. I realized these limiting beliefs had taken root in my younger daughter without me even knowing. By then I had assumed because my life was better overall, she was in a place of positivity. I was mistaken. I don't know how it happens, but as girls sometimes it seems like we are just programmed not to like ourselves. My daughter was being excluded from social groups, and her sense of unworthiness was anchored in this. But she hid it from me, and when I found out it was like a knife in my heart. Both my girls had issues with self-image, being bullied, and trying to fit in — and I saw what a toll it takes on a young heart. With all that came to light with my younger daughter's experience, I felt with more conviction how vital it is to model self-love and teach our girls how worthy they are. I realized I needed to keep digging deeper into my own personal responsibility. I didn't want either of my daughters to be at the age 50 when they realized they needed to change their inner conversation.

We all have inner conversations, many stemming from childhood experiences, that keep us stuck. We all have limiting beliefs that hold us back, even in times when things seem great on the outside. So many of us women have imposter syndrome, the sense of unworthiness that makes us ask, "Who do you think you are?" This had been true for me, and for my girls who meant everything to me.

With added determination in my heart sparked by my daughters, I began to create action steps and guides for women. I discovered what my true vision is; *for women to be empowered through self-love and acceptance to stand for themselves and what they truly believe.* I'm here to tell you that a lot of the thoughts that you're thinking are internal fabrications based on limiting beliefs. They're not the truth to who you are. You can have, do, and be all that your heart desires.

Don't get me wrong, I am still on my journey. I'm on the road right along with you, cheering you on. It's time for you to find what's true for you: who you are at *your* core and what *your* values really are.

The first step is to become aware of the thoughts that you're thinking — how they make you feel and how you're showing up in your life based on them. By addressing the negative reoccurring conversation that you may have going on inside of your head, you can free yourself from all that is holding you back. You can be your own beacon and light the way for anyone around you who deserves to feel greater self-confidence and deeper self-love. That is my wish for all of you.

Start from within yourself, because your superpower can change the world.

IGNITE ACTION STEPS

I believe that anything is possible for you when you learn to manage your mindset. Turn your inner conversations, that 'inner critic' into a superpower!

Do not ignore the negative thoughts or push them down. Instead neutralize the inner critic. This is how you are able to ditch the negative self-talk, when you show your inner-self, love, and compassion, and let it know you are choosing something different. It puts YOU back in control.

You are not your thoughts. Your awareness of what you're thinking and how this has you showing up in your life is your breakthrough!

Embrace these three A's:

1. **Awareness** — become aware of what you say when you talk to yourself. Realize this conversation is on autopilot. Pay attention to the way these

thoughts make you feel, what patterns or behaviors have you created based on this conversation.

2. **Acknowledging** — when you realize that the inner voice is there and that the voice is not going anywhere it's time to create a different relationship with it. What you need to understand about your inner critic is — IT NEVER GOES AWAY and that is not a bad thing because you can CHANGE IT. Love and understand that that voice is there to protect you. Acknowledge it and then choose a different conversation. Just say, "I hear you and I thank you but I now choose _____."

3. **Allowing** — allow yourself to be okay with where you are, to feel the negative emotions. Lean into the fears that are coming up for you. The key is not to stay there! This step is part of the process into self-love! Learning to love your inner critic is the KEY to loving yourself.

BOTTOM LINE: The inner critic is NOT going anywhere so embrace it and turn it into a superpower!

Linda M Parker – United States of America
Mindset and Success Coach for Women
www.itstartsfromwithin.com

Nadia La Russa

*"The harder you work for something, the greater
you will feel when you achieve it."*

**It's natural to want to give your children the best life, but that doesn't
necessarily mean the biggest, nicest house in the most ritzy neighborhood.
Through this journey, I learned that what my children wanted was to be
where I was; everything else was a distant second. Giving them the best
life meant that I needed to give them more of me, and less of everything
else. My hope is as you read this story you realize that achieving financial
freedom is possible, even though it may be uncomfortable.**

The Richness of Being Poor

I put my hands on my hips and assessed the situation around me. I was
standing in the middle of my apartment, trying to figure out which box to start
unpacking. I knew in less than an hour another truckload of boxes would show
up, and I had been trying to unpack as much as I could between loads so we
could at least have the essentials at the ready for the morning.

The day had quickly evaporated and I was exhausted. Further, I was in a
haze of disbelief at my current situation. "My *apartment*," I muttered under my
breath in disdain, and set about opening up another box. I heard my mother's
voice calling me from our office area downstairs. "Up here!" I exclaimed, just
in time to see her enter the room.

"Well," she said, surveying the room. "This is something, isn't it?"

It was the summer of 2012 and the 'something' my mom was referring to was the upheaval I had embarked on with my entire life. A mere six months earlier, my husband Brent and I, and our five children, were living in the newest, nicest area of our city, in a large five-bedroom, two-story house. We had a live-in nanny, two garages full of vehicles, tools, and recreational toys, and a monthly overhead of nearly $25,000.

Then, at the beginning of February, we found ourselves struggling to make ends meet. One evening after sharing a bottle of wine, we came up with what we called the 'crazy idea' to move into an apartment building we owned, relocating our accounting firm to the main floor while living above. Once we calculated the monthly budget, we quickly realized it was financially the best decision we could make for our future.

However, not everyone quite understood this decision — and I think the person who was the most surprised was now standing in front of me, with a look of despair on her face. "Mom," I said softly, "I know this seems like a lot. But we've thought this through, and it's truly the best decision." She didn't believe me, and if I'm being honest, I didn't believe me either. The question everyone in our life wasn't asking out loud was, "What about the kids?"

It was a question I didn't know the answer to. I was moving my young children out of their neighborhood and into a commercial area with no yard, no parks, on a busy street, away from their friends, and out of their school zones. I knew a lot of my friends thought I had absolutely lost my marbles. But what they didn't realize was at that very moment, I had $4.52 to my name. As much as it broke my heart to think of how this would impact the children, I truly didn't have a choice.

Mom crinkled her nose and surveyed the apartment. "I know, it's for the best. I give it a year, and you'll be out of here and back on your feet in no time." I mustered up my most reassuring face, gave her a hug and said, "Yep! A year. It will fly by!"

I think we both knew how wrong I was. Looking back, I now know that when we think about the future, we are often more wrong than we are right.

Brent and I dropped into bed late that night after saying goodbye to our friends who had helped us move. We were exhausted, and we knew we had a long weekend of unpacking ahead of us. "The account is in overdraft," I informed him, "but I had to get the beer and pizza for everyone who helped out today." He leaned over, kissed my head, and said "Sweet dreams, beautiful." I turned away from him so he didn't see the silent tears running down my face. I had never felt so poor, or like such a failure, in my entire life. I couldn't believe he could be so calm and confident while I was feeling like there was no future at all for our family. The despair was overwhelming.

The next morning, I woke to the sound of laughter. Confused, I wandered down the hall toward it. It sounded like… my children. Sure enough, I found them crowded into one bunk bed and giggling away. I was greeted with cheers and hugs as they piled on top of me. "How did everyone sleep last night?" I asked them. "GREAT!" they cheered in unison. "What's for breakfast?" my youngest daughter asked.

I looked at them all in amazement. It was like they had no idea life was turned completely upside down, and that everything was horrible. We were forced into financial ruin, and I had moved from a gorgeous home into this crappy apartment. My thoughts were interrupted by the sound of a firetruck screaming past the building; sirens blaring. The kids didn't even seem to notice the noise. I shook my head and went into the kitchen. Brent handed me a cup of coffee and said, "Well, they don't seem to care about any of this, do they?" I just looked at him in disbelief. Here I was with these five happy kids who were excited and giddy, not realizing their mother was failing them. I figured it was only a matter of time before they figured out the truth behind the facade of this new life I was creating.

Downstairs in my office, I opened up the spreadsheet and reviewed our calculations. No matter which way I ran the numbers, there was no question moving here was the best financial option. We previously had a large mortgage, and were also paying commercial rent for our office space. Moving here had eliminated the commercial rent and cut our mortgage payment almost in half. We were able to go down to one vehicle, since we now lived and worked in the same spot. Our apartment was less than a block from two grocery stores, the pharmacy, and the bank. In addition, there was a bus stop at the front door. Since I now worked on the bottom floor of where I lived, we no longer needed childcare after school for the children, so we laid off our nanny. This also meant that we could eliminate internet, telephone, electricity, and heat bills for our commercial office space. The monthly savings were astounding.

This did not appease my feelings about the fact my future plans and goals had evaporated. Late the year before, my key employee, who was also my best friend, had quit and stolen my largest client, curtailing my normal level of ambition and drive. I had no idea what to do next, and although I knew I was making the best financial decisions, I was grieving the life I had planned out for us. With my bank account in overdraft, I felt like a fraud trying to give others financial advice in my role as accountant, and even after calculating the monthly savings it still seemed like financial freedom would never arrive. My entire identity seemed to be gone. I picked up my phone to get lost in mindless scrolling on social media. Less than 10 seconds later, I saw the quote that set me on a new path:

"Don't wish for it, work for it."

These words snapped me out of my funk and into action. It hit me right then and there; I had just turned my entire life upside down, and I couldn't have it be for nothing. It was like an explosion occurred inside me. I opened my laptop again, and got to work. I might not have had a big house, money in the bank, or a fancy car, but what I did have was my husband, my children, and my skill set. I knew then that I had to put that skill set into action and work harder than I ever had in my entire life.

The first thing I did was email out a revised rate schedule to my clients. It had been over three years since I increased my rate, and it was time to raise the hourly charge. I knew this might cause some clients to leave the firm, but I put a plan in place for that too.

I contacted the business groups I was part of in the city and let them know my firm had capacity to take on new clients and new projects. I attached a screenshot of our rate schedule and a link to my booking calendar.

Then, I emailed our banker asking for an appointment for the coming week to discuss re-mortgaging the building we were now living in. I attached our income statements, prior year tax returns, and some projections I had been working on.

I logged into my online banking platform and recorded all my credit card and loan balances into a spreadsheet. I organized them by minimum payment amount, interest rate, and sorted them by which one would be paid off soonest. Then, next to each payment I put the month and year it was due. As one debt was paid off, I transferred what I was paying on that one to the next one in the sequence. The end of the spreadsheet told me that my debts would be paid off less than three years later. I printed the cursed schedule off and taped it to the wall beside my monitor, titled 'Look here before online shopping.' I snarled at it before moving on to my next task. I knew my life of buying what I wanted when I wanted had to stay behind me if I was going to make any of this worth the hardship.

I wrote down a list of the meals the kids loved to eat, then took those meals and placed them on the June calendar. I calculated out the cost of each meal and set my grocery budget to match that cost. Once I had my food budget planned out, I could estimate how much the rest of our living expenses would be. With this information, I calculated how many hours I would need to work each month to eat and keep the lights on. It was difficult to view this step as freeing rather than restricting, but I was determined.

By the end of the day, I was exhausted and my office walls were covered in calendars, highlighted charts, spreadsheets, data, and figures. My taxed brain had been swimming in a sea of paperwork for nearly eight hours. But the items on my walls were the new road map to my life, and I knew if I didn't have them visible where I could see them every day, I would lose my way.

I hauled myself upstairs to find Brent on the couch with all five kids, each of them eating popcorn. Again, I was greeted with cheers and smiles. Again, I could barely believe what I was seeing in them. "We love it here!" they exclaimed.

"They seem so happy," I said to Brent as we went to bed that night.

"I think they *are* really happy," he responded with a shrug. I was incredulous, but I chalked it up to the newness of the move. I figured reality would set in with them sooner or later. Again, I was wrong.

Less than a month later, we had re-mortgaged the building, were rolling with the new budget, and things were looking up. I had some new clients who I loved working with and a glimmer of hope had returned to my mindset and outlook on life.

I had never worked so hard in my entire life. I started waking up at 4 AM and working until 7 AM when it was time to get the kids up and ready for school. At first, it was nearly impossible to drag myself out of bed at that ungodly hour, but after less than a week, it became easier. I would return back to my desk by 9 AM and work until the kids came home from school. Then, I would prepare dinner, and hang out with them until bedtime at 8 PM. From 8 PM until 10 PM I was working on our family finances — transferring funds into our savings, tracking our spending and bills, and looking for ways to trim even more of our expenses back. It wasn't easy, fun, or glamorous, but it was working. Bit by bit our savings account grew.

As the months passed and life became our 'new normal,' the kids seemed to thrive and blossom. It was like I had unlocked a side of them that I had never seen before.

I marveled over it with Brent one evening. "I cannot understand what is so different for them. We moved to this tiny, old, loud place from a beautiful home, yet they seem so much happier here. What is going on?"

My wise husband smiled as he responded, "I've figured it out. It's us. We are here with them more than we ever have been. They don't care about the walls of the house. They care about us and spending time together."

His words hit me like a lightning bolt. I knew he was absolutely correct. My children didn't care about fancy houses, cars, or nannies. They cared about being with us. Without even knowing it, I was giving them the gift of my very best self. What I realized then was that my biggest hardship was actually my biggest blessing.

We didn't stay in the apartment for a year like my mother had predicted. We stayed there for eight years. In those eight years, my children — and my savings account — grew immensely. When we finally built and moved into our beautiful 'forever' family home in 2020, we did it with a foundation of wealth that was made up of much more than just money. Through the biggest change I ever embarked on came the biggest reward — children who valued family time and relationships over material possessions and status.

Without this hardship, I would have never known the value of hard work. I would still be spinning my wheels in the same house, struggling to make the monthly payments, never getting the chance to enjoy the life I was creating. The eight years in our apartment taught us how to live below our means and create the freedom that comes with building wealth responsibly. It taught our children how to manage household resources and the difference between needs and wants. And, it taught me the most important lesson of all; that I'm not a failure, but rather a tremendous success.

When faced with hardships that seem insurmountable, it's important you remember that these hardships may bring hidden gifts with them. Choose where you spend your money and your time intentionally; keep your plan visible to keep it foremost in your mind as you go about building the life of freedom that you wish to live. Remember always that the wealthiest among us are those who understand the value of our human relationships and give the people we love the gift of our very best selves every day.

Ignite Action Steps

1. Take a good, honest look at your financial situation. Are you in debt? Struggling to make ends meet? Living paycheck to paycheck? If you cannot *save, give, and live* — put money into savings, give to charity, and live comfortably — it's time to make a change.
2. Take a look at your house — is it one you can afford? Is it more than you need? If so, look for something closer to your work, or rent out part of

your space. Consider literally every option, and don't worry about your kids. Remember, they want to be where you are.

3. You need to be the expert on your money. It must be you that knows where each and every dollar you make is supposed to go. Trust me, you can do it. If you feel overwhelmed, get help — reach out to me if you need to.

4. You must be prepared to work harder than you ever have in order to save money. It will give you a reward beyond measure and the freedom you need as you and your family grow.

5. Become addicted to saving money rather than spending it. It doesn't take long to become addicted to savings — even after a lifetime of poor spending habits!

Nadia La Russa – Canada
Wife, Mom, Entrepreneur, and former money stress-case
www.nadialarussa.com

ANNABEL WILSON

"We can allow pain and trauma to define us, or use them
as tools to break free from the prison of our past."

My wish is to awaken within you the belief that we can all heal from unspeakable betrayal, trauma, and fear, and provide you with the tools to alchemize them into infinite possibilities. You'll learn how to unlock the possibility of transcending and transforming whatever situation you're in into an evolution that Ignites your personal fire and ultimate freedom.

CROSSING THE LINE

How do we forgive the unforgivable? When does an act cross the line into something that's so hurtful that we're unable to move into forgiveness? Even though the concept is universal, where this line falls is different for everyone. What do we do when ours is not only crossed, but trampled on and burned?

When we're vulnerable and betrayed by the very people that we trust to keep us safe, when we're pushed to a place where we lose all sense of self-worth, when we've never been taught what healthy boundaries are, how do we gain the ability to feel safe, feel worthy, and trust again?

It took a series of consecutive abusive relationships for me to unravel the multiple layers of toxic beliefs I unconsciously held. At the end of the first relationship, I understood that my unconscious beliefs about men and women were far from healthy. I believed that to be a man was to be powerful and strong: a contributor, a breadwinner, a mover and shaker. To be a woman was to be flighty, dependent, emotional, and weak. I understood that I had a firmly entrenched scarcity mindset, believing that I could lose everything at any given moment, and that competition was necessary as resources were finite.

By the third relationship, I realized beyond a shadow of a doubt that I didn't love myself. Nobody who truly respects and loves themselves would have allowed the repeated emotional and psychological abuse, gaslighting, and manipulation that I did. My abandonment wound was so strong I was like an insatiable addict, desperate and willing to do and accept anything to continue to receive external validation and 'love' from my partner.

Whenever my significant other wasn't able to provide the love and validation I needed; I would try to fill my internal void with extravagant jewelry, luxury goods, and holidays. It was a futile attempt to somehow buy myself the self-worth and love I was so hungry for. I was trying to feed a bruised and battered inner child with extremely expensive temporary distractions that did nothing to staunch her hunger. The problem with all addictions is that we need increasingly bigger doses and rewards to feel the 'hit' — the welcome respite from the overpowering needs gnawing at us. The other problem with addictions is that all externally obtained relief is temporary.

On the surface, it made no sense. I was extremely well educated, had a respectable career doing what I loved, and was financially independent. I was attractive and healthy, had two beautiful children, a glamorous, international, high-flying lifestyle, and was in the prime of my life. Yet under the ultra confident, always-knows-what-to-do exterior sat a dark web of unworthiness that I can only call my inner Gollum. I tried my best to give myself the love and validation that I was so desperately seeking from others. However, something still always felt like it was missing. I could never fully fill the void that gaped like a bottomless black pit inside me.

At my lowest point, I sank to the bottom of a very deep, suicidal depression. I called my sister to ensure that my children would be cared for should anything happen to me. Then, I sat in deep grief for days with the realization that I might not achieve in this lifetime what I had incarnated to become. I mourned with oceans of tears that I might not have the resilience to achieve my purpose. I turned myself inside out, as I thought about my daughters growing up without a mother. As I sat there in my darkest hour, I connected with a voice and presence so clear that it stilled every cell in my being.

My higher self stepped in. She held my damaged, dying, inner child and quietly shared with her, "You're not alone. No matter what happens, I will be with you until the end. Whatever decision you make, I will walk every step of the way with you, support you, and stay with you until the end."

It was at that pivotal moment that I understood what unconditional acceptance and love meant — no judgment. Just pure presence, divinity, and grace. Suddenly, the lashing winds of the internal storm that had wreaked so much damage completely stopped. I had never felt love and safety like this before. It was my salvation and is the tool I use to this day whenever I need to reconnect and self-soothe.

In the fall of 2020, after a particularly challenging year simultaneously juggling solo-parenting with the exhausting hours and demands of my early stage well-being tech start-up, during a pandemic when Covid hit our home and family twice, my children returned to me after a long summer holiday with their father's extended family.

For the preceding five years, I had been holding everything together for my children, solely through my own strength and resilience; often playing mother and father out of sheer necessity. I was confident that despite the overwhelming strain this caused, my efforts to create a nurturing and happy home for my children, and to reach a mutually supportive, respectful relationship with my ex-husband and his family were getting somewhere. I was completely blindsided when in my drained and depleted state, I had unthinkable accusations leveled against me by those very people.

The gut-level betrayal by these family members rocked our little family unit to our core. At a critical time for my business, I had to put everything on hold while we spent the next eight weeks dealing with school, doctors, lawyers, counselors, and therapists. Thankfully, the truth was irrefutably brought to light, and justice prevailed. The perpetrators have never taken any accountability nor apologized for their actions.

As an adult, I can forgive the harm someone causes me, but when their intentional actions harm innocent children, it takes it to a completely new level. My heartbreak at the callousness with which my ex-in-laws had treated my children's mental and emotional well-being was the hardest to bear. I had to dig very deep to overcome repetitive cycles of shock, grief, outrage, and hurt before I could move on.

This unfortunate cycle of distressing betrayal is one that I've been familiar with since early childhood. I learned very early on that I was not safe in my own home. I learned that the very people I relied on to keep me safe could not. I learned that no boundaries would be respected. I began to believe that I had very little value and worth. This knowledge and these beliefs sat like a white elephant within myself, oppressive and larger than life. As this was a most unwelcome feeling, I stuffed it down and started to focus on more palatable external distractions.

Decades later, all that trauma was brought out into the open. When perpetrators happen to be our birth family, taking decisive action to stop contact pushes against the full weight of societal programming; which pressures us to stay, to tolerate, to accept without question. After many months of tortured indecision, I made the gut-wrenching choice to stop contact with my family.

That uncomfortable stalemate dragged on for three years. Cognitively, I accepted what happened and forgave them in my mind, time and time again. Emotionally, I still didn't feel safe enough to be in their presence and held them off at arm's length, declining all in-person contact and virtually any communication. Even once I allowed more virtual contact, my heart remained resolutely closed to them. I could sense the deep pain I was causing my family, but I wasn't ready to move past my need for safety and the boundaries that I thought protected me.

It took the undeniable specter of loss to change this. During a recent visit home, I was present when my sister and brother-in-law almost lost his mother. She has an incredibly strong fighting spirit and managed to come back from the brink. However, with lungs slowly filling with liquid faster than can be drained, her impending death was an inevitable tragic outcome. Faced with the stark reality of my own family's mortality, I became keenly aware that I had a choice. I could resolutely stay where I was, civil but completely emotionally closed to them, or I could finally take off the flea-bitten, shadowy coat of past pain, anger, and grief, and step into the field of infinite possibilities.

I could remain a powerless victim, or I could reclaim my full power to live as a whole, complete being. I could keep punishing and pushing my family away, or I could choose to seize that opportunity to go through the final healing stages of unspeakable betrayal. At that moment, I realized that I absolutely did not want to cause anyone to feel shame and guilt, much less have them go to their deathbeds feeling they had committed an unforgivable crime.

When I chose to throw off the cloak of suffering, I learned what unconditional forgiveness meant. It released an untapped well of tears that wouldn't stop flowing until every last drop was exorcised from my being. I chose to stop pushing my family's love away, and start accepting it with the intention and spirit in which it was given.

I also chose to draw a line under my ex-in law's actions, and be open to reconciliation within safe boundaries. I chose to accept that all these family members, like all of us, were doing the best they could, with the experiences and beliefs that they held. I chose to unreservedly accept the past, and to forgive and love the people who had caused me so much pain.

We can choose to cling on to every slight, every deep hurt we've ever felt, every piece of suffering. We can use them to feed our anger, fear, and hate, and bolster a belief that the world is against us. We can choose to add to this personal library of every insult we've ever received until we've created such a strong victim persona that we're always playing defense or offense against our enemies; real or imagined. We all know a person like this. We might even be one.

Yet, choice goes both ways. We can also choose to acknowledge the pain we experienced: to accept that something traumatic happened, process the pearls of wisdom from these hard-won lessons, and *choose to free ourselves from our past and our pain.* We can cross the line we drew in the sand.

What enabled me to move fully into this final phase, even with people who hurt me the most, was the undeniable awareness that I could actively choose peace and freedom. I did not have to construct a lifetime of pain; both for myself and the people I was protecting myself from. When I realized that I was fully empowered to choose my future, that I wasn't a hapless, unwilling participant in someone else's drama, the choice became effortless and obvious. Why on earth would I keep wearing that heavy coat of misery when I could choose light instead of shadow; peace instead of pain; compassion instead of conflict?

In my journey of forgiving the unforgivable, I had to be consistently mindful. There are no black-and-white rules on allowing people back into our lives. In some cases, it will feel entirely right to open our arms and embrace long-estranged loved ones. In others, it will feel right to establish civil relations within clearly defined boundaries. In certain cases, where continued abuse and violation is likely, it will be entirely right to severely limit or completely cut off contact.

Acceptance is the first significant step in healing. We can choose to rail against what happened; to wring our hands and linger in the deep injustice of it all. Or, we can choose to move past our hurt and grief and accept what *is*. We can find gratitude for the lessons as well as the blessings we receive in life. I am always grateful when people reveal their true intentions and natures, so I know exactly where I stand, and who really has my back. In every moment, regardless of where and who we are, we have the *possibility to choose.* Every choice we make moves us closer to or farther away from peace and freedom.

What's so important to realize, is that we can step into the field of infinite possibilities every single day of our lives. We don't need to have experienced a deep trauma in order to alchemize a life of ultimate freedom. When someone cuts us off in traffic, is short-tempered with us, or takes credit for our work, we can choose to react with anger, asking, "Why me?" — only seeing life as unfair. Or we can choose to forgive; find compassion for others, and look for the lesson and opportunity. That person who cut us off might be rushing to pick up an injured child. That person who was short-tempered with us might have just lost a loved one. The person who took credit for our work might be terrified of losing their ability to support themselves. Choosing not to take things personally brings us closer to peace and freedom.

We can apply our ability to choose to any situation. We choose what thoughts stay in our heads, what sources of information enter our awareness, what intentions we bring to the world. We choose what words we speak, actions we take, reactions we give, and how we spend our time, energy, and money. The power within us to choose enables us to Ignite our personal fire and breakthrough to infinite possibilities.

IGNITE ACTION STEPS

Your steps to Alchemy

1. Center and ground daily so you can create the space between your reaction and actions. Daily breathwork, meditation, Tai Chi, Kundalini, Yin Yoga, or a reflective practice of your choice all serve to center and ground you daily.

2. Become aware of the many choices you make on a daily basis. Ask yourself, is this bringing me closer to peace and freedom? Apply this question and see if you still wish to proceed with your original action. It's ok if you do. Sometimes we just need to vent. It's what we do after we vent that's crucial. Always take accountability for the part you play and always look for the lesson.

3. Remain limitless. We often limit what's available to us, by closing down too early and narrowing our focus before fully understanding the full range of opportunities. The next time you're tempted to shut down or withdraw, practice being still and staying open, inviting the infinite expanse of possibilities into your life.

4. Practice unconditional self-acceptance and self-love. Set aside time in a quiet place where you won't be interrupted. Start small and progress as you feel ready. Visualize your inner child. Ask what he/she needs to feel safe. Visualize your adult self, holding and comforting your inner child in a way that's meaningful to them. Once your inner child feels calm and loved, gently say goodbye for now and return to your adult self. Celebrate your inner child, everyday. The inner child inside all of us isn't a liability. Our inner children enable us to see and marvel in wonder at the magic that's all around us. They are a source of infinite possibility and so much joy.

5. Practice unconditional forgiveness. First forgive tiny irritations, progressing to bigger hurts when you feel ready. You may wish to work with a professional, a trusted friend, or family member on this.

6. Find gratitude for every lesson learned and for every opportunity to heal.

7. Practice unconditional compassion, acceptance, and love. When we find these things for ourselves, it naturally overflows to love for others. Gift the last minute of your meditation or reflective practice by sending love to everyone you know, and to all human beings.

Annabel Wilson – United Kingdom
Founder Director, Living Ashram
www.livingashram.com
⊚ @livingashram

Andrew Kap
- *The Last Law of Attraction Book You'll Ever Need To Read* by Andrew Kap
- Check out my YouTube channel at www.YouTube.com/AndrewKap

Atta Emami
- Go to ChangeFacilitator.com for a free download on the breathing technique
- *Everything Is Workable: A Zen Approach to Conflict* by Diane Musho Hamilton
- *Becoming Supernatural* by Dr. Joe Dispenza
- *The Biology of Belief* by Bruce H. Lipton

Diana Lockett, M.Sc., R-EYT,
- www.dianalockett.com
- Canada's Only Re-Alignment Coach

Donna Lockett, PhD
- If you are struggling with unresolved trauma, stress, or anxiety, reach out to your doctor, your local mental health agency, or a trained mental health practitioner. The website traumahealing.org has an extensive list of trauma specialists internationally who can support you.
- *Waking the Tiger, Healing Trauma* by Peter Levine, PhD (1997)
- *When Things Fall Apart* by Pema Chodron (1996)
- *The Body Bears the Burden, Trauma, Dissociation, and Disease* by Robert Scaer (2001)

Dr. Gerald Curry
- Dr. Gerald Curry is a Tier Two Senior Executive and serves as Director for the Air Force Review Boards Agency and is responsible for the management and operations of 10 Review Boards including the DoD Disability Appeal Review Board (DARB), Air Force Personnel Council (AFPC), Air Force Board for Correction of Military Records (AFBCMR) and Air Force Civilian Appellate Review Office (AFCARO). Dr. Curry has more than 40 years of executive leadership experience in private

industry, federal government, colleges, and universities. He is a retired Colonel in the United States Air Force, and co-owner of The Urban Voice Magazine, based in Las Vegas, Nevada, a successful entrepreneur and serves as the Chief Operating Officer for Curry Brothers Publishing, LLC, and President of PCA Inc., where he provides executive mentoring, lifestyle coaching, keynote, and motivational speaker. Additionally, he serves as an Adjunct Professor in the Criminal Justice and Security Studies Department at Colorado Technical University. His expertise is in assisting leaders accomplish their career aspirations.

Francis Piché
- Thinking Into Results 6-Month Group Coaching Application: https://bit.ly/3v3HtG5
- Private Coaching Free Breakthrough Discovery Session: https://bit.ly/3twuR9Z

Katherine Vrastak
- *The Silva Mind Control Method* by Jose Silva and Philip Miele
- *Letting Go The Pathway Of Surrender* by David R. Hawkins, M.D., Ph.D.
- *Think & Grow Rich* by Napoleon Hill
- *CLEANSE TO HEAL* by Anthony William
- *The Life You were Born To Love A Guide to Finding Your Life Purpose* by Dan Millman
- *Set your Voice Free* by Roger Love
- *The Buddha And The Badass The Secret Spiritual Art of Succeeding at Work* by Vishen Lakhiani
- *Limitless Upgrade Your Brain, Learn Anything Faster, And Unlock Your Exceptional Life* by Jim Kwik
- *A Course In Miracle* by Foundation for Inner Peace
- *Women Who Love Too Much* by Robin Norwood
- *I thought It Was Just Me (But It Isn't) Making the Journey from "What Will People Think?" to "I am Enough"* by Brene Brown
- *Overcoming Unwanted Intrusive Thoughts* by Sally M. Winston, PsyD Martin N. Seif, PhD
- *Evolved NLP* by Ernie Pavan, Laura Cargill Slinn and Kelley Oswin
- *Find Your Why* by Simon Sinek
- *Who Not How* by Dan Sullivan
- *Personality Isn't Permanent* by Benjamin Hardy
- *Ho'oponopono Prayer* by Craig Beck

Kirusha Kulcar

- The work of Jeffrey Van Dyk has helped me connect with and share my message.
- https://thecourageousmessenger.com

Lisa Lynn Eveleth

- If you are living with an autoimmune condition and have any questions or need guidance, my foundation is always here to help. www.livefit-withlupus.org. 844.LFWL.ORG
- A few favorite books I love to share about nutrition are: *The Wahl's Protocol* by Terry Wahls, *MD & The Inflammation Free Diet Plan* by Monica Reingal and Julius Torelli, MD.
- A great resource for learning about the role of vitamin D is www.youtube.com/lisalynnfit (Jim Perry, Compounding Pharmacist ~ District Drugs, Rock Island, IL).
- A healthy gut is important to optimal health. Check out www.facebook.com/mandalaintegrativemedicine.
- I alkaline my body daily with lemon juice, baking soda and an amazing superfood. LisaLynnFit.VimToday.com (Vimtrition).
- You can join me anytime for my exercise classes! Please email me: Lisa@livefitwithlupus.org or ask to be invited to my closed group: www.facebook.com/UFworkoutclan.
- *'Words of affirmation' and 'the power of positivity' are so important to a healthy life. (See Amy Cuddy, Ted Talk ~ Fake it till you make it). www.youtube.com

Marshanelle Horne

- *The Yamas and Nyamas* by Deborah Adele
- *40 Days to Personal Revolution* by Baron Baptiste
- *The Subtle Body* by Cyndi Dale
- *Energy Medicine* by Donna Eden
- *Daring Greatly* by Brene' Brown
- The Seven spiritual laws of Success by Deepak Chopra

Noa Takarroumt

- For French speakers, a book titled *Sept kilos autour du monde* unveiling the full version of this story will be released by June 2021 on Amazon. In an attempt to fully immerse the reader in each country, the book will also include music playlists by country and a dedicated Facebook and

Instagram page @noatk sharing photographs taken on the road.
- Noa's next writing project is an adaptation of these texts in English. As this edition of Ignite Possibilities goes to print, the release date is yet to be defined.

Pat Labez
- *Desiderata* by Max Ehrmann

Reverend Sheila Black
- My webpage: www.beonewithspirit.com
- Spiritualist Church of Canada https://www.spiritualistchurchofcanada.com/
- Lily Dale NY https://www.lilydaleassembly.org/
- Edgar Cayce Foundation https://www.edgarcayce.org/
- Spiritualists National Union https://www.snu.org.uk/
- *Dream Images and Symbols* by Kevin Todeschi

Sorana Pascariu
- *Becoming Supernatural* by Dr. Joe DiSpenza
- Ted talk: https://youtu.be/wzjM21OySv4
- Website: www.mindsetformars.com

Tracy Stone
- I am delighted to share free resources with you, including the 'Borrowing Tractors' exercise from my website here: https://limitlesspotential.co.uk/resources

PHOTOGRAPHY CREDITS

Amy Hackett-Jones - *Luciano Salazar*
Kirusha Kulcar - *Alex Howell*
Lisa Lynn Eveleth - *Scott Denys*
Renee Dutton - *Maria McCarthy Photography*

Thank you

A tremendous thank you goes to all of those who are working in the background teaching, editing, supporting, and encouraging the authors. They are some of the most genuine and heart-centered people I know. Their dedication to the vision of IGNITE, along with their integrity and the message they convey, is of the highest caliber possible. They each want you to find your IGNITE moment and flourish. They all believe in you and that's what makes them so outstanding. Their dream is for your dreams to come true.

Production Team: Dania Zafar, JB Owen, and Peter Giesin

Editing Team: Alex Blake, Andrea Drajewicz, Chloe Holewinski, and Michiko Couchman

Project Leaders: Francis Piché and Traci Harrell

A special thanks and gratitude to the project leaders for their support behind the scenes and for going 'above and beyond' to make this a wonderful experience. Their dedication made sure that everything ran smoothly and with elegance.

A deep appreciation goes to each and every author who made *Ignite Possibilities* possible — with all your powerful and inspiring stories embracing this idea of the possibilities within each and every one of us.

To all our readers, we thank you for reading and loving our stories; for opening your hearts and minds to the idea of Igniting your own lives. We welcome you to share your story and become a new author in one of our upcoming books. Your message and your Ignite moment may be exactly what someone needs to hear!

Join us on this magical Ignite journey!

IGNITE TEAM

JB OWEN
Founder and CEO

PETER GIESIN
CTO

CATHERINE MALLI-DAWSON
VP and Operations Manager

CAROLINA GOLD
Administrative Coordinator

KATIE SMETHERMAN
Brand Manager and Book Design

ANDREA DRAJEWICZ
Manual Editing

ALEX BLAKE
Senior Editor

CHLOE HOLEWINSKI
Editor and Project Manager

MICHIKO COUCHMAN
Editor

MEG HUTHSTEINER
Happiness Manager

TREVOR GOLD
IT & Tech Specialist

DANIA ZAFAR
Manager of Ignite Press

LIANA KHABIBULLINA
Graphic Designer

WRITE YOUR STORY
IN AN IGNITE BOOK!!

THE ROAD TO SHARING YOUR MESSAGE AND BECOMING A BEST-SELLING AUTHOR BEGINS RIGHT HERE.

We make the BEST best-selling authors in just four months!

With over 700 amazing individuals to date writing their stories and sharing their Ignite moments, we are positively impacting the planet and raising the vibration of HUMANITY. Our stories inspire and empower others and we want to add your story to one of our upcoming books!

If you have a story of perseverance, determination, growth, awakening and change... and you've felt the power of your Ignite moment, we'd love to hear from you.

Go to our website, click How To Get Started and share a bit of your Ignite transformation.

We are always looking for motivating stories that will make a difference in someone's life. Our fun, enjoyable, four-month writing process is like no other — and the best thing about Ignite is the community of outstanding, like-minded individuals dedicated to helping others.

JOIN US TO IGNITE A BILLION LIVES WITH A BILLION WORDS.

Apply at: www.igniteyou.life/apply

Inquire at: info@igniteyou.life

Find out more at: www.igniteyou.life

CPSIA information can be obtained
at www.ICGtesting.com
Printed in the USA
LVHW070057180122
708746LV00027B/504